C. Hurst & Co (Publishers) Ltd., New Wing, Somerset House, Strand, London, WC2R 1LA

ISBN:9781805263067 ISSN: 2048-8475

To subscribe or place an order by credit/debit card or cheque (pounds sterling only) please contact Kathleen May at the Hurst address above or e-mail kathleen@hurstpub.co.uk

A one-year subscription, inclusive of postage (four issues), costs £60 (UK), £90 (Europe) and £100 (rest of the world), this includes full access to the *Critical Muslim* series and archive online. Digital only subscription is £3.30 per month.

The right of Ziauddin Sardar and the Contributors to be identified as the authors of this publication is asserted by them in accordance with the Copyright, Designs and Patents Act, 1988.

A Cataloguing-in-Publication data record for this book is available from the British Library

Critical Muslim

Subscribe to Critical Muslim

Now in its fourteenth year in print, *Critical Muslim* is also available online. Users can access the site for just £3.30 per month – or for those with a print subscription it is included as part of the package. In return, you'll get access to everything in the series (including our entire archive), and a clean, accessible reading experience for desktop computers and handheld devices — entirely free of advertising.

Full subscription

The print edition of *Critical Muslim* is published quarterly in January, April, July and October. As a subscriber to the print edition, you'll receive new issues directly to your door, as well as full access to our digital archive.

United Kingdom £60/year
Europe £90/year
Rest of the World £100/year

Digital Only

Immediate online access to *Critical Muslim*

Browse the full *Critical Muslim* archive

Cancel any time

£3.30 per month

www.criticalmuslim.io

CM53

WINTER 2025

CONTENTS

WATER

Photo: Alev Adil

Photo: Ziauddin Sardar

WATER

}

INTRODUCTION:
IMAGES OF WATER

C Scott Jordan

Study chemistry long enough and you are bound to come across this gem. It usually presents as a public service announcement warning you of the next horrible thing we should all fear. It is a spectre – colourless, odourless, tasteless – the undetectable assassin of untold millions. It is dihydrogen monoxide or DHMO because nothing quite scares like an acronym! This relatively simple chemical is the most prevalent of all harmful chemicals to human life. Governments, civic leaders, militaries, corporations, and citizens openly ignore this silent killer, denying the attention we must give it – now! The announcement goes on to explain that dihydrogen monoxide is a major part of acid rain, is found in excised cancer tumours, it corrodes metal, it erodes landscapes, and it is found in every river, lake, and ocean. It is a fire retardant that is also used in nuclear powerplants and in a variety of methods of cruel and unethical animal research. Most deaths from this substance are contributed to excessive inhalation. It improves athletic performance but can cause severe burns and contributes to Greenhouse Effects. Prolonged exposure to dihydrogen monoxide in its solid form can cause severe tissue damage. Symptoms of dihydrogen monoxide ingestion include excessive sweating, urination, and severe electrolyte misbalance. It is also the most addictive substance known to science, withdrawal of dihydrogen monoxide spells certain death.

This pedagogic ruse, a fun way to get you in the mood for writing out chemical equations, ought to evaporate when you work out the equation for dihydrogen monoxide. H_2O. What I like about this fun bit of misinformation (before it was widely fashionable), is that it makes you think about something that we often take for granted as one of the classic 'givers of life'. More appropriately, we might call the ruse 'alternative

information' as it does not necessarily speak lies, but weaponises the truth for the purposes of stoking fear – if, that is, anyone were to take the PSA seriously. There is a beauty to water when we really think about it. It demonstrates a balance that a lot of contemporary thought attempts to detract us from. Water both gives and takes away life. It is both tranquillity and fury. Its beauty is found in such delightful contradictions. Returning briefly to that chemical symbol, H_2O, it is a strange molecule. It is 'bent', quite literally due to the polarity of the bond between the oxygen and hydrogen atoms. Because of that bent configuration, life is possible in the universe, add on a couple other thousand circumstances, coincidences, clever moves, elaborate traps, or elegant architectures (dependent upon your perspective) and the history of the planet Earth was allowed to proceed. Faith aside, that makes this bent little molecule quite miraculous. Thank God for physics. Thank God for the laws of attraction between opposite forces. My ultimate fear in all of this, is that since this molecule is such a beautiful and enduring hunk of atoms, it becomes easy to think it will always be there and thus can, dare I say should, be taken for granted.

I doesn't take a degree from Oxford for one to imagine why so many of the first human settlements and thereafter so many of our civilisations revolve around bodies of water. And because of that existential need for water that our communities possess, it is not hard to imagine why water makes for such a rich character in so many of our memories. The water racing from the hose that waters the garden. Perhaps it is connected to a sprinkler which we ran through as children on a hot summer day. Back when summer was distinguishable from other seasons. An ice cube melting on the skin under a scorching sun that also delivers a long overdue dose of Vitamin D. Condensation droplets crawling on the side of a can of cold drink. Beachy holidays. The spring rain puddles we once splashed in. The childhood baths with shampoo-induced spikey hairdos surrounded by floaty toys. Picturesque, but also in these comforts and vivid memories we have an entry point into water, something otherwise hard to empathise without getting too abstract or scientific about it. Of course it is not always comfort, but equally as cinematographic for our minds is the fears and troubles with water. We might as easily recall quivering in the aftermath of body rattling thunder as we watch dazzling lightning dance across the sky as rain tok-toks on the window. Or recall disasters, such as

floods, that we have seen from our personal experience or from television news broadcasts, or a funny amalgam of the two our hippocampus likes to play at when slicing our memories together for long-term storage.

It was certainly not by design, but the contributors to this issue have largely taken a biographical approach to their essays. Ebrahim Moosa, in the midst of a cosmological analysis of the Quranic experience of water, brings us to his childhood growing up in Cape Town, South Africa, on the coast of the Atlantic Ocean. Luke Wilkinson takes us to the island of Malta, where he lived youthful memories surrounded by the Mediterranean Sea. Christopher Jones, who was born on the Pacific Coast in the US state of California, speaks of his first lessons of water conservation during a great drought in 1977. Ironically, as they lived so near the world's largest ocean, they were still so far away from clean drinking water. His essay goes on to follow his nomadic lifestyle as he went on to live in Costa Rica and Hawaii among other locales that are almost synonymous with water. John Lietchy notes that 'water makes us who we are,' as he recalls his parents' Edenic memories of their own childhood wonderlands in the US near Deer creek in Iowa and along the Ohio River Valley before taking us around our watery world through poetry, prose, and history. When discussing big issues, making that empathetic link is crucial to building a collective sense of a need for action — something we drastically need in terms of water. After all, over 70 percent of the planet is covered in the stuff. As much as we consume and then frequent, often inconvenient trips to the loo at night, might give us a hint that perhaps the water we take is equal to the water we make. Though, if you've had a lot of tea, it might be that you are in fact making more than what is taken! It is easy to take for granted.

I, much like Lietchy, have an intimate relationship with water. My earliest aquatic memories are of my maternal grandfather who served in the US Coast Guard and his tales at sea. His penchant for stories I owe a great debt to for fostering my own capacities and love of writing. He spoke of his epic battles with the real pirates of the Caribbean who he noted were not like Errol Flynn or Johnny Depp, but real nasty fellows. The pirates of the 1940s and 1950s were less swash buckling but no less cutthroat with their pursuits of illicit drugs and trafficking humans. Forget swords clinking and muskets, consider automatic machine guns and their drug-fuelled wielders.

When I was very young, my grandfather would read to me Herman Melville's *Moby Dick* with great passion. He concluded his reading by pointing to his bookshelf where there sat a scrimshaw – a carving made into the side of a whale's tooth – which bore the inky black, detailed image of an eighteenth-century naval frigate. 'I found old Hermie's white whale, and you can bet I didn't let him get the best of me!'

My father severed in the US Navy in the early 1980s. He didn't talk much about it. The only time he spoke openly of his time in the Navy concerned a ceremony and a special mission. The ceremony was a rite of passage for young navy men. They would sail across the International Dateline whereby they suddenly became a day older and had their first experience with time travel. The special mission came up one day when the news announced that so-and-so had won the Nobel Peace Prize. 'Let me tell you how peace is made,' my father began. The mission involved my dad, his close mates, a handful of diplomats from Britian, the US, and Argentina, and a pub somewhere in the southern seas. Several, a pronoun not to be taken lightly here, rounds of beer later a peace was agreed, and the Falkland Island War had ended. For this my dad felt he deserved both the Nobel Prize and a special burial plot in Arlington National Cemetery, the 'most hallowed ground in America', a military cemetery made from land once owned by the defeated Civil War General Robert E. Lee, the ultimate salt-in-the-wound for the vanquished.

While my mother never commanded a vessel on the high seas, to the best of my knowledge, she could never be kept far from a body of water. The beach, a lake, even a hot tub or bathtub were regular necessities. Floating in defiance of gravity was my mother's paradise. Earlier in her life, lived between Omaha, Nebraska and Council Bluffs, Iowa the bordering Missouri River was considered too treacherous for recreational frivolity. Everyone had a tale of that 'one' friend who found a premature watery grave during fun and games by the river. The man-made lake to the south of Council Bluffs, Lake Manawa, made for a suitable substitute for Midwesterners without the experience of 'going to the beach'. Though, the domineering powerplant on one side of the lake always made me wonder if our holidays spent in those waters has increased our chance of cancer and other such health complications. Water shoes were always a necessity for visits to the lake as dumping at one point in its history had left

the mystery of what lies on the lake floor a big enough question mark not to be gambled upon. Many memories, the good, the bad, and the ugly were formed at Lake Manawa. In fact, the only surviving photo I have of my good infant self, accompanied by both my mother and father, all with smiles plastered on our faces, was taken on that beach sometime during the George H. W. Bush administration. While a terraformed lake can bring the 'California' experience to the good folks of Iowa, my mother also noted the limits of water's magic. While serving in the Peace Corps on the island nation of Jamaica, she saw some of the most beautiful beaches in the world, then turned around, looking inland, seeing some of the greatest human atrocities. The political situation of the 1970s and 1980s did not help to advance an already struggling nation with a history of slavery, extreme poverty, and regular hurricanes to boot. Development was a dead-on-launch endeavour. The worse of it was when my mother had to drive a truck around collecting human remains. An extreme view in Rastafarianism holds that if a body is moved after expiry, then the soul will not be able to find it when the Resurrection takes place. Yet for public safety and sanitation, the bodies needed to be put in a proper place. So, as the cries of bereaved loved ones reached ear piercing decibels, my mother could look to the crashing waves on the peaceful beech. Sometimes contradictions can be therapeutic, even sources of hope. And while my grandfather, the pirate-fighting coast guard, had perhaps embellished that my mother was born on the worst of all April showers, she has made it very clear that when her time comes, she is to be cremated, and her ashes dedicated to the ocean. Why must it be dust to dust, when it can be water droplet to water droplet.

While I do not crave the beachy holiday, chlorine and urine rich water parks, recycled watery fun, cruises, or whitewater rafting, I can appreciate water. In fact, I have one distinct memory that solidifies one of the true moments of peace I have found around water. While traveling in the south of Spain, I came to Grenada and spent an entire day in the Alhambra complex. One thing that stuck with me was that all around the complex you hear running water. A complex of streams and fountains always provided for that ambient sound of water trickly in movement. You won't notice it if you don't take the time, but it drowns out the commotion of other tourists. I hope more have memories like this. Instead of reinforcing

the easily taken advantage of existence of water, usually in quantities that would never have our heads wondering what if it runs out, a memory like these forces one to think, what if it wasn't here. I can quickly imagine the Alhambra complex if the water were removed. It would be another shell of history, dry and cracking beneath the wait of far too many tourists over saturated with pursuers of selfies and the annoying cacophony people away from home tend to produce, mostly unconsciously. Films do this to us also.

As a 90s Sci-Fi kid, I was no stranger to the universe of Frank Herbert's *Dune*, watching the late cinematic master David Lynch's version numerous times. In our times of water crisis, it helps to be reminded of what it might be like to have to recycle one's own sweat and urine for sustenance. Liam Mayo analyses the 2011 animated film *Rango*. The story follows a pet chameleon that becomes stranded in the desert after being separated from his family on a road trip. He stumbles upon a town called Dirt, an outpost in lack of law and water. Mayo shows how such situations draw out identities together in a complexifying shared spaces, especially during crisis, perhaps even multi- and permacrisis. The film shares a spiritual connection to the classic 1974 film *Chinatown*, the standard for good screenwriting to this day. Yet those who recall the film may not first associate it with water crisis, the whole backdrop for the film was a real-life scandal where rich elites were buying up and hoarding the limited drinking water available in order to create an artificial drought for profit in 1930s California. It is literally the backbone of the story, yet the film has rich and complex characters interwoven so you may be forgiven for forgetting that is what it was all about. Evil acts are conducted but the moral audience should be saying, 'hey wait a minute'. We need more of this for our present water crisis, and I assure you it is indeed a crisis. Talk to those of Chennai, Cape Town, Istanbul, Cairo. While it can be said that a variety of disaster movies, of varying quality, helped to bring home the threat of climate change, a battle still remains with the water crisis. Of course, the two crises are intimately related, and increasingly more by the day as complexity itself increases in postnormal times. But we can't let the ease of generalisation allow for a discrediting of the very real water crisis before us. Especially because it is not only that water is finite and running out, but that it is becoming the new source of conflict.

While our minds may drift towards more fantastical images, such as those offered by the 1995 polar icecap melted world of *Water World,* the water wars visible in headlines and on news reports are much subtler, but no less catastrophic. The recent conflicts in both Iraq and Syria have given us a more contemporary image of water wars. Water has been weaponised. More accurately, access to water has been weaponised. Over the last decade of war in these two countries, water reserves and infrastructure have been targeted by combatant forces resulting in a diversion of clean water or a cutting off of access to the people. As a result, a seedy underworld of water criminals have arisen, illegally drilling wells or even become devilish private water salespeople. The most desperate have resorted to drinking water from unclean and unsafe areas resulting in a massive uptick of waterborne diseases, including cholera. In Palestine, the weaponisation of water access is a well-honed tool in the arsenal of the Israel Defence Forces, a tried and tested staple of their tactics going back to the 1960s. Now we are seeing the technique implemented in the ongoing war between Russia and Ukraine. The UK water system always seems one disaster away from all the English villages turning into Mad Max fiefdoms warring over guzzoline, water, tea, milk, and eggs! And with the US water disaster in Flint, Michigan, it is not hard to imagine how some national governments could, if they are not already, weaponising access to water. Think of how the price of bottled water itself has increased over the last decade. And this isn't just the water with added minerals, electrolytes, and half a pharmacy for improved vitality, basic purified bottled water itself has been on the rise. Capitalism continues to consume. And it shouldn't be a difficult task to argue access to clean water as a fundamental human right before we even begin talking of Sustainable Development Goals (SDGs)!

The British sustainability journalist Tim Smedley has given us two critical texts in the last five years, 2020's *Clearing the Air* and 2023's *The Last Drop* looking at the global air and water crises respectively. But it is their two respective subtitles that speak loudest: *The Beginning and End of Air Pollution* and *Solving the World's Water Crisis.* While both books are highly accessible, borrowing from his own travel accounts, they are books of action. In *The Last Drop*, Smedley notes that we see this 'crisis' in our own localised way quite frequently, but we can't quite take our local

experiences and extrapolate or sync them to the reality of an increasingly global crisis. We keep the notions separate and therefore do not see a global crisis until something equivalent to a doomsday scenario knocks at the door. Our advantage is that for the most part, especially in the wake of the Covid-19 pandemic, the climate crisis is accepted (even if our approaches to the reality may still differ), but now we need to take these common experiences we have in our day-to-day lives, from the water cuts we might experience during routine maintenance, after heavy flooding, or in the event that our municipal authority closes the main as a result of drought, and see these as mosaic tiles in a much larger global picture.

That is the first step, I would say not only should we take our own brushes with disaster, action demanding as they most certainly are, but to take our own biographical memories with water and imagine if that lake were to run dry, if that river were to die (as we are witnessing in real time with the sick and dying Nile River in Egypt), if the garden hose drew its last drops, if no water was running in Alhambra. Jeremy Henzell-Thomas's resonant essay explores how dreaming is not simply for escaping, but how dreaming is a biologically necessary process that restores the body while resetting the mind and self, especially in a spiritual sense, for the new day ahead. Our dreams, which can quickly shift into nightmares, should not be left as escapist wells to take for granted, but inform how we live our day-to-day lives so that we can begin, in our own small and local ways, to solve our collective water crisis as Smedley proposes we can.

As we build a solidarity between our own experiences and the global experience of the water crisis, we should also note that sometimes our logic, when combined with a reductionist mindset, betrays our appreciation of the real situation. Smedley's book is not just an exercise in cheerleading awareness, he notes that the West is behind on this matter. The cities of Chennai and Cape Town have emerged from their crises, though they do not parade about in hubris. Likewise, Singapore has avoided the catastrophe's California is desperately marred in. Jordan and Ghana are thriving in innovating solutions to their water problems while the US and Europe pray that doomsday scenario can be staved off for another year.

But how do we think of climate change. The average western logical appreciation of climate change precedes like this. We are experiencing global warming, icecaps are melting, sea levels are rising, winters are shrinking, summer is always coming. This makes logical sense. So, in the world of policy, places like Kansas City have cut the budget for snowploughs and other road clearing measures during inclement weather. But this logic has a flawed appreciation of climate change, our climate catastrophe. It is not simply that temperatures are rising and things are getting hot, it is that these changes are creating greater complexity in our weather patterns and thus allowing chaos to take the wheel of meteorology. Greater chaos makes weather events harder and harder to predict accurately. So, while temperatures are generally increasing and the effects thereafter are taking place, the overall weather system of the globe is more and more off kilter. So, yes, sea levels are rising, but this is changing wind patterns, causing more (sometimes simultaneous) hurricanes, increasing the likely condition for tornadoes in places that have never seen such events, increasing the speed and severity of droughts and floods, creating more ideal conditions for cataclysmal wildfires, and occasionally dumping heavy volumes of winter, not seen in a decade, on places that thought this was only possible in the nostalgic past. In light of this, yes, the logic is not necessarily wrong, but it does not give us the full picture. Perhaps the amount of funds given to winter preparations need not be what they were a decade ago, but enough should be given to be ready for such events instead of rushing to build the next sports venue, mega-mall, or other attractor for the one-percenters in a place that has thriven on the fostering of the middle class since the end of World War II! Then again, perhaps the concentrated hate wafting into town with the influx of fascistic nouveau riche Americans looking to settle in the Midwest will raise temperatures enough to easily combat combined freezing rain and heavy snowfall. Then I ask, are we feeling lucky?

Of course, it is not wise to leave such chaotically complex and existential matters to either slot machines or empty prayers. We have plenty of images of the stakes. The clearest one sits just on the edge of Jakarta. Wietske Merison takes us to the Waladuna Mosque: a haunting image of the not-too-distant future. Just outside of Jakarta, a seawall separates the mosque from the city's limits, as the mosque has been surrendered to the

sea, now sitting one meter below the sea. It is the ever-present indication that Jakarta, capital of Indonesia, the most populous Muslim city in the world, is a sinking city. Climate change considered, most Muslim civilisation reside along the equatorial belt and thus face one of two options in the extended present future. Either these cities are swallowed by the waves or become completely deprived, abandoned to desertification. While the climate catastrophe is a global reality, ditto the water crisis, it is the Muslims who will be hit first and hardest – regardless of who did what and who is at fault. This need not be destiny. For it is in the Muslim perspectives and the myriad experiences and ways of thinking found in our various traditions that we might imagine a way out of this. But it is important not to limit ourselves to the thought of Muslims, but also learn from the mistakes made by the West and look with critical curiosity to other ways of thinking, especially in China, Africa, and the various indigenous ways of living that have allowed their societies to weather the choppy waters of time.

At the dawn of the Covid-19 pandemic, Malaysia was preparing itself for a lockdown. I found myself in the company of the British writer and anthropologist, the late Merryl Wynn Davies. Over a cup of coffee in her Kuala Lumpur salon, Merryl posed a problem in her own unique way.

'You', she said, 'as a practitioner of the art of foresight, we, as avid consumers of the news, and we as holders of foreign passports in a foreign land, noting the scourge of virus, do you, I put it to you, do you not see a lurking future problem?'. The problem she was referring to was the renewal of our visas. The government had planned a two-week lockdown. But neither of us believed that this was going to be a such a short interlude, given the ever-rising number of cases and deaths reported. We quickly reasoned this could go on for much longer, like two, three or even four months (we had no idea) and that it would be in our interests to renew our entry visa so as to avoid future immigration problems.

So, plans were made and tickets bought for us to journey to Singapore for a quick stay before returning. And then the Malaysian government of the day, in its infinite incompetence, moved the lockdown date up and new plans had to be made, tickets burned. Thankfully, a friend drove Merryl and I the five-hour car ride to Singapore for an 'afternoon trip'. While I jaunted about and had coffee with a colleague, Merryl checked into a hotel with an

interesting request. She always booked rooms in seaside cities with a view of the bay. I was to learn this was her habit. I knew that we both were from working-class stock. Now, I learned we also descended from sailors and mariners. Although born in different times and places, we were connected through the nautical knowledge passed down from our descendants. For instance: see a red sky at morning, sailor take warning (for rough weather ahead), red sky at night, sailors delight. This, as Merryl pointed out at every opportunity, also draws a tight bond between us and Malaysia, the peoples of the Malay Archipelago having to master both the trials of land and sea in order to see their civilisations grow and thrive. Both these spaces require entirely different ways of thinking to traverse and, in our postnormal times, we need all the different ways of thinking we can get. Those of the terrestrial persuasion take for granted the cardinal directions of north, south, east, and west, where the oceans provide a new host of directional thinking. Think of those under the water, or in the air for that matter, who think not just in planes but in three-dimensional space. Merryl also noted that waking up and seeing the sea gave her a comfort that she could just as easily be waking up and looking out at the Straits of Singapore or the South China Sea or the Bristol Channel or the Irish Sea from her home in Wales. On the sea, Merryl was always connected to home. Of course, she would then go on to explain how Welsh sailors, and particularly Welsh steel, held the British Empire together; and there would be a few expletives thrown in during this discourse.

But it is a nice thought, to be connected. Isn't it? To be part of a world where we have shared homes, shared memories, and shared ideas. And while the differences remain, they have values which help us tackle the collective problems that we face. And while nationalism, and even fascism, leave our global population fighting over home, mother, and fatherlands, why not be connected by water. It is after all, as Naomi Foyle points out, the perfect metaphor for change, for balance, for renewal. We humans are also water. Collectively we can be an ocean for change in our small and great deeds. As we think differently about water, we can think differently about ourselves and our world and make sure the water of our dreams and memories never run dry. And in our new ways of thinking, we can save those streams, rivers, lakes, and oceans that make us who we are.

ENDLESS SHORES

Ebrahim Moosa

'Kinds of water drown us. Kinds of water do not.'

I feel that these two lines by Anne Carson, the Canadian poet and essayist, are addressed to me.

I found deep meaning in these ten words; and can admit they made a great deal of sense to me and resonated with my life experiences.

But why does water, among all the elements humans encounter, occupy such a significant place in both our survival as a species as well as in our imagination? Of course, some might rightfully say what humans, animals, and plants do biologically, and minerals do chemically, need water for their survival and to sustain any kind of existence. But why does air not occupy such a privileged place? For surely, humans, animals, and plants cannot survive without oxygen. Why have philosophers, poets, artists, prophets, and divinities across time given water such a privileged place but did not consider the importance of air? Why has fire, not been valued as much as water, especially since there is almost nothing we can do without heat and energy. Especially our modern world is almost entirely dependent on all forms of energy, what our ancient philosopher forbears described as fire.

Well, it is not entirely true that other than water additional elements were not considered as vital candidates for this privileged role. Ancient philosophers did indeed struggle and agonise about which one of these elements—air, water, fire, earth—was the truly vital one for our continued existence. Known as the pre-Socratic philosophers, some of them said it was 'fire,' others said it was 'air' and the one who earned the highest reputation, said 'water' was the organising 'principle' of the world. So now the question is: how did water win out in the sweepstakes to be the primary organising principle? This is a more challenging question to

answer. The eleventh-century Muslim philosopher and physician Ibn Sina also known as Avicenna, noted that water was the only of the four elements that can penetrate with whatever it is mixed. Given that he was a physician, he also ranked the different kinds of water based on the properties of their sources.

There might be more than a few reasons as to why water captured such a large place in our imagination. My own brushes with water have also deeply coloured my perception of this non-viscous, translucent, and fluid element. It might have to do with our dependence and encounters with water in so many, different ways.

Cosmology of Water

Water, in the twenty first century, is a ubiquitous resource: it is our friend and enemy at the same time. Climatologists and scientists are now agreed that we have entered the age of the Anthropocene, an age in which human activities indelibly influence the earth's climate and ecosystems. Some 11,700 years ago until the present, the previous age was known as the Holocene. That period saw the growth of cities, technological advancement from agriculture, metallurgy to writing. But the new ways of living we have adopted for especially the past 300 years, have now left clear human imprints on the face of the earth.

With climate change literally taking the globe by storm—we find in some places an abundance of water and in other areas of the world there is a paucity of it. Six major global cities suffered drought conditions in the past decade. Sao Paulo in Brazil, Cape Town in South Africa, Chennai in India, Mexico City in Mexico, and Flint, Michigan and Jackson, Mississippi, both in the US, experienced severe drought conditions often with water restrictions or with a caution about consuming hazardous water. An abundance of water in the form of irregular and dramatically violent hurricanes and floods in the US, Europe, South Asia, China, and Australia now afflict the world on a frequent basis. Between 2014 and 2023, the economic impact of flooding in the US alone had tipped to over 1.2 trillion dollars in infrastructure damage as well as loss to housing and agriculture in 173 separate weather and climate related disasters, most of which took the form of floods.

The African American novelist and writer, James Baldwin predicted fire will destroy the world next. He thought that fire will be worse than water, when he wrote, 'God gave Noah the rainbow sign, No more water, the fire next time!'

But it seems that we are still in the age of Noah, with many more violent and unpredictable water and flood conditions. The toll of water-based climate disaster to human and animal life in addition to environmental destruction would possibly have surprised Noah too!

Does water have to do with the way our part of the cosmos is shaped? Or does it have some connection to aspects of existence we cannot comprehend—beyond our physical existence? Namely, is water a metaphysical issue? Water is clearly ubiquitous in both our language and our imagination. If water were a metaphysical question, then it would mean that water plays a role in a mode of thinking that allows us to imagine the big picture of who we are and our place in this cosmos. Water then would be in the mix of how we anchor ourselves here on earth, with values and beliefs and, we might wonder if water has any role in how we imagine the possibilities of the beyond—the afterlife.

The existence of water also remains a scientific question. It has something to do with the composition of our earth and the part of the cosmos to which we belong. Scientists are keen to see if water ever existed or exists on the moon or on Mars. Somehow science—especially the life sciences—thinks of water as elemental to our origins and our survival. Planetary palaeontology is an emerging field that combines planetary science and palaeontology—the science that carefully studies animal and plant fossils. These experts study the surfaces of planets in search of past life and biosignatures looking for life beyond the earth. And the markers they look for are the biosignatures for water.

Long before the advent of modern science, some six hundred years before Jesus walked on earth, a philosopher lived in Ionia, the ancient name for modern-day Turkey, once an ancient Greek colony. Some 30 kilometres from the city of Söke, in Turkey's Aydın Province, near the Aegean coast, is a place called Miletus, an antique city. Here Thales of Miletus was born somewhere between 624 and 620 BCE and where he died between 548 and 545. In Miletus, he flourished as a philosopher, mathematician, and astronomer. Despite his many accomplishments,

Thales is best known for his explanation that water is the fundamental substance underlying all matter. He posited water as the *archê*, the fundamental thing underlying all existence. Believing that the earth was a flat disc, he also suggested that the earth floats on water. He might have been half right in this intuition. Now we know that the largest surface of our planet is covered by water. Yes, what we now do know is that our planet does not ski on water.

Thales is a pre-Socratic philosopher: the name of the era before empirical science became separated from philosophy. In this phase of history, people engaged in 'wonder' and 'curiosity' about certain problems. 'Wonder' and 'curiosity,' as the Jesuit historian of philosophy, Frederick Copleston wrote, were the two intellectual drivers which served as the fountainhead of both philosophy and science. Roughly 2,500 years ago, thanks to Thales, humanity did have some idea that water was in some shape or form indispensable to human existence.

Some 1,200 years after Thales died, this knowledge and wisdom of the pre-Socratics must have circulated in the wisdom traditions of the Near East and possibly known to people in that region. The revelation vouchsafed to the Prophet Muhammad in the seventh century also made a passing observation about the indispensable role of water. Working in the Arabian desert, the Prophet Muhammad laboured hard to persuade humanity to recognise that there was a sovereign Creator of the world. Humanity was invited to look around them and to see if they could behold and recognise the work of a Divine Artisan of the cosmos. In the Qur'an it was stated as:

> Have those who disbelieved not considered that the heavens and the earth were sewn together and we rent them asunder? *And we made every living thing from water.* Will they not then believe? (21:30.)

The Qur'an too is interested in drawing our attention to the earth and the firmament—in other words to the far and beyond, in what we today would refer to as our cosmic dimension. Then almost nonchalantly and parenthetically, the Qur'anic verse states: 'and we made every living thing, from water.' This observation is stated in such a manner as if it was an accepted fact among the first listeners of the revelation that water is the source of every living thing. It was not in a form of a contentious question.

But on further consideration, it is as if the story of the creation of all living things stemming from water is connected to a stack of heavens that were torn asunder. And furthermore, that it points to a direction that we are eminently accustomed to: water pours down from above us, namely the heavens, as rain. Irrespective of the source of water, the question remains: were the people of seventh century Arabia, the audience of the Qur'an, already familiar with this idea of Thales? Did they subscribe to the idea of the centrality of water to all of existence? In other words, would we philosophically describe water as a source of being? Is water only associated to every living thing, meaning only restricted to animals? The philosophically minded twelfth-century theologian and exegete of the Qur'an, the indomitable Fakhr al-Din al-Razi, explains that every living thing comprised of water including vegetation. In short, this verse means that water is included in everything that springs to life, in Razi's view.

Surely, the people of the Arabian desert, the first listeners to the Qur'an, knew how essential water was for human survival and for animals and vegetation to thrive. There is a strong indication that they already subscribed to the notion that water is essential for the creation of every living thing. Perhaps they did not describe it the way Thales pressed the point, philosophically, but close enough. Stylistically the attention of the verse is on the rhetorical question: 'will they not then believe?' It becomes clear that to the best of our knowledge, humanity recognised the integral role of water to life.

Planetary palaeontologists are not obsessed without good reason in trying to find water in other locations and planets in our known cosmos. In the Hebrew Bible, we read in Genesis 1:2-3: 'the earth was a formless void, and darkness covered the face of the deep, while a wind from God swept over the face of the waters.' It is then that God said: 'let there be light'. In the Biblical version water is primordial and it was in existence since the time when the earth was formless and dark.

Poetics of Water

Figures of speech are rhetorical devices that use language in creative and non-literal ways to create a specific effect in the listener, reader, or viewer of texts and art. It is designed to create a deep emotive effect within the

reader or listener, moving them to action, provoking within them certain feelings, and evoking specific desires. Water is frequently used as a figure of speech in multiple languages of the world. Water takes both a literal and figurative form in poetry and literary expression.

Let's take as an example the most famous Arab poet of all time, Abu Tayyib al-Mutanabbi. Mutanabbi, his nickname means to be a 'pretender' to prophecy. He became infamous thanks to his self-professed, but youthful claim, that he was a 'prophet' in his native Kufa in the tenth century. Perhaps no one took note of his childhood fantasy, possibly because everyone admired his eloquence in composing poetry. But in adulthood, this ostensible blasphemy landed him in prison where he was coerced to forswear such heresy of being a claimant to whatever definition of prophecy he conjured. His genius as a wit, drenched in ambition and pride, all contributed to his insightful commentary on the human condition and made him immortal in the annals of Arabic poetry. His memorable lines smack of ambition and self-confidence, when he said: 'if you venture for a lofty aim, do not settle for anything less than the stars'.

Water in Mutanabbi's poetry is a symbol and metaphor for purity and beauty. He could confidently and effortlessly sketch with words:

A face, as if the sun had cast its cloak upon it
And the light of water glistens and reflects upon it.

Water also signifies generosity, benevolence, and open-handedness in Arabic poetry. An object of admiration, especially a generous person, can be described and personified as a cloud. Why a cloud? Clouds provide the life-giving source—water. Like mercy and guidance, some water reaches us from the firmament above us. Arabic poetry and poets love the image of clouds. Patronage in the pre-modern world was essential to the survival of poets and writers. Thus, they had to boost the egos of their patrons and praise their accomplishments in rhymed words.

In one poem Mutanabbi recalls:

When the battlefield is showered by clouds of generosity
Just as the rainclouds nourish the fields.

Note that poetry was the equivalent of the media in the premodern world. News of what transpired in palaces and courts in terms of

accomplishments were communicated by poets. In a sense, court poets played the role of today's public relations officers, except that these men of letters were highly accomplished individuals. Their words in praise of their patrons and rulers soon found a way to literary salons of the time and from there to the lips, hearts, and minds of the broader public. And hard to secure patrons provided the life-giving support that literary figures like Mutanabbi desperately needed.

Another touching expression is where water connects with honour. An expression in Arabic literally means 'he shed the water of his face (*araqa ma' wajh-hihi*)', meaning he sacrificed his honour. Put differently, a truly free person or a person of integrity 'does not shed the water of his face': meaning he or she does not bring dishonour to herself, does not lose face. In other words, they maintain their dignity, they retain the water of their faces.

The inimitable fourteenth-century Persian poet Shamsuddin Hafiz frequently uses water in his poetry. For Hafiz water is often a symbol of the beloved's beauty. If exposed to sunlight, then water always shimmers. Hence this iridescent feature serves as an analogy for the beloved's qualities of physical beauty and spiritual attraction. In Hafizs lines below, the poet blends the love for a mortal friend with love for the Divine. The words used to describe the beloved are also the very same words used to describe the Divine colours and the Divine essence.

> With such love-filled words in praise of the friend
> Every form I paint flows from His water and hues.

In ancient Iranian culture, especially among the Zoroastrians, water was as essential as fire. In their cosmology water was the second of the seven 'creations' into which the world was divided. In Hafiz, water is also a symbol of divine grace, first and foremost. Water by its fluid nature in one form can flow, adapt, and take the shape of its container. Water can flow but it can also carve a rock. Water changes form: liquid can turn into solid ice, liquid or solid ice can turn into a vapour and then the cycle repeats itself. Just as water, in most instances, reaches humans effortlessly, so too does divine grace and mercy reach humans in infinite ways—effortlessly. No wonder when people pray to God, they ask the Divine to pour or rain mercy on them and all of humanity. At most times, gifts and sustenance flow to humans freely: whether through the laws of nature or as acts of

Divine solicitude. All gifts that humans receive flow to them as freely as
water reaches human habitations. Thus, water is life-giving and has a
power almost like fire, but it treacherously appears more subdued in some
instances, before the flood. Hafiz personifies water on a face of a lover,
but curiously it is quietly combustible: it gives a glow, but it does not
consume the blossoms:

> Drunk and drenched, you stroll in the garden,
> Drops from your face kindle flames within the crimson blossoms

Water and wine are sometimes paired in Hafiz: one forms the base for
the other. Water is for purification; it cleanses the body. Wine, in turn, is
the beverage for elevation: it lifts the spirit to celestial heights. Water also
serves as a mirror reflecting the Divine essence and mirrors the inner
reaches of the human soul. It is the clarity and depth of water that
generates the purity needed to perceive the divine truth.

However, few poets can outperform Jalaluddin Rumi with his oceanic
imagination—no pun intended! Rumi is a master in his abundant and
detailed use of the multiple symbolisms of water. In the Islamic tradition
two prophetic figures, Noah and Jonah, are associated with water and
oceans. Noah, however, became the more popular figure in the Abrahamic
tradition, given the account of how most of his people perished in water
because of their disobedience to God. Noah toils to convince his people to
turn to God for a long time, and in the end only a handful of them and
several animals survive God's wrath. Rumi pays little attention to the
details of the event, but rather provides insights into the bigger picture
that unfolds:

> Noah continued to call (the people to God) for nine hundred years: the unbe-
> lief of his folk was increasing from moment to moment.
> Did he ever pull back the rein of speech? Did he creep into the cave of silence?

Of course, Noah continued his task to invite people to God despite his
myriads of detractors. Noah continued in what was his task, just as a
caravan does not turn back from its journey because of the clamour of
dogs. Nor does the moon change its course at full moon, because of a
dog's incessant wailing. Everyone has their allotted task. Then Rumi
continues with his interesting analogies to show how devoted Noah was:

Wrath is like vinegar, and mercy is like honey—together, they form the foundation of every oxymel (a mixture of honey and vinegar).

If the honey can't balance the vinegar, the oxymel will be ruined.

People kept pouring vinegar (wrath) on Noah, but the Ocean of Divine Generosity kept pouring sugar (mercy) for him.

Because Noah's sugar was replenished from the limitless Sea of Divine Bounty, it always outweighed the vinegar of everyone in the world.

It will not be lost on the reader to note how Rumi personifies divine bounty as an ocean and a sea, an inexhaustible source. All negative forces, personified by vinegar, can be neutralised by the sugar, especially if the sweetness came from a boundless source. Embodied with this sensibility, Noah was able to face the harrowing trials and tribulations of his unsympathetic and hostile people. He did so with resilience and determination. He never shrunk from his responsibilities. Just like a good tonic or potion, like oxymel, prophecy becomes resilient due to constant exposure to the vinegar—the taunts of Noah's ungrateful people. But more importantly, it is unrelenting because of the embrace of a divine reassurance to Noah, symbolised by the honey or sugar.

Rumi sums up the notion of resilience in these words:

Who is just one person but has the impact of a thousand? Not just a saint, but a true servant of the Most High (God)—they are worth a hundred generations.

One does not have to be a saint to survive life's trials and tribulations, Rumi believes. All it requires is to be a faithful servant of God, like Noah—who as an individual is honoured and compared to a hundred generations. Why is Noah so special? Because Noah is the equivalent of a jar filled with sea water. All other types of water kneel to that oceanic content out of respect. Listen to how Rumi puts it:

The mighty rivers bow in respect to the humble jar that carries a channel from the vast sea,
Especially this Sea of Reality. When the other seas heard this divine command and powerful call,

They were filled with bitterness and shame, overwhelmed by the realisation
that the Greatest Name had united with something so small.
At the meeting point of this world and the next, this world shrinks back in
humility and shame.

Noah was the vessel of the divine water (the Ocean) and thus was bound
to succeed. Here Rumi points to something profound. As a human being,
as a prophet, you do not have to be a saint who is dedicated to the worship
of God. As a devout saint you will still just be one person among many.
Think for a moment about the huge amount of water in a river: it is
abundant and intimidating. Yet, when you bring water from the ocean,
even in a small amount—in a jar or a container, then by the mere presence
of the ocean water, the river water is intimidated by the water from the
sea! River water bows to the jar of sea water. Why? For the river
acknowledges its limits in the face of the unlimited water of the ocean. So
too the prophet of God, he personifies a jar of ocean water, he stands in
proximity to the Sea of Reality. The saint merely swims for gratification
in a river or a tributary; as a prophet, he works for all of humanity and has
the support of the Greatest Name.

Water was not only limited to poetry, but also had a link to architecture,
if only as a simile. Already in ninth century Arabic poetry the imagery of
water and waves became elements for a simile with polished white marble.
With growing affluence in Abbasid society some spectacular architectural
accomplishments were perfected in the palaces of the caliphs. In some
palaces polished marble was perfected to such a sophisticated sparkle and
glow, that an onlooker thought it was water. We know this from the work
of a renowned Abbasid-era court poet, al-Buhturi. Buhturi in his eulogy
about a palace in the capital city of Samarra, built either by the Abbasid
caliph al-Mu'tasim or his son al-Mutawakkil, draws the following comparison
where marble appears as translucent as water.

As if the glass walls of its interior
Were waves beating upon the seashore
As if its striped marble, where its patter
Meets the opposite prospect,
Were streaks of rainclouds arrayed between clouds, dark and
light, and striped, coming together and mingling.

Water also features in a genre of literature known as the *Wonders of Creation* (*'Ajā'ib al-Makhlūqāt*) going back to the twelfth and thirteenth centuries. These books are rich quarries of information, but they are not often sufficiently mined for material. Meticulously illustrated in rich colours and images, the most famous and well-known of these books is one by Zakariyya b. Muhammad al-Qazwini, author of *The Wonders of Creation and the Oddities of Existence*. Art historian, Persis Berlekamp has done extensive work on this genre in her magnificent book, *Wonder, Image, & Cosmos in Medieval Islam*. Berlekamp draws our attention to another author of this genre about whom we know little, but whose relevance will become clear. Muhammad b. Mahmud al-Tusi is possibly the most reliable name, although he is referred to by other variations of his name. This Tusi was active in the second half of the twelfth century; and also wrote a *Wonders of Creation*, sometimes titled as *The Book of Wonders* (*'Ajā'ibnāma*) and *The World Showing Glass* (*Jām-i Gītī Nāma*). Berlekamp tells us that Tusi wrote about talismans in his *Wonders of Creation*, but guess in which chapter does he discuss it? He writes about talismans in his chapter on oceans, rivers, springs, and wells. It will soon become clear why and what the connection with the ocean is. The story of talismans appears in the entry on the Mediterranean Sea, which our author calls the Sea of Constantinople. This sea extends to the Islands of Felicity and the Valley of the Monkeys, which is the place of the apes, in Berlekamp's analysis.

In this place of the apes, an Abd al-Malik b. Marwan is a revenue collector, not to be confused with a caliph by that name. Abd al-Malik gives orders to divers to get to the bottom of the ocean to bring him gems. One diver comes back with an ewer with some copper pieces coated with tin. The revenue collector demands an account from each diver and each one complained: 'oh, Son of David, for how long will you keep us confined here?' And the story further tells of several thousand ape monkeys emerging, one of them as large as a camel, with a long beard and from his neck was an iron tablet, a talisman, given to him by the great King Solomon. Written on the tablet in Syriac was: 'in the Name of God the Most Significant. This is the writing of demons in this sea: be ye safe from jinn and man'. The ape presented the talisman and demanded that the ewers and pitchers be scattered in the sea, and they be left alone. All

this is partly illustrated in a painting, where small demons with horns and distinct noses can be seen to angrily remonstrate with the diver.

What the description and painting disclose is that these are the demons of Solomon that live in the sea. Medieval Islamic tradition held that in addition to his deep talismanic knowledge, King Solomon also viewed as a prophet in Islam, had knowledge of the stars and was gifted the ability to control the winds.

Qazwini, in turn, in his book of *Wonders* also tells of a story of writing, but this time it is in connection with the river Nile, not an ocean. The incident dates to the first Muslim governor of Egypt, Amr b. al-'As who conquered that land in 641. When the Nile did not flow as usual, the local Egyptians were in a habit of sacrificing a girl to appease the river. When this offering did not bear fruit, Amr wrote to the Caliph in Madina, Umar b. al-Khatib for advice. Umar's advice was prompt and clear. Written on a card sent to Amr was a message to be conveyed to the great river Nile. The message read: 'from Umar, the commander of the faithful, to the Nile of Egypt. As far as you are concerned, you used to flow before and now you do not. God, the One and Almighty was the one who made you flow, therefore we ask Him to make you flow'. Amr threw in the card in the Nile the day before Good Friday, a significant day for the Christians of Egypt. On Good Friday the Nile rose sixteen cubits.

Each story has an underlying moral. The iron tablet as a talisman displayed by the ape exerted power over the revenue collector, Abd al-Malik, since it carried the authority of Solomon himself. The writing of Umar, in turn, did not only have power over the Nile, but also over the Copts who witnessed its efficacy, testifying to the divine will and the power of prayer at the command of the commander of the faithful.

Faith in Water

One of the first textbooks that I studied as a madrasa student in India, once my Arabic was proficient, was titled, *Light of Clarification (Nur al-Idah)* authored by a scholar from Egypt, Abul Ikhlas al-Shurrunbulali, whose last name is even in Arabic, a mouthful. Being able to tap into the writings of the authors who constructed this magnificent intellectual legacy of Islamic scholarship was for me a thrill like none other. Abul Ikhlas became a

renowned professor at the distinguished seminary in Cairo, the al-Azhar. And three hundred years later, tens of thousands of students around the world were still reading his text. The opening chapter in any introductory text on Islamic law focused on rituals would always start with the book of purification. Abul Ikhlas too listed seven types of water authorised for ritual purification. Water collected from rain, sea, rivers, wells, snow, hail, and springs he explained, before going into great detail.

The *Light of Clarification* is among the few textbooks that I still possess from my student days. What happened to the others is still an ache and a loss I feel till today, for it contained my most cherished memories, emotions only books can provide. I had dutifully collected all my textbooks in a metal trunk. And on leaving India I had left the trunk in a basement storage facility at the home of relatives in Mumbai, then known as Bombay in 1981. However, I did not leave my first textbook in the trunk because I carried this one with me to serve as a handy reference to consult whenever I was asked questions on Islamic law after I had graduated. That is the reason I still possess this text from my student days. As to the fate of the rest of my books? Well, I was hoping to earn enough money to pay for the transportation of my trunk of treasured books to South Africa. After several years had elapsed and when I had the means to pay for the shipment, I was informed that my books were soiled and destroyed by periodic floods that afflicted Indian cities and soiled the basement! My madrasa books, in my experience, were the first casualties of climate change.

Few people outside the Muslim community might be aware of how dependent all pious Islamic rituals are on the availability and use of water. Before each of the five daily prayers, a Muslim is required to be in a state of bodily purity. That state of consecration is achieved by washing the hands, face, arms and feet and rubbing the forehead with water, called *wudu*. Some interpretations allow for the rubbing of the feet too with wet hands. That state of consecration is broken by the natural acts of bodily elimination and excretory needs, flatulence, and blood oozing from the body. It is also highly recommended to recite the Qur'an for liturgical purposes, in a state of *wudu*, before touching the revealed book of God. After sexual intercourse, the end of a menstrual cycle, and after childbirth the washing of the full male and female body is a requirement since this is a foundational state of ritual purity. Given the common tradition that

Judaism and Islam shares, the word for ritual purification in Hebrew and Arabic is the same: *taharah, tahara*. In Judaism too there is a requirement to undertake ritual purification involving a full-body immersion in a *mikvah* (ritual bath). In Islam no immersion is required, except that one must ensure that all body parts are washed including the hair, with some exceptions for braided hair. It is enough to pour water over braided hair without the braids being undone. Only in rare instances when water is not available, or water would be harmful to one, does one resort to using earth and soil, to symbolically undertake the ablutions.

Since Islam was birthed in seventh century Arabia, the Muslim tradition annually recalls the story of the Prophet, Ibrahim (Abraham) and his slave wife, Hajar (Hagar) as a basis of the story of the pilgrimage. Hajar was left with her son Isma'il (Ishmael) in the desert by Ibrahim as a trial by God and to soothe the feelings of the then childless other wife of Ibrahim called Sarah. Hajar the mother of Ibrahim's firstborn child soon needed water. Hajar run up and down two hillocks looking for water, but in vain. In the meanwhile, a crying baby Ismaa'il in distress rubbed his feet in the sands and God then miraculously provided water from a source, known as the well of Zamzam. Pilgrims to this day drink this blessed water and bring back jars for their friends and families. And the effort and labour Hajar invested in her panic-stricken search for water for her survival and that of her child—that act is re-enacted symbolically by every pilgrim between the two hills of Safa and Marwa as an essential component of the annual seasonal pilgrimage, called the hajj or when one merely visits the Makkan shrine in a ritual called the *'umra*. That run or gentle jog of Hajar is called the *sa'i*, literally meaning 'effort', a gesture every pilgrim reenacts in their performance of the ritual too.

Water plays an unusual role in the religious imagination as a purificatory element. Through experience we can hardly deny it: the refreshing feeling water has on a face, on a body. Depending on the season the convenience of hot water in winter and cold in summers, each have an impact on the body and psyche.

Yet Islam teaches that water should be conserved not wasted. Islamic ethics based on the teachings of the Prophet Muhammad states that if you are making your ritual ablutions at the edge of a running river, you still do not have a license to waste water!

To the Edge of Water

When I read Anne Carson's words – 'Kinds of water drown us. Kinds of water do not' – they grabbed my mind and soul like a magnet. For I have intimate knowledge of water. As a child I grew up near water. If I stepped out of our family home, in a once multiethnic neighbourhood in the heart of the city of Cape Town called District Six, then to my right was an imposing Table Mountain. Straight, as the crow flies, from our family home to the face of the mountain could not be more than three or four kilometres. To my left, less than three kilometres away, was the expansive Atlantic Ocean. Sights of merchant navy ships, passenger ships, and cranes in the docks of the city of Cape Town, South Africa, were normal to me, it was my everyday visual. Yet, water always intimidated me.

Then in my teens I grew up in a seaside town called, the Strand, some thirty kilometres outside of Cape Town boasting the world's most spectacular beaches: pure white sands, crystal clear water, if you can ignore the occasional sea weeds brought in by the high tide from time to time. If you lift your head on the beachfront, then, at a distance of forty kilometres, you can on a clear day behold the sight of the promontory, a high piece of land falling into the sea, known as Cape Point. This sickle-like piece of land strip geographically turns the surrounding area of Cape Town into a peninsula. This bay, known as the False Bay, has neither the icy water of the Atlantic Ocean nor the lukewarm liquid of the Indian Ocean. It is refreshing.

Even though I lived near the sea, the sound of waves putting me to sleep at night, I could never venture near the sea. First, traditional Indian trader families in South Africa like mine had little time for leisure. Beachgoing and swimming were not their idea of relaxation. Their way of life was different, conservative and restrained. Baring bodies in front of strangers and playing in the water was an entirely different way of life to them. Furthermore, no one in my family could swim from among parents, uncles and aunts and grandparents. The sea and beach were zones of intimidating fear with potential moral terror. But it was also frequently recalled as a site for drowning. We as kids were sternly warned to never go near the perilous waters. Second, the beaches nearest to me were regulated by apartheid South Africa's racial segregation laws. The azure

waters and the powder white sands of the beaches were reserved for people of white pigmentation. Ghastly signboards posted along the shore screamed at you: 'For Whites Only/Slegs Vir Blankes' in English and Afrikaans, the two official languages at the time. As a person of colour, I did not qualify. Putting your foot on the sand was legal trespassing with either a fine or jail time awaiting you, if law enforcement officials who constantly monitored the beaches caught you. The little strip of beach reserved for 'non-whites' were on a neglected and isolated area with deadly rocks, and part of an unsafe and dangerous shoreline.

Years later, I came to know the brilliant poet, journalist, and liberation activist Don Mattera, who suffered the lash of the police on his body when he swam on the wrong side of the beach as a child. That incident in Don's life made him fashion a poem, *Sea and Sand*, whose every word and line struck the very sinews of my being. I only cite the relevant part of his beautiful poem now that I have back the sand and the sea in the South Africa of my birth.

Sea and sand
My love
My land
God bless Africa
But more the South of Africa
Where we live

Bless the children of South Africa
The white children
And the black children
But more the black children
Who lost the sea and the sand
That they may not lose love
For the white children
Whose fathers raped the land.

Apart from the political violence inscribed around water that Don's poem so eloquently captures, my point is to let you know that I had zero aquatic skills, no beach literacy, and could not swim by the time I graduated high school. All the descriptions I have provided of the aquatic

flora and fauna of the beach and the sea, the geography of the land terrain
I inhabited in the land of my birth, is knowledge and experience acquired
much later in life. When I could go on the beach, enjoy its waters and look
at the horizon without racist laws preventing me from doing so. So, at age
eighteen, I embarked on a life-altering adventure to acquire a theological
education in one of India's madrasas. That scholarly sojourn of mine, I had
already documented in my book, *What is a Madrasa?*

During my six-year stay in India, for some strange reason, I kept a diary
off and on, for which in hindsight I am in absolutely delighted. I must have
seen other people in the Tablighi Jamat, the global Muslim propagation
and reform movement which I joined at the time, adopt the habit of
keeping a diary, so I did the same. The Tablighi Jamat helps one to become
devout and committed to Islamic practice and they especially invite fellow
Muslims to adopt a life of piety. Most of my co-sojourners in the Tablighi
Jamat kept a diary to keep track of their spiritual experiences. While I
desired a spiritual life too, I was less fortunate. In the beginning of my stay
in India my daily diary hardly recorded any mystical experiences, but it
noted my everyday events and some thoughts. Later, I dropped the habit
of a daily diary but on occasion made notes in my diary of highlights of a
year in review.

The entry for Tuesday 6 May 1975 reads:

> We went to Shaazli masjid (mosque) near the Shaazli river. We went
> to bathe in the river when I nearly drowned. I walked on the edge of
> the water when my foot slipped. Luckily one of the youngsters came
> to my rescue. *Alhamdulillah* (All thanks to God).

It is rather cryptic. For the very next line says I washed my clothes, then
it mentions that I developed a headache that forced me to sleep after the
afternoon (*zuhr*) prayers. All as a matter of fact. But it was far from such a
mundane event.

First some context. The Shaazli mosque and river is in the city of Bhatkal,
a coastal town along the Arabian Sea in the Indian state of Karnataka, some
750 kilometres from Mumbai and 140 kilometres south of Goa. I
remember the journey from Mumbai to Bhatkal as a very onerous one,
many hours on the train, with the first stop in Belgaum, now Belgavi, also
a city in Karnataka. After several days there, we went by bus to Bhatkal.

My diary entry hardly does justice to my near drowning event. But I remember it as clear as daylight, able to recall every thought and emotion. I recall walking on a ledge of the steps going down from the Shaazli mosque nearest to the flowing river with its beautiful greenery and palm trees on the opposite bank. While walking on the step covered with moss, my foot slipped and the next second, I was flailing in distress in the river. I was wearing a lungi, a traditional waist cloth, for ease of bathing in public, but I was sinking, swallowing water. As I went down, all I could think of was my saddened mother who I knew will be in deep sorrow if I did not return to her. The next thought was that I should recite my declaration of faith in Arabic—'there is no other deity other than Allah and Muhammad is His messenger', as the tradition teaches, that one should die with these words on your lips as a sign of the orientation of your soul to God. As these thoughts went through my mind in nanoseconds, suddenly, I felt someone come under me. And next my head was above water, I recovered, coughed in distress, until I could take in air, my rescuer gently made sure I reached the step from where I fell into the water. Of course, I was relieved to be alive and safe, but I was undoubtedly shaken for the rest of my life.

How I was rescued is a tale on its own. While my Tablighi associates were themselves bathing and washing their clothes in the river, hardly anyone saw what had just happened to me. It turns out that a young kid, no more than ten or eleven years of age, watched the spectacle of me disappearing under the water from his perch on one of the lower branches of the palm trees from where he and his friends were diving and frolicking in the river. I noticed these kids as I approached the river that in hindsight would become the site of my immersion. The lad dutifully dived and swam to where I was and effortlessly pushed me up by turning his body into a submersible vehicle to lift me up to safety. All I remember is the smile on the face of this young lad, proud of his good deed. I owe this nameless boy an eternal debt of gratitude and I pray for his well-being and success in life wherever he may be. And if he or anyone familiar with this incident, which is hardly thinkable, recall this event, to contact me so that I can offer him a more meaningful gesture of gratitude.

Over the years since that episode at age eighteen, I was determined to learn to swim. Over the years in shallow gym pools, I learned to unlearn my fear of water. I learned how to kick and reach the other side of the

pool with the help of a paddle board. But I watched with envy how people effortlessly swam the length of pools. Finally, at the age of thirty, a friend, Siddique Davids, well into his sixties, whom we respectfully called 'Boeta Diekie Pondok' taught me to swim. The first word meaning 'elder brother' in Cape patois, Diekie was a colloquial abbreviation of his first name, and the last signifier was the name of his house, Pondok, meaning a small shelter in the Malay language. He was a master swimmer. I witnessed how he would traverse through rough and high waves in the Atlantic Ocean. For about six weeks I would meet Boeta Diekie at the Kensington public pool at seven o'clock in the morning, more than three times a week for a one-hour lesson. Thanks to his patience and my trust in his skills, within six weeks I could manage myself in the water and my phobia for the deep six-foot end of the pool became something of the past. I knew how to swim: move my arms, paddle my legs, breathe, and move forward as one single coordinated act, which is the essence of swimming. And then to be able to repeat these motions without thinking.

A few years later, in the 1990s, I was delivering a series of lectures in Durban, a city on the Indian Ocean. With time on hand, I ventured out to the beach across from my hotel to take a late morning swim. Before I ventured out into the water, I saw the lifeguard sitting up in the tower. I also saw two flags posted prominently at two ends of the beach. But in hindsight it became clear that I was not beach literate: I had no clue what the flags meant. As I swam out, I ventured left. Very soon I felt a current tug at me. I was battling the waves in a riptide that felt like a whirlpool. I was not making progress in my effort to get out of this imminent danger. Panicked and scared I gave giant kicks and increased my hand strokes, with Boeta Diekie's reassuring voice in my ear: 'Don't panic, Ebrahim.' In minutes I managed to get out of water danger. Once again, a narrow escape-relief. By this time a furious lifeguard was already in the water approaching me in rescue mode. Once he saw I was safe, he upbraided me for ignoring the safe zone between the two flags in which I should have stayed. Embarrassed by my lack of beach literacy I walked out of the water with a false sense of bravado. My body language semaphored to onlookers, that I can handle myself in dangerous water. But once the adrenaline wore off, I realised my catastrophic ignorance. Unlike Solomon who had control of demons in the oceans, I was fortunate enough to have angels who

rescued me, once in a river and at another time, another angel was on standby in the ocean, just in case I needed him.

I can hear Anne Carson say:

Kinds of water drown us. Kinds of water do not.

My journey with water, our journey with water as a humanity teaches us many things. Questions if water is elemental to our existence or if it has any metaphysical proportions, are now all moot. Why? Because water is our life blood, our source of survival, and now it also poses the greatest threat to our civilisation. Over the centuries the imagery of water in language and nature soothed our souls and healed our brows, through its metaphors, imagery, and its gentle caress. Prophets and philosophers taught us about its value as a medium that renews, heals, and explains our world. We respect water just as much as we are in awe of its renewing power and at the mercy of its destructive force.

For me, personally, it is another story. If, God forbid, things went wrong for me in the Shaazli River in Bhatkal or in the Indian Ocean in Durban—if my water angels did not come to my aid in time—just imagine the tragedy that would have unfolded in my family. I dare not imagine. Thinking back, I am blessed in many ways to have escaped sure tragedy— call it fate or destiny. Given my encounters with water, I give the last word to the Greek playwright Sophocles. For him tragedy is an evil to be avoided. What remains uncanny is that I could never have imagined that Sophocles's words in the mouths of the chorus in *The Antigone*, could speak to my predicament so clearly, so powerfully.

Right blessed are they whose life hath tasted not
The power of Evil; for surely if once God's hand
Is lifted against a House, there lacks not aught
In a long moving stream of tribulation,
On, on, from generation to generation,
As waves upon the sand,
When the whole great ocean swells,
And the wind blows cold from Thrace,
And the dark of the deep sea-wells
Steals over the water's face,
Weeds and black oozes sweep

Up from the ocean floor,
And loud against the storm the steep
And wind-racked headlands roar.

RANGO'S ORDEAL

Liam Mayo

'Something you said keeps rattling around in my frontal lobe,' Rango, the chameleon lizard turned town sheriff says to Mayor D.D.F.W., the wheelchair-bound tortoise and mayor of the town Dirt.

'What's that?' Mayor D.D.F.W. enquires. The two are playing a round of golf.

'Control the water, and you control everything.'

'Come now Mr. Rango,' the mayor rebuffs, 'you attribute divine power to me. How on earth can I possibly control the water?' He sinks his putt.

'Well … you've obviously mastered this game,' says Rango.

'Well, I've been playing it for many years Sir.'

The 2011 animated film *Rango*, directed by Gore Verbinski, follows the journey of a chameleon who accidentally falls out of his owner's car and ends up in Dirt, a drought-stricken town of anthropomorphised animals in the Mojave Desert. While ostensibly a children's movie, *Rango* weaves in profound social critiques, cleverly unpacking themes of capitalism, consumerism, and their devastating impact on nature. The film highlights the role of neoliberal water privatisation, depicting how commodifying a fundamental resource exacerbates inequality and leaves the residents of Dirt desperate and powerless. Through this lens, Rango explores the environmental and moral costs of economic systems that prioritise profit over communal well-being.

As Rango, voiced by Johnny Depp, assumes the role of Dirt's new sheriff, he takes on the monumental task of solving the town's water crisis while confronting dangerous adversaries and unravelling the mayor's corrupt plot. The mayor's schemes revolve around the neoliberal principle of commodifying water—a resource essential to life—by privatising it for political and economic control. Neoliberalism posits that publicly owned resources are often inefficiently managed due to regulations like taxes and

price controls, which hinder the market's ability to determine their true value. By advocating for privatisation, neoliberalism turns shared resources, such as water, into commodities subject to market forces. In *Rango*, this ideology manifests through the mayor's monopolisation of water, revealing how the privatisation of essential resources exacerbates inequality and consolidates power. For Rango, the fight to restore water becomes not just about survival but also about challenging the corrupt systems that seek to profit from scarcity.

'I was here before the highway split this great valley,' The Mayor pontificates to Rango. 'I watched the march of progress. And I learned a thing or two. Perhaps it's time you started to take a long view. Begin to appreciate the broad sweep of history.' He directs Rango to a telescope. 'Look out there, son. You can almost see time passing.'

Rango bends down and sees the construction site in the distance. 'What are you building out there?' He asks.

'The future Mr Rango. The future.'

The Mayor of Dirt, voiced by Ned Beatty, has a straightforward plan: by privatising the town's water supply, he aims to turn the surrounding land into a barren wasteland. Once the townspeople are desperate enough, he plans to buy their land cheaply and construct his own modern city, displacing its inhabitants and erasing the desert. As both a landowning entrepreneur and government official, he stands at the convergence of corporate and state power, at the intersection between nature and the city, surfing the wave of progress from the past into the future. He embodies the essence of neoliberal policymaking, the visionary corporate entrepreneur, and proprietor of the future.

'One day soon all of this is going to fade into myth,' the Mayor continues. 'The frontier town, the lawman, the gun slinger, there's just no place for them anymore. We're civilised now. That's what the future holds. You can either be part of it, or you can be left behind.'

Dams and Myths

Myths depict moments when the boundary between the visible and invisible worlds are crossed. Around these moments, societies craft stories,

establish cultural frameworks, and build belief systems that shape their understanding of origins, purpose, and their relationship to the cosmos.

What is often referred to as Modernity's Promethean Project, borrows its name from the Greek myth of Prometheus; the Titan who stole fire from the gods, giving it to humanity, and igniting our quest for knowledge and power. Prometheus, in Friedrich Nietzsche's view, embodies the rebellion against divine authority that characterises human exceptionalism. The Promethean Project is the ambitious and hubristic endeavours of modern societies to exert control over nature, reshaping it through technological and scientific advancements. This symbolises a fundamental belief in human ingenuity and innovation as tools to transcend natural limitations and create a world better than that which already exists.

There is no clearer testament to the success of Modernity's Promethean Project than its treatment of water. Water lies at the crossroads of nature and society, moulded by human innovation while sustaining life itself. Massive reservoirs and precision-engineered canals channel vast quantities of water to fuel cities, nourish farmland, and facilitate global trade by streamlining transportation routes. Intricate pipelines transport water seamlessly from reservoirs to homes, industries, and farms, ensuring essential supplies for drinking, sanitation, and production.

Water is the primary resource for maintaining beautified, vibrant, and safe urban landscapes, playing crucial roles in firefighting, street cleaning, and nurturing lush parks. It is also a symbol of leisure and status— backyard pools, fishponds, and birdbaths don't just delight, but demonstrate one's socio-economic standing in the world. Adventurous spirits and thrill seekers ride the tides, conquering waves, rapids, and depths; from surfers taming colossal swells to freedivers exploring the ocean's depths, water is both a challenge and a medium in the relentless pursuit to excel. And of course, the bottled water industry has turned this necessity into a symbol of luxury, health, and lifestyle.

Dams, the geographer Maria Kaika tells us, have a particular place in the mythology of modernity. At the crossroads of nature and society, the dam stands as humanity's triumph over nature; a monumental modern spectacle that captures and controls vast quantities of water, harnessing its power and transforming it into a valuable resource and commodity. They are a heroic endeavour, deeply rooted in the social and cultural aspirations of

progress. Dam building is shaped not only by the aspirations of urbanisation but also by the specific historical and geographical contexts in which they are constructed. They embody the tension between imagined geographies and the material practices of the modern project. They highlight the power dynamics involved in their creation and the ultimate domination over nature. They are, as the environmental historian Margaret Cook puts it, the ultimate solution to the problem of nature, the keystone in shaping water's flow according to human logic.

The intricate technological systems that transport water from dams to our homes play a critical role in shaping how we view the relationship between our built environments and nature. Water flows seamlessly into cities and homes, masking the complex processes that make this connection possible. This blurs the boundaries between nature, urban life, and human control, creating a socio-spatial continuum where nature and society appear to be deeply interconnected. According to Anglo-Irish political scientist Benedict Anderson's concept of imagined communities, these structures—physical and political—help perpetuate the belief in the continuity and permanence of the nation-state. The myth of the nation-state is sustained by systems like water infrastructure that maintain the illusion of natural order and control.

Modernity cleverly convinces us that we are both masters of nature and at harmony with it. As American novelist Henry Miller aptly puts it, we are 'one with nature and against nature at the same time.' This paradox highlights how modernity fosters a dualistic relationship with the environment, where the very systems that sustain life also distance us from the natural world, reinforcing the idea that human progress and nature's exploitation go hand in hand. The result is a worldview that continues to endorse urbanisation and the nation-state as inevitable, enduring constructs, even though they are historically contingent and deeply shaped by human intervention.

Moreover, this continuum, the one that distortions the boundaries between nature and urban life, not only sustains the concepts of imagined communities but also transforms water into a thing, *an entity*, positioning access to it as an inalienable human right. *In What Is Water?: The History of a Modern Abstraction*, Jamie Linton argues that modernity reduces water to 'modern water'—a simplified, chemical compound, H_2O, and confines it

to the hydrologic cycle. The spatial logic of dams means that modern water management abstracts it as a mere resource, shifting focus from its life-sustaining force to the infrastructure that controls it.

Dams, at the capture, control, and harness end of the continuum, are the embodiment of this conceptual reduction, demonstrating how modernity applies scientific principles and socio-political goals under the guise of natural law. And in doing so, modernity affirms the notion that the flow of water to our homes is a fundamental human right, essential for sanitation, health, and prosperity. Reliable water access not only prevents disease and promotes public health but also cultivates an engaged and resilient citizenry that drives economic growth and prosperity.

'Modern water' is both an abstraction and a political construct. What emerges from dams is not simply a natural resource but a network of administrative systems and commercial partnerships. These entities apply empirical and scientific methods to simplify, quantify, and standardise the complexity of natural ecosystems, aligning them with political objectives and economic development strategies. Through these efforts, water is reframed as a commodity, integrated into intricate human-made ecosystems that assign value to it in various forms and functions, ultimately packaging and selling it back to society. This process underscores the entanglement of environmental systems with governance and commerce, revealing how water is reshaped as both a product and a symbol of modern control over nature.

This is more than a sleight of hand; like a magician placing a ball under one of three cups, shuffling them back and forth, lifting one cup—no ball, another—no ball, the third—still no ball. Then, with a flourish, he reaches behind your ear and reveals the ball; it was there all along.

Modernity's illusion, executed with such precision, enchants us with spectacle, while the truth slips away behind smoke, mirrors, and hidden trapdoors. Water, that exists naturally in our world, that is of nature, is captured through the myth of modernity, transformed and repurposed and re-presented as something that is entirely different, in a way that we are told, convinced of and believe is a process that is natural. The magic trick of modernity doesn't simply lie in masking its own contradictions, but in the way it persuades us that its reshaping of the world is not just inevitable, but the best and most harmonious order of the things. The cunning of

modernity rests in this duality. We know the magician had a spare ball tucked up his sleeve all along, but we've bought our ticket, enjoyed the spectacle, and we're so eager to believe in magic that we acquiesce.

Nietzsche juxtaposes the figures of Prometheus and Dionysus, each embodiment of different aspects of the modern condition. While Prometheus symbolises the striving for knowledge, mastery, and control over nature, Dionysus celebrates life's chaotic and primal unity. Dionysus's intoxicating essence dissolves boundaries, inviting immersion into a greater, unrestrained whole. The allure of the Dionysian lies in its power to reconcile humanity with itself and with nature, transforming alienation into harmony. In this vision, nature—once dominated, estranged, or subjugated—rejoices in reuniting with its wayward child, man, restoring the bonds severed by the Promethean quest for dominion. Lest we forget, as E.R Dodds, the Irish scholar of Greek classics, so eloquently put it, 'Dionysus [is] the Master of Illusions, who could make a vine grow out of a ship's plank, and in general enable his votaries to see the world as the world's not'.

The South African author Rob Nixon believes the illusion of modernity obscures the long-term consequences of our dominance over nature. A gradual erosion of nature, which he terms 'slow violence,' occurs as the destructive impacts of political and economic decisions unfold over time. As Nixon explains, whilst we commonly associate violence with immediate, explosive events that are visible and have clear causes and effects, 'slow violence' is far more insidious; it can take years or even centuries to manifest, often leaving no distinct origin point. This makes it challenging to recognise and address the harm before it becomes irreversible. And while a particular set of modern values and processes supports the development of imagined communities, they also actively produce 'unimagined communities'—those systematically excluded from narratives of national identity, progress, or development. These marginalised groups are often rendered invisible, suffering directly or indirectly from the political and economic decisions that benefit the 'imagined' national community.

Nixon is particularly interested in the communities affected by environmental degradation, such as displaced indigenous groups or rural populations impacted by dam construction. It is these populations that do

not fit into the narrative of progress or prosperity. Instead, they exist outside this narrative as part of the 'unimagined'.

The magicians gradual reveal means that the cycle of exploitation is deeply ingrained; by the time we realise we've been hoodwinked by the magic show, it's too late—the curtain falls, the lights come up, and we're left with the aftermath. The myth of modernity is buttressed by the Promethean will to wrest control from the gods and take on the burden of creation, and the Dionysian celebration of destruction and renewal. The cunning duality of modernity can be an uncomfortable reality.

In the opening of *Slow Violence, Neoliberalism, and the Environmental Picaresque*, Nixon refers to a confidential memo, penned by the then president of the World Bank, Lawrence Summers, in which he advocates for the bank to develop a system whereby the garbage, toxic waste, and heavily polluting industries of wealthy countries, are exported to Africa. Lawrence assured his colleagues that such a scheme would offer dual advantages: it would economically benefit both the United States and Europe while simultaneously addressing the growing discontent among wealthy environmentalists who were campaigning against garbage dumps and industrial effluent that they condemned as health threats and found aesthetically offensive. Summers's arguments posited a direct connection between aesthetically unpleasant waste and Africa, characterising it as an out-of-sight continent, distant from the areas of concern for green activists.

I'm reminded of the gruff speaking tortoise Mayor of Dirt in *Rango*.

Nixon goes on: as we indulge in the comforts of modernity, we are blind to the unforeseen repercussions of our actions—diminished ecosystems, displaced communities, and the gradual erosion of the natural world. He points out that our focus on spectacular crises, which yield instant, dramatic images, makes it difficult to sustain attention on the long-term impacts of slow violence. This distraction is intensified by media and political structures that prioritise what can be sensationalised or addressed within a quick news cycle. As imagined communities become engrossed in the comforts of modernity, they are complicit in the creation and persistence of unimagined communities, failing to recognise that both groups share a common vulnerability to the slow violence inflicted upon their interconnected ecosystems.

As *Rango* shows us, while Rob Nixon identifies 'unimagined communities' as bearing the primary burden of modernity's slow violence, 'imagined communities' are yet to properly realise the magician's gradual reveal. Rango was quite contented, living in his rectangular glass tank, in a controlled, artificial environment, he had control and was safe, insulated from the unpredictability of the outside world. He was an aspiring thespian, with a close circle of friends, a headless Barbie doll and a plastic wind-up fish. However, when he is accidentally ejected from this existence into the Mojave Desert, landing in the town of Dirt, his worldview collapses. He is now thrust into a harsh, chaotic environment where he must confront the unpredictability and existential challenges of life.

Benefiting from modernity's comforts along the socio-spatial continuum, imagined communities remain largely oblivious to the hidden degradation accumulating within natural and social systems. Whether or not they're aware of the plight of unimagined communities, their focus on short-term gains distracts them from recognising the slow degradation impacting everyone's future. While they believe themselves to be part of nature and its master, they are caught within a myth that obscures their vulnerability; imagined communities are sustained by modernity's narrative but remain blind to how they, too, are ultimately enmeshed in a cycle of ecological and social instability. In this way, the postnormal creep quietly transforms the imagined into the unimagined, though they remain unaware, ensnared by a myth with far-reaching consequences.

The intricate interplay between the slow violence inflicted upon both imagined and unimagined communities unveils a sobering truth: as we indulge in modernity's comforts and illusions of abundance, we develop a dangerous blind spot to the environmental degradation that underpins them. These dynamics form a cycle where the systems meant to support us ultimately erode the foundations of our shared future. The infrastructure that fosters our perception of endless resources enables ongoing exploitation and degradation, concealing the environmental and social costs tied to our entitlement to water. In this way, the myth of modernity intensifies our detachment from the ecological realities essential to our survival.

In January 2011, heavy rainfall carpeted southeast Queensland in Australia, causing what was described by the media as an 'inland tsunami'. I remember this because I was in Germany at the time. I was sleeping on

the floor of a one-bedroom apartment in Frankfurt, rented by my friends Max and Manu. Max had the bedroom, and Manu had established a makeshift bedroom behind a large curtain that divided the living room in half. I slept on the living room floor on a large foam mattress that we stowed between the wall and the couch during the day. We, the three of us, sat tight on the two-seater couch watching the events in Queensland unfold on the German television news. I saw footage of familiar places devasted by brown skies, brown water, brown mud. I listened to the German words I could not understand. Every now and then Max or Manu would translate for me: 'It's bad... people are dead... more rain coming... no power, no clean water...' Some more German... and then clearly in English, 'inland tsunami.' Max and Manu looked at each other, and then me, and in unison said, 'what tis an inland tsunami?'

The media coined the term 'inland tsunami' to describe the sudden, violent wall of water that swept through Queensland's Lockyer Valley during the 2011 floods. Moving with overwhelming speed and force, it caught residents off guard, tragically trapping and killing many. The Queensland Floods Commission of Inquiry later found that the Wivenhoe Dam, located upriver from Brisbane, had been severely impacted by the rainfall, leading authorities to release large volumes of water to prevent the dam from failing. However, delayed releases and deviations from the Flood Operations Manual intensified downstream flooding, particularly in the cities of Brisbane and Ipswich. It was a profound reality to face for a community that believed it had total control of its water.

Cities and Heroes

The Mayor of Dirt sits high, surveying the town below him: 'You see them Mr. Rango, all my friends and neighbours. It's a hard life here. Very hard. You know how they make it through each and every day? They believe. They believe it's going to be better. They believe that the water will come. They believe against all odds and all evidence that tomorrow will be better than today. People have to believe in something.' He looks at Rango deeply. '... Right now, they believe in you.'

Between Prometheus of the Greeks and the modern Promethean Project, the Enlightenment crafted a blueprint for the modern hero. A

cultural icon shaped by myth. This blueprint took the power once ascribed in pre-Enlightenment to divinity—an omnipresent God existing outside humanity—and shifted it to a power residing within us: humans. For Enlightenment thinkers, this hero was embodied in the scientist, engineer, or bureaucrat, standing steadfast against nature's wild unpredictability, equipped with reason and rational knowledge.

The philosopher Marshall Berman wants us to understand that the influence of modernity is intricately tied to our relentless pursuit toward progress, rooted in the notion that our imagination, creativity, and ingenuity will get us where we want to go. The modern hero embodies a bold desire to establish order against disorder and is marked by a defiant yearning to reshape the world in their image.

No hero embodies modernity with more potency than the sheriff of the American West. He (and they are almost exclusively men) is the rugged individual who stands for order, justice, and moral authority. Rooted in American frontier narratives, the sheriff represents a power grounded in control and surveillance, wielding a perceived righteousness that justifies dominance over untamed lands and diverse communities. He epitomises a distinctly Western form of modernity—one that glorifies conquest, enforces law on its own terms, and advances with an unshakable belief in manifest destiny.

The sheriff isn't only a lawman but a cultural symbol of self-determined mastery, drawing clear lines between civilised society and the chaos to be subdued. Because of this he is estranged from the townsfolk. This distance allows him to be both saviour and enforcer; a symbol of stability in one sense and of domination in another, holding an ambivalent legacy within the modern narrative. This frames the structures of modern statehood, echoing ideas that humanity, too, can and should be controlled, ordered, and 'civilised' according to specific ideals. Just as mythology brings order to water, so too the hero brings order to society.

If dams are the manifestation of humanity's triumph over nature, cities represent the heroic structures of modernity, where capitalism, rationalism, and industrialism converge. Just as the heroes of the Enlightenment—the scientist, the engineer, and the bureaucrat—conceived and built dams, cities serve as the stage where the heroes of modernity live, innovate, and create. As embodiments of modernity's vision of nature as perpetually

transformable, cities offer a space where individuals can aspire to become heroes of their own lives, continually shaping the world around them in the relentless pursuit of progress and control.

The philosophers Gilles Deleuze and Félix Guattari describe cities as dynamic circulatory systems, perpetually in flux and undergoing continuous transformations in social relationships, physical infrastructures, and symbolic meanings. Emerging from the manipulation of natural resources through human labour and social organisation, cities stand as hybrids of nature and culture, environment and society. Water, essential to urban life, acts as the lifeblood of this evolution, enabling the intricate exchange between natural resources and human development. It powers industries, sustains agriculture, and shapes infrastructure, weaving itself into the fabric of urban machinery and embodying the interplay between natural and constructed worlds.

The historian Karl Wittfogel coined the term 'hydraulic society' to describe civilisations that organised themselves around centralised control of large-scale water management systems, using governance to ensure agricultural productivity and societal stability. Modern cities embrace the idea of the hydraulic society as it exemplifies our ability to control and reshape nature through anthropogenic ingenuity while reinforcing ideals of urban progress and environmental mastery.

The management of water profoundly determines social hierarchies, economic activities, and cultural practices within cities. Commodification, the cultural process by which essential resources like water are inserted into market relations, reduces them to marketable goods evaluated primarily in terms of their financial worth rather than their intrinsic qualities or social significance. This transformation strips water of its essence, rendering it a commodity subject to the forces of the market. As a result, access to water becomes increasingly framed as an economic issue, where inequality and social hierarchies dictate success and control.

This process mirrors the fetishisation the economist Karl Marx described, whereby commodities acquire value disconnected from their origins and production processes. Instead of recognising the labour, resources, and social contexts involved in the creation of commodities, people come to perceive them as independent objects with intrinsic worth. Commodities, like water, are no longer seen in relation to their social relationships or the

human effort behind their production. Instead, they are elevated to the centre of our lives, shaping our understanding and identities.

Once water is commodified, the labour and environmental resources that transform it from a natural resource into a marketable good are concealed. This leads consumers to overlook the socio-economic and environmental conditions underpinning its production. By reducing water to a commodity, we obscure not only its true nature but also the ecological and human labour involved in its extraction, purification, and transportation. The detachment from its origins diminishes our recognition of water's intrinsic value, reducing it to a mere product in a world driven by exchange value.

This shift in perception obscures the environmental costs of water's extraction and the human labour embedded in its treatment and distribution. In urban environments, where clean, commodified water is an assumed fixture of daily life, this consumer mindset prioritises convenience over the labour and ecological realities tied to water's commodification. As a result, access to water becomes increasingly unequal, reinforcing social divides between those who can afford it and those who cannot. Water, as a resource, ceases to be a collective good and instead becomes a transactional entity—its life-sustaining nature eclipsed by its monetary value.

The process of commodification occurs alongside Marx's concept of fetishisation, where water is transformed into an object of exchange, stripped of its social and ecological context. The city, as a microcosm of modern capitalist systems, reflects this transformation. Water becomes a commodity in the urban landscape, reducing a vital resource to a marketable good. This shift exacerbates social inequalities, as those who are economically privileged gain greater access to water, while marginalised communities face scarcity or substandard conditions. The commodification of water, then, is not only an economic issue but also a cultural one—one that privileges market-driven values over the recognition of water's fundamental, shared role in sustaining life.

Thus, the fetishisation of water in cities creates a disconnect between the natural world and the market, reinforcing social and economic divides. Water, once a common resource essential to life, becomes an object of

consumption—an abstracted entity whose true value is obscured by its status as a commodity. This detachment, influenced by capitalist logics, perpetuates a cycle in which access to water is increasingly governed by economic means, sidelining the ecological and human contexts that sustain it.

Rango is standing in the Dirt bank, looking at the large glass vault of water - nearly empty.

Gasp!... Rango whispers to himself.... 'Mercy'

He swings around to address the crowd of upset towns people who have followed him in.

'Alright, listen up... I've been thinking and I believe I figured something out: you folks have a water problem.'

Everyone grumbles in agreement.

'Now pay attention everybody, I'm trying to make a point here... Let's say this fella here were to take a drink of water, just one little drink, no harm, no foul, right?' He takes a swig of water from the vault. 'And you! Why you're just as dried up and parched as a jackrabbit in July! So, you belly up here and you take you a double shot' He takes another swig, '... Stay with me...' and another, 'What do you think happens then?... Why we'd all be drinking! And before you know it there wouldn't be any more water and then where would we be?... We'd be thirsty... real thirsty! We'd turn on each other like a bunch of animals!'

The philosopher and sociologist Henri Lefebvre argued that the exchange value of commodities is deeply rooted in the specific social relationships and production methods that define them—encompassing labour dynamics, economic structures, and broader social systems. This transformation of natural resources through human labour, often referred to as socio-environmental metabolism, reflects the process by which cities metabolise and commodify nature, turning raw resources into goods while embedding these transformations with social, economic, and environmental implications.

In this process, imagined communities—urban populations privileged by economic policies and infrastructure—are prioritised in resource allocation, ensuring consistent access to commodities like water. These groups become central to the city's official narrative, benefiting from the commodification of natural resources, which positions water as a reliable, purchasable product. This dynamic highlights the fundamental disconnects

that modernity imposes on our interaction with nature. While the natural environment remains essential to commodity creation, economic systems obscure the connection between raw resources and final products—such as turning water into carbonated beverages sold in plastic bottles in urban supermarkets—thereby masking the environmental and social costs behind production and consumption.

Unimagined communities, marginalised and invisible in urban planning, experience the commodification of water as a stark symbol of exclusion. Reduced access to clean and affordable water underscores the inequalities embedded in socio-environmental metabolism, relegating these groups to spaces where resources are harder to obtain, costlier, or of lower quality.

Water in the city, counter to the myth of modernity, is not a human right, but a commodity, stripped of its natural origins and the labour necessary for its distribution. The modern hero, who establishes order against disorder, maintains the illusion of progress and control, but is complicit in entrenching inequality and fostering a false perception of abundance. The hero, in playing their heroic part, inadvertently mark the harsh socio-environmental realities that shape value and availability of water.

This accentuates Lefebvre's idea that exchange value often overshadows the intrinsic value of resources, creating stratified urban landscapes where imagined communities thrive on resource accessibility, while unimagined communities bear the ecological and social costs of these urban processes. In this light, commodification in cities fosters an environment where power dynamics dictate who benefits from the transformed natural world and who is left to navigate its consequences.

So, where have we arrived?

Well, the power of myth of modernity is such that it reduces water to 'modern water', abstracted and politicised under the guise of natural law. Hydraulic societies, with their focus on water management and social hierarchies takes modern water and further strips it of its essence, through the parallel processes of commodification and fetishisation, having us perceive these as procedures of nature. Water of modernity represents a severing between humanity and nature. Modern water thus demonstrates the profound mythological power of modernity, a narrative that positions humans as masters over nature. It celebrates as heroes those who can mediate the divide between the chaos of nature and the order of civilised

society, maintaining the illusion of progress and control. Yet in doing so, it reinforces a disconnection, both ecological and social, that perpetuates inequity and obscures the deeper, life-sustaining relationship between humanity and the natural world.

Floods and Nature

I will always associate the Queensland 2011 floods with Julian Assange.

That German Christmas was my first white Christmas. I had been travelling a long time and had run out of money. I needed to stop somewhere, find a job and write something. Me and Max and Manu had found a lovely, domesticated cadence. They introduced me to Lidl and carbonated water. Weekly we would slide together through icy Frankfurt streets toward the local Lidl to replenish the fridge and kitchen cupboard. And then, with large fabric bags overflowing with goods and produce tucked under our arms, we made our way home again a throuple of back slapping lanky two-legged mules. We reserved the largest bag, filling it to the brim with plastic bottle of economy brand carbonated water. *Wasser mit Gas*, in German. Bubbly water, we called it. The boys taught me about Pfand, the German recycling scheme. It worked like this: every plastic bottle of carbonated water we bought cost 65 cents. But once emptied and returned, each bottle earned us a 25-cent refund.

One night, as we were stacking our collection of empties in the corner of the kitchen, Manu clapped me on the shoulder. 'Look,' he said, eyes bright with amusement, 'we're practically drinking for free.'

They'd figured out a simple system. We'd start with a few bottles of bubbly water each week, but along the way, we would keep an eye out for stray empties. Parks, sidewalks, benches near the tram stops—there were plenty of half-forgotten bottles to be found. Each extra bottle we returned chipped away at our costs. By the end of the week, it was as if every new bottle was only costing us a handful of cents.

'And the beauty of it,' Max chimed in, 'is that people don't bother with them. If they leave a bottle behind, they're practically giving us our next drink.'

This wasn't just frugality—it was a little rebellion, a way of outsmarting the system. A playful act of defiance perhaps. 'Think about it,' Manu said,

grinning. 'Pfand wants us to recycle. We're doing exactly what they want, and eventually we'll be getting paid in bubbly water to do it.'

In their minds, we weren't just economising. We were playing the game to our advantage. There was nothing illegal, immoral, or unethical about it. There was nothing particularly ingenious about it either. But with each empty bottle, we edged a little further ahead, sipping our bubbly water, feeling like we'd cracked some hidden code.

Recycling is when resources are repeatedly processed, assigned value, and reintroduced into circulation. Yet, for Max and Manu, this wasn't about grand theories. They found a way to utilise a system that naturalises commodification to their advantage. They were, in some small way, turning the capitalist mechanism into their own source of sustenance. A small triumph in a rigid system.

I reflect on this now, and I think about how Max and Manu's subversive scheme would probably be called a 'hack'. And someone would probably be posting about it on social media. And I think about abstraction and how the water itself is so far abstracted that it is not simply the vessel that is commodified and fetishised, but the processes of recycling. And that in turn, this distance par abstraction means that recycling is not even about the preservation of nature, rather the preservation of the capitalist market conditions that allow water to be bottled, carbonated, distributed, and sold on mass at an economic price point.

Was this a rebellion, or merely an elegant compliance with the rules? Can subversion exist in a system that commodifies everything, even dissent?

Max and Manu first introduced me to Julian Assange. By January 2011, his name was dominating headlines, though I'd missed the buzz while travelling. They filled me in: Assange, an Australian, had become a hero to online activist movements, challenging authority and sparking global debates. Through WikiLeaks, he had inspired a generation of digital activists by exposing hidden truths in a shadowy world. They showed me *Collateral Murder*, a grim, shaky video leaked by WikiLeaks, revealing a U.S. helicopter attack in Iraq.

Assange stood at the precipice of the emerging social media age—positioning himself as a figure defying entrenched power to reveal uncomfortable truths. Around the same time, movements like Anonymous,

Occupy Wall Street, and the Arab Spring were gaining momentum, fuelled by decentralised digital platforms that empowered global protest and rebellion. WikiLeaks, an indicator of the emergence of postnormal times, exposed the fragility of systems reliant on secrecy, galvanising a generation to reimagine activism in the digital age.

I think now about the word 'leak', and I think about a dam at capacity, under strain.

Yet Wikileaks highlights the paradox of our postnormal world. While leaks disrupt systems and erode trust, they don't dismantle the power structures they expose. Instead, the flood of information overwhelms us, deepening alienation rather than fostering empowerment. Transparency, therefore, becomes a double-edged sword: a tool of rebellion that simultaneously magnifies the chaos and fragmentation of the postnormal condition. Assange's piracy reveals the cracks in modernity's façade, but the resulting deluge leaves us disoriented, forced to navigate an uncertain and rapidly shifting reality. Nostalgia develops.

It would be another thirteen years before Assange is able to emancipate himself from global arrest warrants. In that time, the rapid expansion of technology—particularly artificial intelligence (AI), electric vehicles (EVs), and digital infrastructure—has provided a new kind flurry toward resource consumption, especially water. Mining critical minerals like cobalt, nickel, and copper—essential for EV batteries and AI systems—requires massive water usage, often in regions already suffering from scarcity. Cobalt mining in the Democratic Republic of Congo, for example, depletes local water supplies while polluting them, intensifying environmental crises in vulnerable areas. Similarly, the vast AI data centres powering cloud computing and machine learning rely heavily on water to cool servers. These facilities consume billions of gallons daily, often in water-stressed regions, exacerbating competition for limited fresh water.

While these innovations are marketed as sustainable, their production and maintenance impose significant environmental costs. An exacerbated reliance on finite resources exposes the hidden water footprint of modern technologies. And let's not forget the way in which the financialisation of resources like water and air—through mechanisms like carbon markets—threatens to further privatise and commodify these things in more profound and complex ways. Framed as solutions to global crises, such

systems often consolidate power among elites while neglecting broader environmental and social needs.

The cunning of modernity is that we are once again lured by a dual promise: emerging technologies will sustain our lifestyles through supposed sustainability, while social media platforms offer unprecedented access to critical information. Yet, the uncomfortable reality of our postnormal times is that the convergence of these two forces—finite resources and digital platforms—amplifies instability. As the demand for dwindling natural resources grows, fuelled by the unsustainable expansion of new technologies, social media magnifies grievances, accelerates misinformation, and intensifies social unrest. The very tools that claim to unite and inform us often sow division, creating chaotic conditions that undermine the possibility of equitable, sustainable solutions.

The Pfand scheme wasn't Max's first racket. In high school two detectives had shown up at his mother's doorstep. Authorities were cracking down on online piracy, and Max had been deep in it, downloading and sharing music through websites like Pirate Bay, LimeWire, and Napster. But the police had tracked his IP, forced him to delete everything, and threatened him with fines he could never afford. It scared him. And his Mum. This was the reason, Max will tell you today, that he ended up, at the bottom of the globe, in Australia, not far from Brisbane, where I first met him.

Now, music is not downloaded but streamed. Max wouldn't attract the ire of the authorities these days; music is no longer owned, but rented. The shift to streaming platforms like Spotify and Apple Music has fundamentally changed how we interact with music, moving from ownership to access. Rather than collecting files or physical albums, we now pay for temporary access to vast libraries of content, a transition that reflects a broader cultural shift from possession to experience. In this new reality, the value of music is increasingly determined by its convenience and *streamability*, not its permanence in our personal collections.

I think about the word 'stream', and I think about how capitalism strips things of their essence and replaces it with value. And I think about how if Assange and WikiLeaks were to emerge today, he would be just another opinion in an ocean of opinions, screaming for attention on insidious social media platforms. And I think about how his video *Collateral Murder* would be just another grim spectacle of violence carried out on innocent people,

in the perpetual flood of videos from across the world. What was once a potent, world-shaking revelation has become just another instance in the relentless barrage of disturbing content we scroll past every day. In the end, everything becomes an abstraction, even human suffering. Just as a stream is no longer a stream, violence is no longer violence.

The Brisbane River system, the Australian historian Margaret Cook tells us, is approximately 40 million years old. The Brisbane River catchments that contribute to the run-off to the river are 13,560 square kilometres, skirted by vast mountain ranges that channel the weather, capture the rain, and control the flow of the water overland to the ocean; an ancient hydrological symphony. For 60,000 years the Turrbal and Jagera people, the First Nations people of the region, were in harmony with this symphony. The British colonisers of 1824 brought with them a plan to settle a city on the floodplains, imbued by the myth that nature is a trove for human progress. Within the Brisbane River catchment, the towns of Kilcoy, Fernvale, and Lowood, and the city of Ipswich on the Bremer River, trail down to Brisbane city, Queensland's state capital. The Brisbane River flows right through the centre of the city and into the ocean, the mouth of the river, the Port of Brisbane.

The British colonisers understood the challenges of settling on a riverine, that flooding was not a chance, but a likelihood. But as they had done for centuries in Europe, hydraulic engineers were employed in Australia to control, tame and harness the vast Brisbane River catchments to mitigate floods. As Cook argues, Australia evolved into a quintessential 'hydraulic society,' heavily dependent on technology to manage its water resources. In response to the challenges posed by the Brisbane River system, technocratic solutions were employed to control its flow, ensure the supply of potable water, and mitigate flooding. British colonial engineers initiated a profound transformation of the Brisbane River by dredging, straightening, and reshaping it. This process marked the river's evolution into an 'envirotechnical landscape'—a hybrid of ecological and technological systems that interwove culture with nature, redefining the relationship between the environment and human intervention.

Floods are not unfamiliar to Brisbane. Before the inland tsunami of 2011, major floods had impacted the region in 1841, 1893, and 1974. The Brisbane River catchment has a unique flood history shaped by the region's

climate, geography, and hydrology, characterised by a subtropical climate with wet summers and dry winters. The river experiences extreme variations in streamflow, influenced by natural phenomena such as the El Niño–Southern Oscillation and La Niña, which cause prolonged droughts or intense rainfall and flooding. Cyclones, such as Cyclone Wanda in 1974, have historically contributed to severe floods, with record-breaking rainfall events highlighting the area's vulnerability to extreme weather patterns.

In January 2011, heavy rains and extreme weather events overwhelmed Brisbane, culminating in catastrophic flooding. Fuelled by a La Niña phase and record-breaking rainfall, the Brisbane River catchment was inundated after four major weather events, including a flash flood in Toowoomba. The Wivenhoe Dam, typically relied upon for flood mitigation, reached capacity, leaving authorities and residents unprepared for the immense flow of water surging toward Brisbane, devastating communities and resulting in tragic loss of life.

My Mum rang me from Brisbane in those early days of January 2011: You've been away a long time. It would be nice to see you. Can you come home? I rung a friend in Dublin. After my failed attempt at job hunting in Frankfurt, and lack of meaningful writing, I had organised to hop across and stay with him. He had arranged for us to get away to his parent's home in the Irish countryside for a few months. I told him I was now probably going to go home. 'I don't understand,' Chris said over Skype, 'why would they build houses where it floods? It doesn't make sense to me.' I didn't really know how to answer him.

After the 2011 floods, frustrated residents sought answers and accountability for the devastation of their properties. Public attention turned to the dam's management and the decisions of its flood engineers, questioning whether operational errors contributed to the disaster. The Queensland Government established the Queensland Floods Commission of Inquiry, to investigate the state's preparation, response, and management of the floods, including dam operations and planning. Its final report, released in March 2012, criticised inconsistent floodplain management and inadequate historical flood data but largely absolved governments and councils of blame. The Commission prioritised forward-looking recommendations, such as flood studies and updated floodplain management plans, but decided not to lay accountability for past

development decisions and allowed floodplain development to continue largely unchanged.

Since 2011, Brisbane has progressed unabashed. The Howard Smith Wharves, a heritage listed site that sits on the banks of the river, were redeveloped into a mixed-use precinct with public parklands, dining, and entertainment venues opened to the public. 1 William Street has become a dominant feature of the city's skyline, a 44-storey office tower was designed and constructed, quite ironically, to consolidate Queensland Government offices into a single location, providing a central hub overlooking the Brisbane River. And Brisbane's jewel in the crown, Queens Wharf, a multi-billion-dollar project that incorporates a casino, luxury hotels, retail spaces, was opened in 2024 right on the northern banks of the Brisbane River.

I wonder what my friend Chris would say about these.

I might borrow from Miller again, who says that whatever is created beyond the normal limits of human suffering acts as a boomerang and brings about destruction. Because the joy of living is unnaturally acquired, it becomes a poison which eventually vitiates the whole world.

Bodies and reflections

The Greeks hypothesised that the Universe is comprised of four elements, fire, water, earth, and air. What we learn from Greek thought of antiquity, the French philosopher Gaston Bachelard tells us, is that water is essential. It is the truly transitionary element, the ontological metamorphosis between fire and earth. He points to Heraclitus, who pondered that one cannot step into the same river twice, because it is not the same river, and they are not the same person. The human being, Bachelard concludes, shares the same destiny as flowing water; a being dedicated to water is a being in flux.

Along with Prometheus the Titan of forethought and fire, and Dionysus the god wine and ecstasy, Narcissus has a distinct place in Greek mythology. It is no mistake, Bachelard reminds us, that it was with a still body of water that Narcissus fell in love with the reflection of his own image. The fact that the body of water is still, without flux, is one thing, that's for sure. But what is important to note, Blanchard stresses, is that a mirror would not

have worked for Narcissus. Mirrors are too civilised, too geometrical, an object that is too easily handled. If he were to use a mirror, Narcissus would see himself behind a cold rigid surface, trapped in a second world within the mirrors frame. If he were to peer behind the mirror, Narcissus would discover the truth: that which the mirror holds is merely an abstraction of his image, it is not really him.

I'm reminded of dams, those grand tools for the abstraction of water. And I think about phones, the cold rigid mirror like objects we hold in our hands and up to our faces.

Because water is of nature, Narcissus perceives unity between himself and his image. He is not just fascinated by his reflection but is absorbed by the water's capacity to transform his self-image into something captivating. Narcissus does not just see the ideal self-image; he experiences the seamless connection between the person who is and the person who he sees himself as. The image is both a part of him and separate, symbolising a tension between self-awareness and self-obsession.

I'm thinking about those intricate technological systems that enable a smooth socio-spatial continuum between nature and cities. And I'm thinking about social media.

But because the water is still, stagnate, Narcissus is captured, in that moment, forever entranced by the image of himself, an image that although he feels connected to, he can never attain. And there on the water's edge, either by his own hands or by wasting away, Narcissus dies.

And I find myself thinking about Brisbane. And modernity.

There is something else happening here though, Bachelard argues. The myth of Narcissus is not just a case study in narcissistic pathology, but an exploration of deeper, more poetic layers of self-awareness. While modern interpretations often pathologise narcissism as a form of self-destructive obsession, Bachelard emphasises the reflective, intimate interaction between Narcissus and his own image in the water. This reflection isn't just a mere vanity; it's an essential part of his being, offering him a moment of existential recognition. For Bachelard, narcissism is not inherently pathological but speaks to the complexities of self-reflection, where Narcissus contemplates not only his own image but his very connection to nature.

Rather than viewing narcissism as a neurosis, Bachelard invites us to see it as an interaction that holds potential for introspection and a deeper

understanding of the self. This aligns with his broader philosophical ideas, where the natural world—particularly water—plays a critical role in our perception of self and existence. In this light, the myth of Narcissus becomes a powerful metaphor for the tension between self-awareness and self-delusion, highlighting the fragile balance between the ego and nature. Bachelard challenges us to rethink narcissism as more than a pathology, as a complex, reflective process that reveals both the beauty and limitations of the self in relation to the world.

Here, the reflective surface of water symbolises an ongoing dialogue with one's own image and ego. This process is not inherently destructive but can reveal the limits of the self while illuminating its connection to nature, particularly through water as a metaphor for transformation, fluidity, and impermanence. By my reckoning, Bachelard's interpretation enriches the myth by focusing on its creative and introspective dimensions, showing how the act of self-reflection fosters a deeper understanding of the human condition. He challenges the traditional moralising view of Narcissus as a warning against vanity, suggesting instead that this myth speaks to our existential need to confront ourselves in relation to the larger world. In this light, narcissism becomes a space of possibility—a creative engagement that enables individuals to grapple with their vulnerabilities, potential, and limitations in a world that is both interconnected and unstable. Indeed, it was Herman Melville, in his classic work on the human condition, *Moby-Dick*, who said, 'as everyone knows, meditation and water are wedded forever.'

The story of Rango is not just a story about water. Sure, it talks to the oppression of the poor by the powerful, the suppression of the masses by the opiate of mythology, and the making and meaning of a hero. But more than this, it is the tale of reflection, identity, and transformation. The narrative uses the absurd—a lizard stumbling through the desert with a fabricated identity—to dig into profound truths; it asks who we are and whether identity is something we construct in isolation, or something forged through our relationship with and responsibility to the world around us.

Rango begins as a figure in existential freefall, a creature of imagination and performance. Within the confines of his tank, he is everything and nothing at once—a blank slate yearning for meaning. It is only when his

tank shatters and he is cast out into the indifferent desert that he begins to confront the question of his existence. For Rango, the town of Dirt offers a stage, and he scripts his identity as the classic Western gunslinger, conjured entirely from his fantasies and a need to be seen. His manufactured self is convincing, even to him. Until it is not. And when Rango's façade is exposed, he is again sent into a spiral of self-doubt and searching. Rango leaves the town of Dirt and wanders into the desert, passing out from heat and exhaustion. When he wakes up, he spots a figure:

'The Spirit of the West?' he says, approaching the figure. 'Excuse me, Mr. Spirit, sir?'

The figure is digging in the dirt and holds up an item he's found, 'Ah, there's a beaut. Sometimes you gotta dig deep to find what you're looking for.' He spins around and looks at Rango, 'So you made it?' (The figure looks and sound distinctively like Clint Eastwood, although he is voiced by Timothy Olyphant).

'Is this heaven?' Rango asks.

'If it were, we'd be eating Pop Tarts with Kim Novak.' The Spirit of the West replies.

'Yeah, no kidding. What're you doing out here?'

'Searchin', same as you.'

'I don't even know what I'm looking for anymore. I don't even know who I am. They used to call you 'the man with no name'.'

'These days they got a name for just about everything. It doesn't matter what they call ya'. It's the deeds that make the man.' He turns and walks back to his golf cart.

'Yeah, but my deeds just made things worse,' Rango laments. 'I'm a fraud, a phony. My friends believed in me, but they need some kind of hero.'

'Then be a hero.'

'Oh, no. No-no. You don't understand. I'm not even supposed to be here.'

'That's right. You came a long way to find something that isn't out here. Don't you see? It's not about you. It's about them.'

'But I can't go back.'

'Don't know you've got a choice, son,' The Spirit of the West uses his finger to draw a rectangle around Rango, framing him. 'No man can walk out of his own story.' He then drives away in his golf cart.

The rectangle is a recurring and poignant symbol throughout the film. Rango repeatedly draws a rectangle around his own head. At first, it's a self-imposed frame of significance, a way of carving himself out from the chaos around him and marking himself as the protagonist. But when the Spirit of the West draws the same rectangle, it shifts perspective. Rango is no longer alone in the frame—he is surrounded by the empty space of his community, the people who rely on him to lead and protect them. This simple gesture reframes the film's thesis: identity is not self-contained but shared, constructed through the connections that bind us to others.

This is Rango's reckoning, the pivotal moment where his identity, crafted from illusion and bravado, dissolves, leaving him to confront the core of who he truly is. Identity, the film suggests, is not rooted in the performance of self, the stories we tell, or the roles we play, but in the essence of our relationships—to others, to community, and to the world we inhabit. Rango's journey becomes a profound reflection on the idea that we are not self-contained beings but interdependent participants in a broader ecology of life.

What makes Rango unique is its rejection of the hyper-individualism that dominates contemporary narratives of self-discovery. The film does not frame Rango's transformation as an isolated, inward journey but as an outward-facing recognition of his place within a network of connections. His eventual heroism does not stem from asserting his fabricated identity but from embracing his relational responsibilities. This relationality extends not just to the people of Dirt but also to the environment they inhabit—a dry, desolate town on the brink of collapse due to water scarcity.

The inclusion of the environment as a key aspect of Rango's reckoning feels particularly resonant in an era of ecological crises. His journey highlights how human identity is deeply tied to the environment—not just as a backdrop to human drama but as an active participant in shaping who we are. The film's narrative underscores the notion that the commitments we make are not solely social but also environmental, emphasising the interdependence of human life and the natural world. In this sense, *Rango* quietly but powerfully advocates for humility, interconnectedness, and the profound significance of care.

THE SEA AND THE QUR'AN

Luke Wilkinson

I grew up in Malta, where one struggles to go a day without seeing the sea. That startling blue, or shimmering grey, lies still, or slowly rumbles, from any vantage point across the soft hills of home. Now I live in Cambridge, which is beautiful, and, on crisp spring mornings, serene. Yet, from what my grandparents tell me, it is one of the furthest cities from the sea in England. If I think about this too much, I start to feel a little claustrophobic. There is something about the sea that calls out to me. My heart soars upon seeing that horizon and, upon nearing it, I find myself rushing, running, towards it. I yearn for the sea air to clear my capillaries of the grit acquired over days, months, or years of life ashore.

Talking with my fiancée and a close friend about the sea and scripture, the first example we landed upon was Jonah and the whale. The story that recurs across the Old Testament and the Qur'an tells of a prophet fighting the destiny that God has revealed to him. Fleeing by boat from the lands where his quest must unfold, his ship soon becomes overwhelmed by the sea. Knowing that the sea has been thrashed into a storm to prevent his escape, he eventually jumps overboard to save his fellow sailors from the raging waters. He then finds himself in the belly of a big fish, or whale, where he calls out to God for aid and for forgiveness. This leads him to return to the land, travelling to the town of Nivaneh, where God had decreed that he should endeavour to guide people to the Path. In the story, it seems that the sea acts as the catalyst for Jonah to wilfully submit to the divine and rediscover his selfhood. The Qur'an questions how Jonah 'thought We had no power over him' before it narrates his trial at sea.

In the *surah* entitled *Yunus* (Jonah), the Qur'an tells a broader story about seafaring that may be familiar to all of us. While confident of our self-dependence on land, we find that when travelling upon the sea—or in the modern era perhaps through that different element, the air—we may

become aware of our complete vulnerability and our reliance upon some 'thing' else. Remind yourself of the last time you were on a boat or, more likely, plane that was struck by a storm.

> He is the One Who enables you to travel through land and sea. And it so happens that you are on ships, sailing with a favourable wind, to the passengers' delight. Suddenly, the ships are overcome by a gale wind and those on board are overwhelmed by waves from every side, and they assume they are doomed. They cry out to Allah ⌜alone⌝ in sincere devotion, 'If You save us from this, we will certainly be grateful.'
> But as soon as He rescues them, they transgress in the land unjustly. O humanity! Your transgression is only against your own souls. (10: 22-23)

As a sixteen-year-old on a small plane taking off through a raging storm in Rome, I felt utterly helpless in that shaking cylinder of metal, alone in the vast expanse of the sky. Afterwards, I soon filed away that feeling of complete fear in the overwhelming power of nature to a recess in my mind, only to re-emerge when encountering air travel.

How are we to understand the divergence of human experience when on land and aboard a ship or plane? The Qur'an offers various dialectical responses. It describes our life in this world with the Arabic term *al-dunya,* which literally means something akin to 'the near' or 'the lower'. This is contrasted to *al-akhirah*, which means 'the last', an eternal 'now' of existence beyond this world, both spatially and temporally. The human can come to know and experience *al-dunya* through two modalities, *zahir* and *batin*. These two ways of knowing relate to the One, who is both *Al-Zahir*, the manifest or the outward, and *al-Batin*, the hidden or the inward. *zahir*, then, refers to the human capacity for knowledge that is self-evident in nature, what I will call exoteric knowledge. *Batin* points to the equally important faculty of knowing the unseen, which, as we will see, encompasses psychological and spiritual knowledge. We should refrain from neatly mapping the epistemological distinction of zahir and batin onto the ontological division of al-dunya and al-akhirah. When we assume that al-dunya is exclusively interpreted through the zahir, the unseen becomes unknowable in our world. Among those who identify as religious, this can all too often lead to a complete focus on al-akhirah, resulting in a future-bound temporality that drags the believer from the presence of the divine

in this very moment. The Qur'an does not suggest that the zahir should only be used to interact with the present world; we should also employ exoteric, or empirical, knowledge to consider existence beyond al-dunya.

And strike for them the similitude of the life of this world: It is as water that We send down out of heaven, and the plants of the earth mingle with it, and in the morning it is straw that the winds scatter. (18:45)

Through its stories of seafaring, the Qur'an warns against solely viewing al-dunya through the zahir; a trap into which the positivism of modern science and much of our Zeitgeist has fallen. In the stories of seafaring the land might represent the zahir, in which the solidity of land enables us to grasp it and stand upon it. Meanwhile, the sea here may represent al-Batin, a mysterious reality replete with hiddenness. Except for the prophet Jesus, humans cannot stand upon water. Of course, both land and sea exist in this earth and our life upon it, al-dunya, meaning this world can be approached through both forms of knowledge. Voyaging through our life in this world, we may try to cocoon ourselves from knowledge of the unseen by constructing ships, creating the appearance of solidity amongst the fluid expanse of the sea. When the waves spill over, we are terrified by this reminder that we have been disregarding another dimension—which points us to the fact that our existence is a stream that extends beyond al-dunya. The sailors instinctively cry out to Allah, suddenly seeking the knowledge of something beyond their sheltered existence aboard the ship. A typical sceptical response would argue that this was an exceptional moment of desperation. But was it not a stark realisation of the limits of the visible world? Commenting safely from the land, it is easy to dismiss that calling out.

Why do we seem to attach ourselves so fixedly to outward knowledge, zahir? Why does this sometimes lead us to believe that our life in this visible world is the sole level of reality? Recall that the word for the latter is al-dunya, which literally means 'the near'. The Islamic model of the human personality identifies a part of us that is 'near': the nafs, often translated as soul or ego. As the twelfth century theologian and mystic, Imam al-Ghazali narrates, the human nafs pursues its own desires, at the expense of others, for its exclusive satisfaction. To justify placing the individual needs above all others, the nafs aims to convince the human subject that they are a self-enclosed monad, that their being has no relationship to other beings,

negating selfless action. This is undergirded by the deeper commitment that the human has no intimate relationship to the process of being itself—before the embryo developed, the person was nothing, and they will die, becoming nothing once more (though even this materialist position cannot avoid using language that suggests a return to nothingness, inadvertently placing the human within a deeper cosmological plane). So, the nafs aims to convince us that we are solely defined by the events that make up our life in this world. The nafs fixes our feet solidly to the land and encourages us to believe resolutely in the stable truth of the ship, disregarding the sea.

Yet, the human personality consists of something distinctly that stems from beyond the 'land'; a wind that carries the fragrance of the sea. Although modern psychology often treats the self as a material entity, there remains a mystery to human consciousness. Refer to the original etymology of psychology in Greek: the study (λογία, logia) of the soul (ψυχή, psyche). On these grounds, American Muslim psychologist, Abdallah Rothman, shows that *tasawwuf*, Sufism, was an essential science of the self in the Islamic past, offering a method for an individual to understand unseen drives within their soul. From this perspective, knowledge of the unseen, batin, refers to the hidden, psychological dimension of the self.

Carl Jung, the twentieth-century Swiss father of psychoanalysis, had a profoundly different understanding of the ego, but similarly held that it had a tight relationship with the outer world. Jung, however, believed that there was a central hidden element to the human personality—what he called the unconscious. The unconscious was for Jung informed by both personal experiences across one's lifetime and elements inherited by previous generations of humanity. Since one did not choose the unconscious elements inherited by previous generations, the subject did not necessarily understand these elements that constituted their personality and, thus, when encountering such drives within themselves, could become bewildered and overwhelmed. The goal, as Jung makes clear in his *Liber Novus*, was to confront these unconscious elements within oneself to ultimately carve out a distinct selfhood.

Drawing together a Sufi psychology with the different concept of the unconscious in Jung, we might reflect on how the Qur'an challenges the human to see the depth of their being-ness beyond the nafs. If I see my

egoic drives as constituting the full depth of my personality, when an ugly thought spontaneously arises within my consciousness, I perceive this thought as defining my being and respond with bewildered horror. The metaphor of seafaring might point to the ego as a ship and the sea as the deeper elements that inform the ego. When smooth sailing, we are quite content with accepting the ego as constituting the full truth of human experience. Invariably, however, we suddenly are struck by an incomprehensible egoic drive that crashes over the ship, making us aware of the sea around us. As you read these words of the Qur'an, recall the last time you felt submerged, alone, in the waves of your thoughts.

> Or like the darkness of a fathomless sea, covered by waves with waves above them and clouds above them—darknesses, one above the other. When one puts out one's hand, one can hardly see it. (24:40)

In fear of drowning in our ego, we, like the sailors, call out to something beyond the ship. Jonah ventures further, choosing to throw himself from the ship into the sea. Jung interprets the sea as the depths of the unconscious into which Jonah voluntarily dives. Here Jonah 'cried out in the darkness', where the Arabic for darkness is *zulumat*, in plural form, as in the above Qur'anic passage. Discovering the complete darknesses of the ego, and therefore its false multiplicity, Jonah finds the One, the singular light, which dispels the multiplicity of darkness. In plunging into the sea of his self, Jonah actualised the inner meaning of what the later prophet, Muhammad, stated: 'he who knows himself, knows his Lord'.

Alongside emphasising the terror that the sea can induce, the Qur'an also underlines the beauty of the sea. Does this not appear contradictory? It has long been a hallmark of critical Orientalists or Christians to highlight the contradictions in the Qur'an as a way of disproving its divine origin. They neglect that the Qur'an is not simply a book but a collection of signs, or *ayat* (which is often translated into English as 'verses'), that mirror the kaleidoscope of signs in nature. Just as nature is full of opposing forces, so too is the divine word. These apparent contradictions sing like the *harmonie* of Heraclitus's lyre, where the string is pulled in two opposite directions, producing music. While terrifying us, the sea, as it exists in nature and in the Qur'an, simultaneously gives us a direct, felt experience of the beautiful unity of the One.

Medieval narratives and maps of the world, such those by the thirteen century Iranian jurist and cosmologist, Zakariyya Qazwini, were suffused with miraculous creatures. In the modern day, when all lands have been mapped and brought forcefully under Coordinated Universal Time, we may feel that there is no wonder left. The twentieth century German sociologist Max Weber argued that the modern is defined by the 'disenchantment' of the world, where humans no longer see nature as replete with the mystery of the divine. This has a drastic impact on the mood with which we encounter the world. In his diagnosis of the modern, the nineteenth century German philosopher Friedrich Nietzsche argued that the Apollonian drive of mankind, the organising traits of logic and reason, had triumphed over the Dionysian, the playful, creative element within us. The enchantment within Islam has also been heavily pasteurised. Reeling from what the late Palestinian-American critic Edward Said has traced as the portrayal of Islamic religion and cultures in Europe as fanatical and fantastical, Muslims have felt that they must present their religion to the modern world as divested of wonder. Islam has become now well known among much of the educated west as the tradition that translated Greek philosophy, the pillars of rationality, and invented much of the theories and devices of modern mathematics and science. How are we to rediscover the wonder? Perhaps by looking beyond the land. The sea remains hidden beyond empirical knowledge of man. I remember being shocked to learn at a young age that only five percent of the sea has been discovered by mankind. While the mythical beasts roaming the earth that are depicted in Qazwini's Wonders and Rarities seem impossible now, who knows what watery creatures may occupy the depths of the sea?

The Qur'an calls us to wonder at the beauty and expanse of the underwater world. Remember 'the One who made the sea of benefit to you: you eat fresh fish from it and bring out jewellery to wear' (16:14). This comes during a series of ayat that call us to observe the 'diverse hues' of nature (16:13). Here, then, having elsewhere highlighted the terror of the sea, Allah calls us to reflect on the beautiful kaleidoscope of different forms of life in this world, which all breathe with *al-Hayy*, the Living. In his *Mathawi*, Rumi marvels at the 'existence myriads of seas and fishes [that] prostrate themselves in adoration before the Munificence and Bounty'. Why would God bother telling us to reflect on how the seas are full of shells of different colours from which we make jewellery? When I

was young, I remember my *padrino* (my loving godfather from Madrid) giving my sister and I a jewellery kit. I marvelled at the diversity of the different rocks and shells that we could use to create endless variations of necklaces and bracelets. The waves of the sea, the rising and falling chest of the divine, soften different rocks and shells into cool, smooth beads of many colours, which we craft into a chain of different stones, a creative energy flowing through us as we string them together, as they keep breathing with our chest memories of their ongoing evolution by the sea and our patient fingers. 'God is beautiful, and he loves beauty.' My parents sometimes remind me, with a smile, of how I used to spend walks collecting so many shells or stones that my shorts would start falling down with the weight of my pockets. I think this is why I love prayer beads; they also remind me of the beauty of stones and shells, their tactile softness and gentle 'click-clack' as they connect with each other.

'If all the trees on earth were pens, and all the seas, and seven more seas besides, were ink, still God's words would not run out'. The sea, full of wonder, enables the pen to speak forth life. *Al-Batin*, the seas as ink, rushes through *al-Zahir*, the pens as trees rooted to the land. It seems significant that the Qur'an describes the sea as the ink that allows the pen to write in this metaphor. A pen without ink can only carve lines on a page. Rumi complains, 'I tried to write *'ishq* (love) but my pen broke'. Yet, the sea, when it breaks, falls back upon itself in a loving embrace. The sea moves with currents rushing over one another, like ink gushing through a pen, spilling out through the needle point. If, as the American musician Amir Sulaiman voices, the universe is a poem, an ongoing love poem, then the flow of the sea records its verse. The Qur'an, then, makes a direct link between the sea and the words of *al-Bari*, the One who is spontaneously creating within nature. The motif of the sea or the ocean is used repeatedly in Sufi literature to evoke the Oneness of the loving, creative force in the world. When I plunge into the sea, swimming beneath its waters, I can feel oneness washing my skin. The sea cures our deep scars of separation and isolation. The child cries upon breathing its first oxygen like the reed moans at being plucked from the riverbed, where the water flowed through and around it. Feeling separate, we yearn to fall back into the One, a wave yearning to find itself within the sea once more, the drop finding its ocean heart again.

Why do we humans, bereft of gills and thus feeble in water, also feel very much at home in the sea? Why does the feeling the sea around us innately remind us of our deeper oneness? The Qur'an provides us with an ontological explanation: we are made from water. On a literalist reading, the modern scientist would have to agree given modern medicine tells us that at least 55 percent of the human body is composed of water. Nor are we in this sense unique; the Qur'an explains that all beings are made from water. This has a deeper symbolic meaning. As Ibn Arabi expounds, water remains the best metaphor for the suffusion of all life by the Divine. As Toshihiko Izutsu, the well-known Japanese scholar of Islam, explains, the divine name al-Latif (the 'soft' or the 'subtle') is central in Ibn Arabi's cosmology. This name explains the nature of all things, 'the materiality of which is in the extreme degree of rarefaction, and which, therefore are capable of permeating the substances of other things, diffusing themselves in the latter and freely mixing with them'. Al-Latif symbolises how Allah playfully creates through weaving life across itself. This can be hard to picture. Therefore, Ibn Arabi, inspired by the Qur'an's ayat that describe all life as made of water, expands that the permeation of the Divine through the universe is like water. Water, even if in very small amounts, flows through all things. The divine, then, is subtly creating all life like water gently lapping over itself, currents flowing over themselves, gurgling. With this universal flowing of water, we can better understand the oft-quoted Hadith Qudsi: 'when I love him, I am his hearing with which he hears, his seeing with which he sees, his hand with which he strikes and his foot with which he walks'. The divine life joys in rippling over itself with emanations of its life in us. In turn, the gushing waters of al-Latif within us thrill at rushing over other currents of water. When swimming in the sea, this seems natural. Next time you swim, feel the water of life within you rediscovering itself in the water around you. As Rumi says:

You think yourself merely a drop in the ocean
But you are also the entire ocean in a drop.

Of course, when we only view the dunya through exoteric knowledge, we feel separate. Having briefly called out to the unseen in moments of isolation or experienced the divine in moments of blissful wonder at the beautiful unity of all life, we turn away again. Return your attention to the Qur'an's metaphor of the sailors calling out to Allah, being saved, and

finding land again to then abandon God once more. You may notice that they are not described as betraying or letting down God; Allah is *ar-Rahman*, the One whose very nature is mercy, which flows through every atom of existence, and thus has already lovingly responded when someone calls to Him. Rather, the 'transgression is only against your own souls'. The sailors briefly felt themselves become porous to the divine water within them, calming them in the surroundings of the sea, only to pour cement over their heart again, losing the opportunity to feel at one with all life. The ego's exclusive attachment to the outward mode of knowing our life in this world separates us from the sea of wonder within us. Then, sometimes, there is a beautiful, spontaneous moment: we feel the water within us pouring out. Sometimes, we may find this literally happen, shedding salty tears from our eyes. Perhaps this is why something in our heart runs towards the sea. Just like the systole and diastole of our hearts in each beat, we find ourselves becoming compressed by the outward appearance of the world, only to then free ourselves at sea again. The contraction is necessary for there to be expansion. Sachiko Murata, the American Japanese religious scholar, describes contraction as the response of fear at the majesty of God, the masculine quality of *yang*, while expansion is the response to the beauty of God, the feminine quality of *yin*. The Qur'an describes this feeling, as follows:

> Then your hearts hardened thereafter, being like stones or harder still. For indeed among stones are those from which streams gush forth, and indeed among them are those that split and water issues from them, and indeed among them are those that crash down from the fear of God. (2:74)

The gushing forth is an apt image for the divine smiling, laughing, at finding itself; the sea marvelling at one of her pearls of water. Ibn Arabi explains the original and ongoing act of creation as the 'breath of the Merciful', which, as Izutsu glosses, can be compared to how 'the creative drive of Existence gushes forth out of the depth of Absolute'.

How do we find that oneness again? Simply by taking a dip in the sea? Maybe. At the age of sixteen, while on an incredible holiday with my family in Barbados, I discovered surfing. Hooked, I have spent many mornings and evenings in Malta sitting, waiting, for the expanding of the ocean's breast, to briefly flow with it as it exhaled into the embrace of the land. Once in

Cambridge, crammed into a library and separate from the horizon of the sea, I began to struggle with increasing anxiety, particularly revolving around health concerns about my heart. With the onset of Covid-19, these moments of spiralling anxiety increased, finding myself aboard a ship rocked by waves, where my chest, compressed into stone, felt as if it would drown beneath the surface. I yearned for control, to steer the ship, but my hands kept slipping. Through these storms my fiancée stuck lovingly by my side. Eventually, having learned about Islamic philosophy and Sufism during my undergraduate degree, I had a series of openings. One day, reading an ayah of the Qur'an in the Eranos library that looks onto Lake Maggiore, I experienced water gushing into my heart. Just before bed, when I usually meditated, I tried instead going into the physical position of prostration that I had seen Muslims do in films. I surrendered all control. Peace.

I could breathe again. Although a completely new experience, I think, with hindsight, notes of the sensation felt familiar. When surfing or swimming in the waves, I had learned through experience that sometimes, when a wave was moments from breaking, I had to completely relax and be consumed by its power. There is no use in resisting. Similarly, I think the physical positions of prayer mirror the 'breath of the Merciful' as she inhales and gushes forth from the sea. The all-encompassing name for Allah cannot be said properly (which requires lingering on the 'l', like saying Al-lah) without a small inward and outward breath. Beginning the prayer, standing upright, surrounded and suffused by Allah, I realise I am like a 'needle dipped into the sea', in the words of the Prophet. I then lower halfway, bearing witness to being completely encompassed by the sea, opening my pores to the seawater so that water may pass freely through me. Taken by the rhythm of the sea, you rise up, and you feel the sea expanding, swelling, until you crash onto the floor. We are now flotsam, helplessly washing with the breath of the sea.

There are other times in my being Muslim when I experience a suffocating contraction. My heart tightens when a sermon exclusively addresses the 'uncles and brothers', effacing the hundreds of women in the crowd, or when I feel despair that I am not 'good enough' at following the practices. When this happens, I can feel again that I am lost in a raging sea within me, struggling with darknesses, zulumat. This opens up the dual nature of the sea in the Qur'an. As we have seen, there is a consistent

interplay in the Qur'an of dunya and akhirah, which Ibn Arabi extends to a 'worldly state of being (al-nash'ah al-dunyawiyah)' and the 'otherworldly state of being (al-nash'ah al-ukhrawiyah)'. As I have underlined, zahir and batin each can be used to relate to interpreting the dunya and akhirah. These two forms of worldly and otherwordly being sit in productive tension with the dual epistemology of zahir and batin. Let us approach the worldly and otherworldly states of being from the perspective of inward knowledge, batin, which we said can relate to the inner psychology of a human. A seeker can internally experience fana, in which one's self is annihilated in the presence of God—and therefore one tastes the otherworldly state of being—and baqa, in which one has experienced this annihilation and thereafter subsists in the presence of God in this world. While there is continuity across all life—as all beings are created from water—there are also two distinct categories of existence, dunyawiyah and ukhrawiyah, which are bisected by two modes of knowing. 'He mixed the two seas, such that they meet one another'.

What are these two seas? 'And He it is Who mixed the two seas, one sweet, satisfying, the other salty, bitter, and set between them a divide and a barrier (barzakh), forbidden'. Reflecting upon this verse in nature, we can find the intermixing of 'sweet' river water and 'salty' sea water in an estuary. In the latter, as the ancient naturalist Pliny realised, and modern science has cemented, fresh and salty water, when meeting, do not initially blend but rather remain separate, rapidly circulating due to their different densities. The description of some form of barrier, barzakh, between the two seems accurate then. Moving from the apparent to the symbolic, this indicates that, while all the universe is suffused with the water of life, there is a distinct barrier between the seen and unseen that is not crossed. Similarly, from an ontological perspective, there is a barrier between the dunya and the akhirah that no person can cross. Still, as in an estuary, the two waters run up against one another, swirling over each other. which might suggest that these epistemological and ontological dichotomies might become 'mixed' but never blend into one.

'Not equal are the two seas: one sweet, satisfying, pleasant to drink, and the other, salty, bitter. Yet from each you eat fresh meat, and bring out ornaments that you wear. And you see the ships therein ploughing through, that you may seek of His bounty, and that haply you may give thanks'. (35:12)

The above *ayah* brings together many of the themes that we have discussed so far—the significance of ships, the wonder of underwater life, and the two seas. What might it mean that these two seas are not equal? The nineteenth-century Moroccan Sufi, Ahmad ibn Ajibah (d. 1224/1809), who entitled his Qur'anic commentary, *al-Bahir al-madid* (the 'Vast Ocean'), interprets the water that is 'pleasant to drink' to be the exoteric forms of worship in this world, such as following the law, which requires comparatively little striving, while the bitter taste of the sea indicates the path of the spiritual wayfarer, which is much more directly challenging the ego. Ibn Ajibah expands that, given one can find fish and jewellery within both, that they each have their benefits. 'From the ocean of the Law "one obtains the sweetness of proper conduct", while from the ocean of Reality one tastes "the sweetness of witnessing [God] and of spiritual knowledge".' In the premodern world, where potable water was generally river water, Rumi says the following:

> Silence is the sea, and speech is like the river. The sea is seeking thee: do not seek the river. Do not turn thy head away from the indications given by the sea.

Rumi is not suggesting abandoning the revealed practices of the law, but rather that we should not worship the law itself; we should seek out the purpose of the law, the One. The river offers a path to the sea, but if we get too attached to its sweet water, observing practices without presence, we will be rendered stuck among its banks. In fact, the very nature of the river is to seek—for it seeks out the sea—which inculcates in us a similar seeking attitude, drawing us away from the divine presence in the now. Rumi tells us that we do not need to seek but rather allow ourselves to be sought, to be swept up by the ocean waves.

Consider the story of Moses in Surah al-Kahf. The Qur'an tell us that Moses sought out a mysterious figure at the 'junction of the two seas'. This figure is often known as Khidr ('Green one') perhaps a prophet that lived for many lifetimes. Fakhr al-Din al-Razi, the great twelfth century polymath and theologian, takes Moses to represent the form of exoteric knowledge, the law, and Khidr to represent esoteric knowledge. The Qur'an says Khidr had been 'taught knowledge from Our presence'. This may suggest that he exists in a state of annihilation in constant presence of God, *fana*, while Moses had experienced *fana* but had a divine mission in this world to spread

and uphold the revealed law, therefore living the state of *baqq*. Khidr is reluctant to take Moses as a companion because he argues, or perhaps even playfully suggests, that the latter will not remain silent but instead question Khidr's actions. 'How could you be patient in matters beyond your knowledge?', he asks Moses. Although the latter promises that he will remain silent, when they begin to travel in the sea by ship—which may symbolically suggest the departure from the exoteric realm that Moses usually inhabits to the beginning of esoteric knowledge—Moses questions, aghast, why Khidr strikes a hole in their vessel. Khidr knowingly responds, 'did I not tell you that you would never be able to bear with me patiently?'. Abd al-Razzaq al-Kashani, the fourteenth century Sufi mystic, a student of Ibn Arabi and commentator on the Qur'an, interprets Khidr's breaking of the vessel to equate to the subjugation of the desires through ascetic exercises. We might add that the creation of a hole in the ship enables the seawater to flow in, bringing them closer to the Oneness of the sea. Moses is bewildered at this suicidal act of self-annihilation. Or perhaps it triggered memories of his own relationship to water. As a baby, he was thrown into the Nile to escape death and was miraculously saved by Pharaoh's wife, leading to his own destiny to confront the Pharaoh. Significantly, perhaps, it was the river rather than the sea into which he was thrown. His prophetic knowledge and mission would largely revolve around the exoteric practices, to guide people to the sea, rather than seeking the sea itself.

Returning to Jonah, we might now see his decision to dive into the depths of the sea to symbolise a pursuit of mystical wayfaring, which almost destroys him, surrounded by darkness, but then prepares him fully—as with Moses seeking the junction of the two seas—to reveal and spread the laws of the divine path, armed with the spiritual knowledge of its depths. Both prophets, then, undergo the mystical process of annihilation (fana) and subsistence (baqa); unlike Khidr who cheerfully smiles in the divine presence, otherwordly being, they must wearingly strive to guide others to the path in this world.

Moses and Khidr are unable to journey together for long because Moses continues breaking his promise to remain silent and Khidr grows tired of his companion's outward focus. The barzakh of the two waters, different ways of being and knowing, cannot be held together for an extended period. Moses is well-known among Jews and Christians for parting the

Red Sea. The waters that mix in an estuary do not linger there but instead new waters constantly feed in from either side of the sea and the river. Yet, it is at this place of frantic swirling that the crashing creativity of prophecy occurs—it is perhaps no coincidence that estuaries are some of the most biodiverse habitats on the planet.

It seems significant that the final prophet, Muhammad, unlike many in the chain of prophets before him, had little experience with the sea; the natural expanses that he knew well were the desert and the sky. Water was a scarce and incredibly precious resource. He grew up in the valley of Mecca, where Hagar, the concubine of Abraham, had, long before, desperately looked for water for her son; until water burst forth from a spring. A desert appears as a sea without water, where only the sand of the seabed remains. And yet, Muhammad received revelations that called, and continue to call, upon humanity to reflect on the signs of the sea. The jewel of the desert was thrust into the churning currents at the junction of the two seas. What are we to make of this gulf between his own experience and the words that gushed forth through his heart? It is difficult for us to relate to how bewildering it must have been for him. As I try in vain to picture his position, I like to read the following lines from Rumi while imagining the Prophet watching the desert and reflecting upon those many ayat about the sea that had somehow trickled from his tongue from beyond the desert plain before him.

> Our speech and action is the exterior journey: the interior journey is above the sky.
> The sense saw dryness, because it was born of dryness: the Jesus of the spirit set foot on the sea.
> The journey of the dry body befell on dry land, the journey of the spirit set foot in the heart of the sea.
> Since thy life has passed in travelling on land, now mountain, now river, now desert,
> Whence wilt thou gain the Water of Life? Where wilt thou cleave the waves of the Sea?
> The waves of earth are our imagination and understanding and thought; the waves of water are self-effacement and intoxication and death (faná).
> ...
> Outward speech and talk is as dust: do thou for a time make a habit of silence. Take heed!

WATER IS GAIA

Christopher Burr Jones

Water is essential to human life support and the general sustainability of life. Yet, it is facing profane abuses and disrespect. Water is essential to building and growth of ecology, biology, and civilisations. Yet, it is vanishing, threatening the very ecology and geology of the planet. Water is everywhere. Yet, our understanding of ecologies of water are limited; and awareness of epistemologies of water almost non-existent. Water shaped evolution. Yet, we still need to fathom the evolutionary role of water in mediating solar radiation and sustaining life over aeons.

Life first emerged in the oceans, and we have ocean water sloshing around in our bloodstream. Water has been a planetary lubricant, from the top of Everest and the highest peaks to the depths of the deepest ocean trenches. The story of Earth is about climate ice eras and glacial cycles over geologic time, our Goldilocks position in Earth's orbit around the sun, the chemistry and physics of water, and our connections – personal, as well as that of flora and fauna – to water. To truly understand water, we need to surf the spiritual, metaphysical, and deeper cultural meanings of water, explore the sacred aspects of water in our modern world, realise the importance of clouds and rainbows, and pose some existential questions about our relationship with elemental water.

Water in the Anthropocene

'When the well's dry, we know the worth of water.'
— Benjamin Franklin

Our relationship with water is 'in the moment' a part of our daily routine, of washing, drinking, food preparation, and cleaning and we rarely consider the long-term consequences of our water use. That has changed

given growing freshwater shortages, and drought across the globe. I learned water conservation in California during the drought of 1977. We learned new ideas like 'if it's yellow, let it mellow' (toilet flushing behaviour), rationing, and reuse and recycling of water. I was born near the Pacific Ocean in California in year of the Water Dragon according to Chinese astrology. Growing up in the San Francisco Bay Area, I learned the phases of water from: the Sacramento River, the bay and sloughs, the ocean, and fog. Snow was rare, but I experienced the fluffy stuff in the mountains, the Sierra Nevada, on my way to grandma's house for Thanksgiving in Idaho. My first white Christmas was in Boise, Idaho.

Our family journey took me to Costa Rica for a year, where I learned about monsoon rains and storms that marched up the valley like clockwork. I learned how the lunar cycle and tides drove the eruptions and ash clouds from nearby Irazu volcano. It was an early lesson in fire and ice, magma and ground water collisions. I was transformed into an island boy after living a year and a half in Puerto Rico where I got my first surfing lesson and the tropics got under my skin. That certainly played a factor in my move from California in my twenties to Hawaii; a decade and a half living and working in the Pacific taught me serious respect for the ocean and the spirits within. My first futures research project involved 60,000 or so miles of air travel over the South and Central Pacific.

I have come to realise that our ocean and freshwater futures are bleak. We are polluting and abusing water systems and sources without much thought. Our ingenuity and creativity are being applied to maximise ocean resources (think magnesium nodule mining, overfishing), but our industrial society is threatening to transform the oceans through ocean warming and rising acidification. We appear to be influencing the Atlantic Meridional Overturning Circulation and could face ocean circulation collapse within a few years. Mining of aquifers and geologic water has reportedly caused the Earth's axis to tilt nearly a meter due to displacement across the planet's surface, therefore impacting sea level rise and slowing the planet's spin. That human creativity is also being applied to geoengineering strategies using the oceans that could have counter-intuitive or unanticipated consequences.

Theories that humans were once aquatic have not held water, but our species clearly has evolved along coastal areas and near water. Sixty

percent of the human body is water and significantly, we spend the first nine months of our life suspended weightless in fluid. Water is considered by many cultures to be sacred, however, our industrial technological civilisational attitude toward water is profane, if not insane. Human water violations include overfishing, particularly industrial scale gill-net fishing. Miles-long drift nets catch indiscriminately both desirable and unwanted species and the latter is discarded. According to the UN's Food and Agriculture Organization, around one-third of global fish stocks were considered overfished in 2024 – in other words, ninety percent of global fish stock have been either fully exploited or overfished.

Ocean mining and exploitation of manganese nodules are nascent, but critics and Island nation representatives are concerned about resource extraction processes, wealth distribution, pollution, or worse – ocean ecosystem destruction.

Systems of water

'Water is the driving force of all nature.'

— Leonardo da Vinci

Water makes our planet blue seen from space, we live on a water planet. Water comes in many different forms. It is a vapour or suspended in clouds, it is liquid, and it is frozen at the poles and mountain tops. Accelerating global warming means that the atmosphere can carry more water and energy – that, in turn, exacerbates hurricanes, flooding events, and drought as the jet stream meanders and shifts. Arguably, to counterbalance global warming, we want more of Earth's water contained in ice sheets and glaciers to increase albedo and reflect more of the sun's energy into space. The form matters.

Entire ecologies of water are being lost. When I was a kid, the Aral Sea in Central Asia was the fourth largest freshwater lake in the world, but it has been almost completely drained by diversion of water for agriculture. That has led to regional ecological, economic, and cultural disaster, particularly for former fishing folk. The resulting desertification and toxic dust clouds have created a vast public health and economic crisis. Lake Chad in central Africa has shrunk by roughly ninety percent over the past

fifty years, due to the changing climate, population growth and overuse of water for agriculture. The disappearance of the lake has had negative impacts on millions of people in bordering Nigeria, Cameroon, Niger, and Chad who historically depended upon it. Moreover, it is a significant loss of freshwater in a region of considerable population growth and has generated conflict in the region.

Sometimes called the 'lungs of the Earth,' the Amazon River and its South American tributaries are facing threats of deforestation, overdevelopment, and climate change. Areas that were once humid, dense jungles, have become savannah and grassland. There are legitimate concerns that the loss of the Amazon monsoonal rain cycle will have global impacts that are not currently defined, let alone understood. Rainforest is also being converted to agriculture. I was horrified to read that it requires ten tons of water of Latin American water for one pound of the coffee that I drink.

Other great river systems such as the Yangtze, Mississippi, and Indus systems are threatened by overuse and climate change. Drought has been a recent problem for the Mississippi due to low water levels that resulted in serious delays and congestion in river navigation. The agricultural runoff from the river has created a dead zone in the Gulf of Mexico has grown to over 17,000 square kilometres.

Other endangered water features are the frozen ones: alpine glaciers, Greenland, and Antarctica, particularly Pine Island and Thwaites in West Antarctica, face rapid melting. These are Gaian elements but have very real impact. Melting of Himalayan glaciers pose both threats of catastrophic flooding, but also eventual diminishing of flows in the Indus River Valley. Alpine glaciers in the US's Glacier National Park are forecast to be completely melted by 2030; the glaciers on Mount Kilimanjaro will be gone by 2050.

Glaciers are, of course, also forms of water entertainment – skiing. Other forms of water entertainment use a lot of potable water for fun. One of my most vivid memories of water used for entertainment was the waterpark in Costa Rica called Ojo de Agua, 'eye of the water,' that was formed from an artesian spring that fed a circular structure resembling an eyeball. There were Olympic-sized swimming pools, high diving boards, wading pools, and other water features. Water parks continue to be

popular around the world. Other uses of water for entertainment have been questioned, such as the prolific use of water on golf courses, including in the middle of deserts. The aesthetics may have started in Scotland, but developments have been resisted in Hawaii and elsewhere hoping to put an end to 'golf curses.'

Rising ocean temperatures have been dramatic and have had compound effects given that warmer water expands, therefore raising sea levels. Rising sea levels accelerate coastal glacier melting, and could potentially untether large running glaciers in western Antarctica, raising sea levels even more. Loss of Greenland ice has been one of the largest contributors to sea level rise since 2002, now 63 millimetres higher. Rising temperatures are not mitigated by melting glaciers and continue to rise. The last few years have been record years and has resulted in coral bleaching, putting other global water features, such as the Great Barrier Reef in jeopardy. The degradation negatively impacts marine biodiversity, and the livelihoods and economy for millions of people.

At the same time, the Earth's ocean pH has also continued to decline. Acidification further damages corals and can eat away at the minerals used by bivalves such as clams and oysters, lobsters, shrimp, and perhaps more importantly, the microbiota of the oceans: phytoplankton, zooplankton, and foraminifera. The latter particularly matter because they are at the bottom of the food chain and disruptions in the microbiota could have catastrophic impacts for plants and animals that feed on them. Thus, the 'web of life' has its origins in the oceans and they are intrinsically connected to life and the flows of water on the land surfaces.

Gaian Water

'In one drop of water are found all the secrets of all the oceans.'
— Khalil Gibran

There is both evolution as a chronological process and the evolution of Gaia, the term coined by the late maverick British scientist James Lovelock, at the level of deep time, that is, over millennia and aeons. The Gaia theory argues that the biosphere and geology function as a self-regulating system, where life and the environment interact to 'maintain

conditions favourable for life.' In other words, Gaia is a water being. Water plays a central role in the system, and operates as a solvent, but also as a medium that helps regulate the planet's chemical and geological cycles. It is important to remember that the Earth has maintained a stable average temperature, within a narrow range, for more than a billion years. The planet has cycled between ice ages and warmer periods, but has never frozen over completely, turned to desert like Mars, or the hell of Venus's surface. This temperature moderation happened during a period that the Sun's total output of radiation has increased by 30 percent. Thus, water's role in helping maintain Earth's temperature is significant and has contributed to both the chemical and thermal balance of the living planet.

Water's role in Earth's chemical cycles has been central in carbon, nitrogen, and oxygen geological cycles – particularly the carbon cycle – in temperature regulation, ocean circulation, and heat distribution across the planet. Water's unique properties, including heat capacity, solvent ability, and role in chemical reactions have been vital for life and helps regulate the composition of the atmosphere and oceans. Water has an impact on carbon dioxide levels in the atmosphere through long-term processes, including weathering and ocean circulation. Water facilitates the breakdown of rocks and absorption of carbon dioxide in the oceans. Carbon dioxide is stored in ocean creatures, such as the foraminifera mentioned earlier. This indirectly helps regulate Earth's temperature by controlling the amount of carbon dioxide in the atmosphere.

Over deep time, millions of years, weathering serves as a thermostat to help regulate the Earth's temperature. In warmer periods, weathering, and deposition speeds up, and carbon dioxide is drawn out of the atmosphere, which then helps cool the planet. On the other hand, planetary cooling reduces weathering and sequesters more carbon dioxide and warms the planet again. In fact, this is the general pattern over the last few million years of repetitive cycles of glaciation every 100,000 years or so. Geologists argue that we are at the end of an interglacial warm period – at the end of one of those cycles. 'Normal' would be a return to more ice soon.

Water's high heat capacity allows the oceans to be a vast heat sink and enables distribution of heat around the planet. Ocean currents, driven by wind and the planet's rotation, transfer heat from the equator to the

higher latitudes helping to moderate the Earth's temperature and overall climate. The oceans and atmosphere are a coupled, integrated system that prevents diurnal extremes in temperature and moderates seasonal differences due to the tilt of the Earth's axis.

Water is also integral to geological cycles, involved in both the formation and recycling of Earth's crust and tectonic activity. In terms of plate tectonics, water is involved in the subduction process, where oceanic crust is pushed under continental tectonic plates. Water and other active chemicals interact in the mantle, resulting in melting and volcanism. Volcanic activity and outgassing of water vapour and carbon dioxide into the atmosphere, then contribute to the greenhouse effect. The interaction between water and the geological cycles, through hydrothermal circulation and volcanism have helped to both reshape the landscape and also to alter/ regulate the temperature and climate of Mother Earth.

Water is a universal solvent, both for its chemical and physical abilities to weather rocks. Chemical weathering, where water and atmospheric gases interact with minerals, helps breakdown rocks to form soil. This, in turn, facilitates the carbon cycle, where plants play a role. Plants also contribute to the breakdown of rocks and the creation of soil, adding another contribution to the chemical recycling of the planet surface. Over geological time, water is the force behind the creation of sedimentary rocks, from the breakdown on the land surface, transportation, by rivers, and deposition in oceans and seas. These sedimentary rocks serve as carbon sinks that sequester carbon in limestone formations, such as the White Cliffs of Dover.

Water's ability itself to maintain a stable temperature is one of the key factors that helps Gaia. Those chemical properties include a high heat capacity, latent heat, and evaporation in the water cycle. For a liquid, water has an exceptionally high specific heat capacity. In other words, it can absorb or release large amounts of heat with only a small change in temperature. This physical property allows large bodies of water, like oceans and lakes, to act as buffers, absorbing heat during the day and releasing it at night, preventing drastic temperature changes between seasons as well, particularly for coastal areas.

The physical properties of evaporation and condensation are other key factors in temperature regulation. As water evaporates, it absorbs heat,

latent heat, from the environment which cools moist surfaces. On the other hand, when water vapour condenses (when clouds form or when it rains), it releases heat to the surrounding air. This physical property allows for the distribution of heat, globally, and contributes to the movement of the jet stream and regional weather patterns.

The continuous movement of water through the atmosphere, oceans, and across the land – the water cycle – plays a critical role in regulating temperature. Evaporation from the oceans and evapotranspiration from plants contribute to cloud formation, which can reflect sunlight or trap heat. The balance between these two processes, the cooling effect, and the greenhouse effect, helps maintain a relatively stable climate. We need to remember that we operate within the boundaries of these planetary regulatory systems, and messing with them may not only create problems such as accelerated warming, but that the lag time, the geological cycle time is often beyond human awareness. What we set in motion now will take centuries if not millennia to play out and to rebalance.

Cosmic water

'Water is life.'
— Ancient Proverb

Astronomer Carl Sagan wrote and spoke of earth as the 'pale blue dot' — a phrase that both acknowledges Earth as a water planet and that we are seemingly alone in the vastness of cosmic space. Water is not unique to Earth. Our curiosity in exploring outer space has revealed evidence that water is ubiquitous in the cosmos. Space telescopes and sensors have detected water on comets and asteroids and in gaseous form. Water molecules have been detected using the Hubble Space Telescope from the ejected atmosphere of a dying star in the Helix Nebula. Hubble and Spitzer telescopes have found water in the atmosphere of an exoplanet, WASP-39b, 700 light-years from Earth. According to the Jet Propulsion Laboratory, the largest and most distant reservoir of water contains the equivalent of 140 trillion times all of the water on Earth. There, a quasar is responsible for both creating the water but also feeding it to a large

black hole. In our own solar system, water has been discovered on Europa, a major moon of Jupiter, and on Enceladus, one of the moons of Saturn. Water is also implicated in the origins of life. It has been theorised microscopic life, or at a minimum amino acids, the building blocks of DNA, have been spread through asteroid and comet impacts, a process called panspermia. Comet impacts could carry primordial elements onto the planet's surface, and serious impacts also eject biological material into space. Mars once had oceans and likely hosted life. Billions of pounds in research have been devoted to the quest for life on Mars and elsewhere in the solar system. While all of these findings and observations are of the physical evidence of water in the cosmos, life and water are synonymous in many spiritual and religious traditions.

Water has been revered in spiritual and religious traditions across the planet, particularly the symbolic uses for purification, transformation, and association with the divine. Water is considered a sacred gift in many cultures and sustaining its sources is essential to maintain balance and harmony between humans and nature. The growing trend of extending human rights to rivers and bodies of water reaffirms this fundamental belief. For example, the Ganges River in India is considered to be the embodiment of a goddess and a place for spiritual purification. Water is a symbol of cleansing, renewal, and fluidity. The very quality of water itself is seen in some cultures as having a direct effect on the energy and vibrations of spaces, people, and places. For Muslims, who are required to purify before prayers five times daily and after elimination, water's ability to cleanse and purify makes it central to cleansing rituals. Therefore, protecting the purity and sanctity of water is vital to maintain planetary balance, both at the material and spiritual level.

Water is sacred and ceremonial. Water rituals have played a role in my own life experience. I was baptised on my tenth birthday in the religious tradition of my parents. A seasonal ceremony that I attended recently combined indigenous and traditional European music but began with a ritual offering of fire (a candle) and water. As one might expect, indigenous traditions in the US Southwest place great value on honouring water given its scarcity and importance in sustaining community. Groundbreaking work on water futures in Muslim communities by

sustainability expert Mariya Absar stresses this spiritual connection in Islam. Water is a vital element in cleansing and purification before prayer.

Thus, water is far more than simply a molecule or resource. Water is central to the diversity of life, ecology, culture, and the spiritual aspect of existence on Earth. In postnormal times, accelerating warming, climate change, environmental degradation, and geopolitical tensions and conflict, protecting and sustaining water resources are not simply practical or ethical problems, they are moral imperatives. The fact that water is connected to virtually every aspect of our planet, from the Gaia perspective of hundreds of millions of years to the immediacy of the functioning of our household and community water systems – all should remind us of our responsibility to care for Mother Earth and Mother Ocean. It is not simply a question of our own survival, but for the well-being of all life on Earth.

Who Speaks for Water?

'Thousands have lived without love, not one without water.'
— W.H. Auden

The United Nations identifies access to clean water as a basic human right and two Sustainable Development Goals (SDGs) directly address water: SDG 6, Clean Water and Sanitation, and SDG 14, Life Below Water. In the past decade, the number of people who lack access to fresh water has nearly doubled, to approximately two billion people. Many billions more people lack access to safe sanitation. Access issues are compounded by water contamination due to industrialisation and agriculture, depletion due to climate change, and mismanagement. Safeguarding water systems, reservoirs, and ensuring equitable access to freshwater will be pivotal in adapting to accelerating climate change and mitigating the effects of flooding, drought, and sea level rise.

Until recently, there have been few voices advocating for the rights of bodies of water, rivers, or oceans. In spite of the abuse of water and it's conversion to a neoliberal commodity, there have been positive trends establishing rights for parts of nature. The Whanganui River was granted legal status as a person by the New Zealand government in 2017 in

recognition of the Whanganui Iwi (tribe), who consider the river a living ancestor. In that same year, the Ganges River and the Yamuna River, its tributary, were granted personhood by the Uttarakhand High Court in India (later overturned by the Supreme Court in 2019). The Yasuní National Park and the Yasuní-ITT Initiative came under legal and constitutional protection under Ecuador's Constitution of 2008. Binding votes in 2023 supported the efforts of indigenous communities to stop all oil exploitation in a significant block of the territory under policies protecting these areas. In the United States, in 2019, voters in Ohio passed an initiative calling for a Lake Erie Bill of Rights (LEBOR). It gave individuals legal standing to sue on behalf of the lake's health and well-being. While it is not a binding constitutional measure, the initiative was groundbreaking in the Great Lakes region as recognition that water bodies are legal entities with rights. These actions lay the foundation for future policy and litigation on behalf of water, its sources, and stakeholders.

Legal protections now exist both in Brazil and internationally for the Amazonian rainforest region, including its rivers and tributaries. These protections encompass the sustainability of sources of freshwater, biodiversity, and carbon deposition and storage. Indigenous communities in the region continue to advocate for even stronger protection against exploitation for mining, ranching, and conversion to agriculture. The Narmada River in India was granted legal rights in 2017 in the state of Madhya Pradesh that mandated its legal protection. While short of full legal protection as a person, other major water systems have established integrated management systems, for example, the Murray-Darling river basin in Australia, the Colorado River system spanning the United States and Mexico, and the Limpopo River system in southern Africa that is protected by a multilateral commission to enable cooperation between Zimbabwe, Mozambique, South Africa, and Botswana.

The growing movement of granting legal rights and arrangements to rivers and bodies of water is part of a broader trend towards recognising the intrinsic, not just commercial value of parts of nature. The goal is not simply to protect ecosystems, but to acknowledge the importance of water in sustaining human life and cultural traditions. These are important examples of substantial progress and protecting water, but significant challenges remain in implementing and enforcing rights and forging

cooperation across borders. The chaos, complexity, and contradictions of postnormal times and the major driving forces of change conspire to encourage more water use at a time when we need to explore alternatives and look at it from Gaia's point of view. The movement to grant legal protections to water bodies is a hopeful sign of a more holistic, sustainable approach to environmental stewardship.

Ice 9

'Water is the most perfect traveller because when it travels it becomes the path itself!'

— Taoist Proverb

Any consideration of the futures of water should consider the fictional material invented by Kurt Vonnegut in his 1963 novel *Cats Cradle*, ice-nine. Ice-nine is a form of water, a *polymorph of ice,* that melts at 45.8° Celsius. Each ice-nine molecule would serve as a seed crystal that would convert any regular water molecule to its freezing point. Contact with ice-nine would kill instantly because one's body would turn solid. It is a relevant thought experiment to imagine the doomsday scenario where the oceans freeze solid. End of Gaia. While the actual invention of ice-nine is unlikely, an equally frightening possibility is the release of experimental 'mirror cells' – left-handed DNA that might also spread via the oceans. One previous mass extinction, the 'great Dying' at the end of the Permian period 252 million years ago was due to the ocean becoming anoxic.

Postnormal times analysis also suggests that cascading water crises will be certain to drive the futures discourse. Emergent technologies could be devastating. For example, geoengineering projects could adversely affect the water cycle. Cloud seeding has already created cross-border conflict and suspicion. Plastics present problems currently, from coastline pollution to large mid-oceanic gyres the size of islands. There are emerging concerns about micro plastics that seem to be ubiquitous now in the environment and in our bodies. The impacts of microplastics are poorly understood at best. The postnormal menagerie avatar, the black jellyfish, represents the unexpected proliferation of growth of something normally in the background, like jellyfish clogging power plant intake

pipes. Explosive growth occurs in response to excess nutrients or input of energy into a system. Coral bleaching caused by the dieback of coral polyps has been occurring planet wide as ocean temperatures spike. Black jellyfish are examples of emergent postnormal bursts when dramatic transformations can happen and they can be disruptive or even existential threats.

We have a lot to learn and to practice from traditional people and cultures. For example, the ancient Hawaiian land use strategy of *ahupua*, an integrated agriculture, aquaculture, and hydrology from the tops of the mountains down to the fishponds and reef. In *Waves of Knowing*, Hawaiian Political Scientist Karin Ingersoll advocates an ocean and surfing epistemology that could inform our policies, production and application of programmes grounded in water consciousness. We need to move beyond managing water as a commodity, and shift it to a place of sacred trust, from the clouds and their rainbows to the rivers and streams, to the lakes, to the Mother Oceans, and the waters of the Cosmos. We must turn down the heat and mind the greenhouse. We need to slow the production and release of carbon dioxide, methane, and other greenhouse gases. We need to extend rights, before it's too late, to the ice lands. To the Arctic tundra and permafrost, to the Alpine glaciers, to the icebergs and Greenland, and Antarctica. We need to honour the ice, too.

Cool it, says the Earth. If only we would listen.

SHARIAH IN A SINKING CITY

Wietske Merison

Between the walls of the Waladuna Mosque in Jakarta runs a remarkably stunning carpet. It changes colour depending on the time of day, reflecting the sky up above. It moves with the rhythm of time and sways with the wind. It is nothing less than the source of all life: water. Located just outside of the city's sea wall, the Waladuna Mosque is submerged in about a meter of seawater.

The scenic mosque used to be a vibrant place of worship. Initially built for fishermen and port workers, it quickly became beloved by residents of the wider Muara Baru area. But then, fifteen years ago, Muara Baru was struck by a flash flood. The government decided to build a sea wall in an attempt to prevent further flooding of the area but the most strategic place to build this wall was behind the Waladuna Mosque, sacrificing the house of worship to the waves of the steadily rising water. And so, since 2001, only the creatures of the sea and the occasional swimming child have uttered joyful praises within its walls.

Many coastal cities across the world are faced with the challenges of rising sea levels due to climate change. But Jakarta has an additional problem: it is sinking. Between thirty and sixty percent of Jakarta's eleven million inhabitants depend on groundwater for their daily needs. In the absence of reliable municipal piped water, the majority of Jakartans get their water from wells, draining the aquifer. As the aquifer is slowly consumed, the ground shrinks like a dry sponge, causing Jakarta to sink at unparalleled speeds. In certain parts, such as the area of the Waladuna Mosque, the city has subsided more than four meters in the last decade, slowly fading in the embrace of the Java Sea.

Aquifers are not easily drained in natural circumstances, especially in wet areas like the Jakarta region. After all, whenever the tropical rains come, they refill the aquifers and ensure that the equilibrium is

maintained, and the cycle of water steadily progresses. The problem is that ninety-seven percent of Jakarta is covered in concrete. Just about every area of wetland and forest where rainwater could trickle down to the aquifers has given way to air-conditioned malls, endless apartment complexes, and sky-scraping hotels forming Jakarta's famous concrete jungle. At the same time, millions of inhabitants and daily commuters consume immense amounts of groundwater, often retrieved from illegal wells. As such, Jakarta sinks at an annual rate of up to twenty-five centimetres in the north, fifteen centimetres in the west, and ten centimetres in the east. With tides rising at a rate of about five centimetres per year, the picture is clear: the city is drowning.

There are many discussions about the causes and possible solutions to Jakarta's environmental challenges. Most of them fixate on identifying technical causes, such as a lack of protective dams and an excess of impenetrable concrete. Technical solutions are then proposed, such as constructing dams and digging vertical drains to allow rain and flood water to reach the aquifer. But the issue at the heart of the sinking city is not technology—it is morality. Injustice is causing Jakarta to sink.

When the Dutch first arrived in what was then Jayakarta, they burned it down. Prince Jayawikarta, the local ruler, had granted the Dutch permission to build a warehouse to facilitate the trade in spices. But the Dutch East India Company (*Vereenigde Oostindische Compagnie*, or VOC) cunningly turned that warehouse into a defence stronghold. In 1619, under the command of Jan Pieterszoon Coen, they attacked and destroyed Jayakarta and expelled its population. On its ashes, they built Batavia—a settlement named after the Batavi Germanic tribe, who in folklore were perceived as the brave and fierce ancestors of the Dutch.

Batavia quickly transformed into a tropical version of Amsterdam, with tall buildings, canals, and, of course, segregation. In fact, water was used as a means of segregation right from the digging of the first canals. The Dutch were far outnumbered in Batavia by Chinese, Indian, Indonesian, and enslaved populations. Carefully planned segregation was a part of the very blueprint of the old city of Batavia, or Kota Tua as the neighbourhood in the heart of Jakarta is called today. Colonial hierarchies were quite literally set in stone through the building of city walls to exclude enslaved

populations, and the digging of unbridged canals to separate the Dutch from the Asian populations.

But the canals were a stinky business for many other reasons. Whereas canals were a vital part of Dutch architecture in the Netherlands, used for transportation, drainage, and defence, their construction in Batavia showed a lack of understanding of the Jakartan ecosystem. Whereas in the Netherlands, well-functioning canals are regularly flushed out by the steady flow of Dutch rivers, the flow of the thirteen major rivers in Jakarta is highly irregular. As such, for most of the year, Batavia's canals were stagnant and shallow, unable to properly handle the sewage from the growing city. Consequently, the canals omitted a horrendous odour and were a threat to public health. Dysentery and typhoid rapidly spread among the inhabitants of Batavia. The odour of the canals was, in fact, so horrendous that it was even thought to be the cause of another tropical disease: malaria (from 'mala aria', meaning 'bad air'). Mosquitoes thrived in the shallow, still waters of the canals. After 1733, an average of two to three thousand VOC employees died every year of various diseases relating to water mismanagement, resulting in a total of around 100,000 deaths in the eighteenth century alone. The number of deaths among non-European populations in Jakarta was never officially recorded.

By the eighteenth century, the canals had become so polluted and dilapidated that many of the wealthy Dutch Batavians had built new luxurious residences several kilometres south of Batavia, in a place that became known as Weltevreden, and is now Pasar Baru. In Batavia, the canals were not improved or treated—they were simply left behind by those who could afford to do so. The Dutch population slowly moved away from the problem they caused in Batavia towards Weltevreden, where they created a centralised piped water supply. Of course, this centralised supply of clean water was never meant to be accessible to all. Unsurprisingly, it was almost exclusively the Dutch who had access to clean water and indoor bathrooms. Local populations often remained dependent on the polluted canals, had to buy water from street vendors, or resorted to a different strategy: digging wells.

And like that, a legacy of unequal, class-based access to water was established in Batavia, a legacy that would continue long after Batavia became Jakarta. Almost half of Jakarta's subdistricts have *kampungs* (urban

villages with simple and often poor living conditions, sometimes referred to as 'slums'), out of which most are located in North Jakarta, the fastest sinking area closest to the rising sea. In many of these kampungs, people have no choice but to get their water from local, informal wells. Since contemporary water regulations in Jakarta have sought to stop the problem of land subsidence by prohibiting the extraction of groundwater without a permit, many of the inhabitants of the kampungs now have to break the law to access clean water, risking fines. In some areas, the municipal government justifies the practice of fining because these areas have recently become connected to the piped water system. But not all piped water is made equal. Even when piped water does reach the kampungs, the quantity and quality of the water flow is often unreliable and, as a general rule, unsuitable for cooking and consumption.

When I told a colleague at my university that my main field of interest is Islamic environmental ethics, he said, 'oh, that's nice. I like nature as well. But my research interest is politics'. So often, we perceive the environment as something that is 'out there', safely kept in the songs of the birds, the deep green of forests, and the royal blue of oceans. But environmental ethics relate just as much to the songs of the oppressed, the deep green of the Hereafter, and the royal blue of the uniform of a nurse tending to a child with malaria, or leukaemia as a result of pesticide spraying to combat malaria. Perhaps issues relating to water make this point most clear, because both the majority of the planet we inhabit, as well as the majority of our own physical bodies, consist of water. There is no permanent, impenetrable barrier between our bodies of water and all other bodies of water. Rather there is a constant relation, a constant exchange. Our bodies are a part of the cycle of water, not just the bodies of trees and clouds and rivers. In that sense, we are 'the environment' just as much as these other bodies are. And in that sense, environmental pollution can also be violence, racism, colonialism, and genocide, just as much as environmental restoration and protection can be charity, mercy, forgiveness, and resistance. Beyond narrow perceptions of the modern fragmentation of the world, environmental justice is *simply* justice.

When Joseph explained the dream of the King of Egypt and predicted seven years of prosperity followed by seven years of famine, this was surely a spiritual affair. Yet it was just as much surely an economic,

political, and environmental affair. Still, the Qur'an does not present Joseph as a great environmentalist for preventing an ecological disaster, but rather simply refers to him as one of those who do good (*al-muhsinin*). Similarly, the plagues of Egypt in the time of Moses were, to our modern understanding, environmental—floods, locusts, frogs, lice, water turning to blood, diseased livestock, and prolonged darkness. But nowhere does the Qur'an describe these issues as 'environmental'. In fact, the Qur'an does not even mention the concept of 'nature' in its discourse. Rather, the Qur'an speaks of the interconnected web of life as 'creation', including both humans and other creatures.

Perhaps one of the greatest ethical failures of our current time is the creation of 'the environment.' In the twentieth century, the term 'environment' was first used in the West to abstractly refer to 'the natural world' as something other than 'us'. Before the relatively new field of environmental studies, there was the field of ecology. Ecology is a term that stems from the Ancient Greek words for 'house' (*oîkos*) and 'study of' (*logía*). The 'house' that is studied is the house of creation, containing all living organisms under its wide roof. Ecology focuses on the study of relationships within the various ecosystems or smaller rooms in the bigger house of creation.

The crisis facing our world today is not a crisis that takes place in 'the environment'. It is a crisis facing *everything* and *everyone*. In Jakarta, that crisis stems from exploitative, colonial, and classist immorality. While blaming climate change for some of Jakarta's problems is not incorrect, it is pointing at a symptom rather than the true cause. Climate change, after all, is caused by increasing immorality, greed, and sin on a global scale, predominantly in the Global North. The true environmental problem we are faced with, in Jakarta and in the world, is a problem of *kufr* (denial) and *shirk* (idolatry) that can only be solved by *shukr* (gratitude) and *tawhid* (oneness).

In the discourse of 'environmentalism', we have denied the truth of who we are as mere inhabitants of the house of creation who can either do right or wrong in their relationships with themselves, other living beings, and their Creator. We can make this crisis as complex and compartmentalised as we want, but from an Islamic perspective, it simply boils down to sin. Too many human beings in positions of relative privilege have become lazy

worshippers of the idols of power, wealth, and ego. Instead of treading lightly and gratefully upon the earth, they have come to spread corruption upon her surface, and have come to deny, divide, and pollute the oneness of the *oikos*—the oneness of the house.

In *Surah Saba* of the Qur'an, the story of the Dam of Ma'rib is related. Like so many other Qur'anic narratives, the story of the Dam of Ma'rib is a story of both ecology and economy—of both spirituality and practicality. It is a story from a world before these fragmentations of understanding.

With the dam, the people of Saba regulated and guided the water of the episodic floods to farmlands beyond the natural reach of the Wadi Dhana. In the dry desert climate of the Sabaean Kingdom and its capital city Ma'rib, which was located in modern-day Yemen, this dam was at the heart of the nation's prosperity. It was significantly different from many modern damming projects in the sense that it did not aim to create a reservoir from where the water would be distributed throughout the year. Rather, it simply aimed to divert the water of the episodic flood, ensuring that no areas were overflooded, and the floodwaters reached as large an area of farmland as possible. The Dam of Ma'rib was an ecologically sound project of a remarkable scale and impact. It was over six hundred meters long and reached a height of sixteen meters at its tallest point. Archaeologists estimate that the labour of around twenty thousand workers would have been necessary for the dam's construction. A similar amount of workers was noted in historical records for later reparations and renovations.

As a result of the episodic floods of the Wadi Dhana and the infrastructure of the dam, two prosperous areas of agriculture thrived in the valley of Ma'rib. The Qur'an refers to these prosperous gardens as a verse in the book of creation, a sign from God: 'Indeed, there was a sign (*ayah*) for Saba in their homeland: Two gardens, one on the right and the other on the left. Eat of your Lord's provision, and be grateful to Him, for your land is good and your Lord most forgiving.' (34:15).

But then, disaster struck. An environmental disaster, our modern minds might propose. A great flood struck the people of Ma'rib and overwhelmed their dam, causing the land and settlements to be flooded, the dam to be destroyed, and the agricultural and economic systems to collapse. The Qur'an narrates: 'but they turned away, so We sent upon

them a flood that overwhelmed the dam *(sayl al-'arim)*, and We replaced their gardens with others yielding bitter fruit, tamarisk bushes, and a few lote trees. This is how We requited them because of their ingratitude. And never do We requite in such a way except those who are ungrateful *(al-kafur)*' (34:16-17).

The story of the Dam of Ma'rib is commonly interpreted and narrated as a story of God's great might, punishing those who are ungrateful for the blessings bestowed upon them. But to many modern readers of the Qur'an, God's recompense strikes as rather harsh. Some argue that rather than ingratitude, *kufr* here must be read as disbelief—the theological denial of the existence of God. I object to this modern attempt to make a distinction between the spiritual and the practical, between the theological and the ethical, which I perceive to be entirely at odds with the Qur'anic discourse.

Ingratitude is not merely a small individual failure to express thanks. Ingratitude creates systems of injustice and inequality and is, in that sense, nothing but a practical testimony of denial of the existence of God. The Dam of Ma'rib did not fall in one day due to one flood. As the stability of the Sabaean Empire slowly deteriorated, there was not enough social cohesion to keep up with the maintenance of the dam. The ancient Incense Road that had brought much wealth to the Sabaean Empire was outcompeted by sea-based routes, which meant increasingly fewer caravans passed through Ma'rib. Ma'rib's economy, which had become increasingly focused on profits from the incense trade, was faced with a great challenge: as the source of abundant wealth slowly vanished, how would the people respond? Would the Sabaeans stick together, be mindful of the blessings and wealth of their gardens, and restructure their economy to ensure communal thriving and self-sufficiency? Or would Ma'rib's elite be unable to let go of the memory of the abundant wealth of the Incense Road, and descend into conflict, corruption, and fierce competition to preserve the wealth they perceive as rightfully, truthfully, and inalienably theirs?

The environmental disaster of the flood of Ma'rib was self-imposed. With the downfall of the land-based Incense Road, morality, too, fell in Saba. Corruption skyrocketed, and different traders resorted to ruthless strategies to try and monopolise whatever was left of the old routes. One such strategy was to eliminate rest stops along the caravan routes, which would make it more difficult for small traders with fewer resources to

compete against the most influential and successful traders, whose ample supplies enabled them to complete longer routes. These aggressive strategies of competition, rooted in ingratitude, were denounced in the Qur'anic text: 'and We placed between them and the cities We had blessed towns within sight of one another. We had made their journey easy: "Travel safely, by night and by day!" But they said: "Our Lord, increase the distance of our journeys." They wronged themselves, so We turned them into stories and scattered them. Truly in that are signs for all who are patient, thankful' (34:18-19).

Instead of rising to the challenge of gratitude and patience, many of the powerful people of Saba resorted to ingratitude and denial, exploiting and dominating their human and non-human environments. In a rapidly individualising society of political unrest, the Sabaeans failed to perform the necessary maintenance of the Dam of Ma'rib. As such, in desperately clinging to the wealth of the past, they lost the wealth of the present. They saw the cracks in the dam but covered them with denial instead of fixing them with gratitude.

Jakarta's sea walls are already showing cracks. Many inhabitants of the kampungs fear the moment an earthquake will bring their modern-day *sayl al-'arim*— the flood that breaks their dam. I lived in Jakarta for several months when I was working on issues of ecological ethics at the Center of Islam and Global Challenges of the Indonesian International Islamic University. On a visit to the Muara Baru area, we stopped our boat about a mile away from Waladuna mosque to enter Kampung Luar Batang, an urban village in the fish market district. From our boat, we climbed a ladder onto the sea wall, and immediately, we were greeted by a kind young lady with Down syndrome. Her room was built right on top of the three-meter-high sea wall, overlooking her mother's shop down below. I carefully stepped down the slippery stairs to descend into a flooded street. Two slippers were floating in the water. They belonged to Ibu Fitri, who was busy trying to get the water out of her flooded shop, bucket by bucket.

The sea wall was leaking, sending a constant stream of water into the kampung's streets and into her shop. Ibu Fitri told us that government officials had come by a couple of times now, but they had not yet sent someone to fix the leak. 'So I just keep draining my shop,' she said, 'we

have nowhere else to go.' Her daughter was looking down at us from up the sea wall.

As we sat down to eat and drink together, Ibu Fitri showed us her noticeably swollen feet. 'When I clear the water from my shop,' she explained, 'my feet always get itchy.' While we were out on the water near the Waladuna mosque, at times, a strong odour of metal and sulphur arose from the water. The water of many of the thirteen rivers flowing through Jakarta, as well as others flowing into the Java Sea near the bay of Jakarta, are severely polluted. Plastic pollution is a big problem, contributing to flooding and various public health and ecological hazards. An arguably even bigger problem is chemical pollution, caused by industries upstream, such as the notorious textile factories in West Java, manufacturing synthetic fabrics for global fashion giants like H&M, Adidas, and GAP.

The moral framework of *Surah Saba'* can be applied to our contemporary interconnected world, on both a local and global scale. Locally, in the face of Jakarta's environmental problems, the Indonesian government has decided to build a new capital city, Nusantara, on the island of Borneo. The ethical considerations of the new capital city are complex and deserve a thorough, nuanced analysis. That being said, as a response to the environmental crisis in Jakarta, it is a policy of denial, not unlike the denial of the cracks in the wall of Ma'rib, or the Dutch leaving behind the polluted canals of Batavia to settle in Weltevreden. Moving the government away from Jakarta will not change the fate of Ibu Fitri and her daughter in any meaningful way. Rather, as the institutional and physical bodies of power and influence move away from the smog and floods of Jakarta, there is a risk of Jakarta's ecological problems becoming even more so merely problems of marginalised communities as opposed to problems of the nation as a whole.

Globally, it is not hard to draw a parallel between the wealthy traders of Ma'rib and their aggressive strategies of competition and various monopolising capitalist enterprises. Global chains like H&M slowly outcompete small boutiques by partnering with textile giants like PT Gistex Group. They do not hesitate to pollute rivers, promote mega shopping malls, monopolise food chains, and encourage rampant

consumerism – all to outprice the competition, and lengthen the trade routes to exhaust the caravans of opponents.

But luckily, the Qur'anic narrative is not one of despair. Even the story of the Dam of Ma'rib is a hopeful one. It is hopeful, because in presenting the poison of ingratitude, it also presents the antidote of gratitude. With the gaze of ingratitude, the flood, the *sayl al-'arim,* is nothing but a cruel punishment. But with the gaze of gratitude, it rather becomes an opportunity. After all, the Qur'an describes that the flood does not destroy everything. Rather, it brings change, creating space for a very specific kind of vegetation to thrive: bitter fruit (*ukul khamt*), tamarisk bushes (*athl*), and a few lote trees (*sidr*).

Why does the Qur'anic narrative highlight these specific plants, rather than describing the valley of Ma'rib as dead or lost? Some Qur'anic commentators argue that these plants are simply chosen to describe the return of a desert climate to the valley of Ma'rib. I do not argue that this interpretation is anything but true. In fact, these plants are ecologically sound examples of the type of vegetation that may have naturally grown in the valley of Ma'rib after the flood. Yet just because this interpretation may well be true, the search for truth is not necessarily over. Often, the Qur'anic discourse contains multiple layers of truth. One such layer of meaning may be that these verses, beyond portraying a story about gratitude, are actually an example of the power of gratitude themselves.

Although bitter fruit is perhaps not as appealing as sweet fruit, the growth of bitter fruit does not have to be interpreted as exclusively negative. Most often, when fruits are bitter, it means that they are simply not yet ripe: patience is the missing ingredient to their sweetness. Other bitter crops, be they 'fruits' or other 'foods' (both appropriate translations of *ukul*) such as vegetables, may not be as appealing or addictive as sweet fruits, but are not necessarily negative or evil. Ginger, for example, is famously bitter, but is actually mentioned among the foods of Paradise (76:17). The growth of bitter foods in the newly changed valley of Ma'rib may then just as well be read as a call to return to a prophetic lifestyle of simplicity and gratitude—a lifestyle that exudes sweetness for those who approach it with patience.

Similarly, tamarisks do not necessarily come with any negative associations either. They are unique trees that can grow in the harshest,

most saline, and desertified regions of the world, such as the Dead Sea shore. They are able to do so because they grow exceptionally long taproots, obtaining water meters below the surface of the desert soil. The plant secretes salt during the day, which absorbs water during the night. This water then evaporates upon the rising of the morning sun, providing a cooling effect upon their immediate environment. As such, tamarisks were historically often used for shade and shelter. According to Biblical sources, a tamarisk tree likely sheltered Ishmael when Hagar sought water, and the spring of Zamzam appeared (Genesis 21:15). Abraham likely planted a tamarisk at Beersheba, where he worshipped the Lord (Genesis 21:33-34). When Moses led the Israelites, wandering in the desert, they were saved from starvation by the appearance of *manna,* a mysterious white flake-like substance that arrived with the dew during the night (Exodus 16:14, 21, 31). Some have linked *manna* to the tamarisk manna scale (*trabutina mannipara*), a small mealybug that produces a sweet honeydew on the tamarisk tree. Far from a meaningless desert shrub, then, the tamarisk has the potential to be a great source of blessings for those willing to look with patience and gratitude.

Lastly, the positive connotations of the presence of lote trees (also known as 'thornbush') perhaps require the least explanation. After all, it is a lote tree (*sidrat al-muntaha*) that marks the utmost limit of the seventh heaven. This blessed tree is described as the final celestial barrier between the realms of the angels and the all-encompassing presence of the Divine. In Islamic spiritual traditions, the tree is often used to symbolise Divine presence. Many lote trees bear fruit, known as jujube fruit or red date, which is considered a delicacy in many Middle Eastern communities. Like the tamarisk, lote trees also provide shade and coolness in the midst of the heat of the desert.

When we approach the valley of environmental crisis and injustice with ingratitude, we will find only death and despair. But when we approach the flooded valley of Ma'rib, or our ecologically corrupted world, with gratitude and patience, in full awareness that lote trees in this world have thorns, unlike the thornless trees of the Hereafter, and that light in this world comes with darkness, unlike the light upon light of the Hereafter, we may just find blessings as great as those found by Joseph in Egypt. After all, the Qur'an proclaims that no one is ever requited with anything but

what they themselves produce. The real ethical pursuit—the challenge for shariah in a sinking city—then is no different from the ethical pursuit in any other case of injustice: to be amongst the *muhsinin* – those with gratitude who beautify and enrich with their actions and conduct others and their environment—regardless of the outcome of the fight, and regardless of the identity of those who commit injustice. And the embodiment of *iḥsan*— gratitude—may take many different shapes in many different bodies.

In the body of a government official, it may look like hours of work, attempting to push forth the administrative process of fixing and reinforcing the sea wall outside of Ibu Fitri's shop. In the body of Ibu Fitri, ihsan may look like simply continuing to give care for her daughter and not losing faith in the face of the flood. In the body of the owner of a severely polluting textile factory, ihsan may look like shutting down or taking other drastic changes to prevent any further violence and harm. In the body of a member of the environmental orange army of Jakarta, ihsan may look like the structural cleaning of rivers. In the body of an ecologist, ihsan may look like supporting projects to conserve and restore the mangrove forests along the coast of Jakarta. Ihsan may take many different shapes in many different bodies, but one thing is clear: the collapse of the Dam of Ma'rib was caused not only by individual sin but also by a lack of social cohesion and collective striving for ihsan. Therefore, to stop the breaking of our contemporary dam, to stop the flooding of our *oîkos*, we will need every single body of water to step up and realise that they are the flood.

So which will we be: the flood that irrigates the valley of Ma'rib, or the flood that destroys it?

OCEAN DREAMS

Jeremy Henzell-Thomas

I have had many dreams!

My dreams, however, are very much centred on the metaphysical symbolism of traditional cosmology, astrology, and alchemy including those of oceanic expanses of water. It was Empedocles who proposed, around 450 BC, the set of four elements (fire, water, earth, air) to be adopted by Aristotle who believed that all matter was made up of these four elements in varying proportions. Hence the division of the twelve signs of the Zodiac into three each of the four elements (comprising Cancer, Pisces, and Scorpio as Water signs). I should add that I am aware that astrology has been truncated and has lost much of its spiritual significance in modern times, and I very much value the deeper 'mystical astrology' expounded by Ibn 'Arabi.

I have always given great attention to my dreams throughout my life, and I have learnt to distinguish between different types of dreaming. There are those arising from leftover impressions of the day (it's common to equate this kind of dream with too much cheese before bedtime!), and then there are those one might call psychological dreams drawing one's attention to unresolved issues or conflicts in the psyche. Then there are dreams of archetypal psychology dealing with universal symbols pointing to deeper integration of the psyche (which in its Greek sense of course refers not only to the mind but also to the soul). Then, beyond all these, there are metaphysical dreams which offer spiritual inspiration and guidance, and these are attested to in all spiritual and mystical traditions, including that of Islam. We shouldn't regard them as special or privileged experiences. Many people (perhaps most people) have what one might call big dreams of this kind, and some have shared them with me in groups devoted to work on dreams, but whereas in traditional societies such dreams might have been shared with the whole community, we live in an age of general

disconnection from the imaginal dimension of life. One can see this disconnection not only in the scientific materialism (scientism) which pervades modern life, and the spiritual illiteracy this creates, but also in the literalism which permeates many strands of formal religiosity and the taboos and fears about deviation which they generate. One dream that immediately comes to mind is one of thirty years ago, which distilled for me the essence of divine revelation and opened the door to my love affair with Islam. In the dream I had received a love letter from a profoundly mysterious and numinous feminine presence in 'the Gulf'. The Arabian and Persian Gulf came to mind, but beyond that the Gulf is etymologically Greek *kolphos*, 'cleft' or 'bosom', and it was on a cleft in the rock that the Delphic Oracle stood to reveal her prophetic wisdom. The provenance of the love letter therefore suggests a locus of divine revelation, and this is confirmed by the fact that in the dream I opened the love letter to reveal a page of beautiful Islamic calligraphy in blue and gold. In 1993 when I had the dream, I associated this page with an illustration in Laleh Bakhtiar's illustrated book *Sufi: Expressions of the Mystic Quest*. But it was not until 1998, the year I embraced Islam, that I realised that the page in question was a calligraphic illustration of *Al Fatiha*, the opening surah of the Qur'an, also referred to as *Umm al-kitab*, the Essence of the Divine Writ. So the love letter from the Gulf was none other than the opening and transmission of divine revelation, the supreme act of love. I am in awe of this whenever I recall the dream.

In a recent discussion with James Morris, Professor of Islamic Studies in Boston University's Theology department and Islamic Civilization and Societies programme, I have learnt of the insights of Ostad Elahi, the twentieth century Iranian philosopher, mystic, jurist, and musician, who affirmed that 'the true devotee of God is the person who is in love with God', and 'until a person has become a lover of God, they will never know what "God-seeing" really is'.

I was aware in the dream that the mysterious female writer of the love letter was 'submissive', and I knew that it was of the greatest importance to affirm that this quality had nothing to do with feminine submission to dominant masculinity but referred solely to submission to the Divine.

The blue and the gold of the love letter held a special meaning for me years before I came to associate these colours with formal calligraphic

texts of the opening surah of the Qur'an. I saw the ocean in the blue and the sun in the gold, two elemental images that I had seen in a visionary experience when I was nineteen years old. In my natal horoscope my fiery Sun in Aries is in opposition to watery Neptune, but in my vision, I saw, to the audible accompaniment of what I can only describe as 'the music of the spheres', the sun moving around my chart until it was no longer in opposition but in conjunction with Neptune – fire with water, the union of the opposites, the *rubedo* or culmination of the alchemical process. Years later, I understood this *coniunctio oppositorum* to be the guiding *mythos* of my life, the confirmation of the first dream I remember in this life at the age of eight. I was driving a chariot through the sky, a chariot drawn by a white and a black horse, and my task was to guide the horses to a state of perfect balance between them. By careful use of the reins, I managed to achieve this, and as I did so a powerful influx of energy from the union of black and white caused the chariot and horses to soar in a great arc into the heavens.

What stands out for me in the various images in the dreams I have related is the deeply felt awareness that the soul in submission to the Divine is immersed in an ocean in which all opposites are united. Such is the source of Divine revelation, which is also the place of self-knowledge, for, as the Prophet said, 'he who knows himself knows his Lord'.

The ocean beckons, and in entering the ocean, one becomes more than just a drop, for the ocean fills the drop. Or, as Rumi said, 'you are not a drop in the ocean. You are the entire ocean in a drop'.

Two more striking dreams of an ocean of water come to mind. In the first of them, I saw myself as the archetypal lover Tristan ardently setting off into the ocean in a flimsy canoe in search of his beloved Isolde. There was a pilot in the prow of the canoe, but I could not see his face as his back was turned towards me. I had not gone very far when the whole ocean seemed to rise up from the depths in an immeasurably vast and scintillating golden wave which towered above me, but I awoke before I was engulfed by it. I have always interpreted the dream as an imaginal representation of the *hadith qudsi*, 'if you come to Me walking, I will come to you running'. The Beloved is always aware of any sincere desire to come closer to Him/Her.

The second dream occurred the night after my return to England after I had said my shahada, embraced Islam, and taken hand with Shaykh Safer Effendi at the tekke of the Jerrahi-Halveti Order of Dervishes in Istanbul

in 1998. In my dream I was in the tekke again, but it was a completely different place, a simple room with bare whitewashed walls devoid of any cultural or formal religious identity. There were none of the traditional Islamic artifacts I had seen in the tekke, no calligraphy, no oriental rugs or cushions, no cigarette smoke so indicative of Turkish dervishes! There was a complete absence of any Middle Eastern cultural flavour to the setting. There were dervishes, but they did not wear dervish robes, and they sat around simple square tables (four to a table) drinking from ordinary white mugs. The most striking feature of the room was a large picture window which took up the whole of one side of the room and looked out onto a vast, blue, simmering ocean. Nothing else, only this ocean. The room appeared to be small in dimensions but the scale of the view imparted a sense of almost limitless spaciousness. It reminded me of the stunning view of the vastness of the Pacific Ocean I had seen as I trekked along the mountains in Big Sur in California. I had a sense of pristine clarity uncluttered by any formal accretions. I realised that my experience in Istanbul had actually not been about joining a brotherhood in any specific place, but about opening a window to the universality of Islam.

In the dream, I seemed to have the role of waiting at the tables of the dervishes. I circulated the room picking up their empty mugs and taking them to the kitchen. In doing so, I always picked up four mugs at a time, for there were four dervishes at every table. To pick up four mugs, you have to use the thumb and three long fingers of your hand, and in doing so you make a cube of four cylinders, with the four circles of the mug openings forming a square. I knew in the dream that the geometric symbolism of this was important. Four circles forming a square – the containment of the infinite within the finite, the embodiment of the formless within form. Then I inwardly 'heard' these words, absolutely clear and impossible to forget: 'this is a station on the way to meeting Ibn 'Arabi'. I was reminded of *An Ocean Without Shore*, the title of Michel Chodkiewicz's book on the writings of Ibn 'Arabi.

At this point, it might well be asked what guided me to embrace Islam in 1998. In other words, what motivated my conversion? Well, it will probably not surprise you to learn that my path to conversion was itself the outcome of a dream, one that further expanded and gave concrete expression to my awareness that my dream in 1993 of the love letter from

the Gulf had opened a window to Islam. As I have explained in relating that dream, it was not until 1998 that I realised that the love letter was a calligraphic illustration of Al Fatiha, the opening surah of the Qur'an.

In 1997, I had been Director of Studies at a well-known independent school in Glastonbury in Somerset, England for several years. My haven was the Recital Hall in the Music School, where I often used to go to play the piano as a keen amateur classical pianist. One night, I dreamt that I was standing at the entrance to the Recital Hall holding in my hand a black box in the shape of a cube, and I knew it was a gift for my wife, who symbolized the feminine, and all that meant to me on a spiritual level, including love, mercy, beauty, creativity, receptivity, and what I can only describe as the fragrance of the essence. I opened it to see what it contained, assuming it to be a precious jewel of some kind, or an expensive fragrance in a fancy bottle. But the box was completely empty. I looked into it and the more I looked the vaster became the space within, until it seemed to become an infinitely expansive space, like the dazzling darkness seen by astronauts as they looked into the deep space of the cosmos. The feeling as I gazed into the depths of the box was very similar to the sense of awe and mystery that pervaded the oceanic depths of the source of the love letter in my dream of the Gulf. There was a paradoxical merging of intimacy and remoteness in the sense that, as the Qur'an says, God is 'closer to you than your jugular vein' (50:16) yet 'utterly remote in His limitless glory' (59:23).

I awoke from the dream and lay awake for some time reflecting on what this might signify. Unable to go back to sleep, I went downstairs and switched on the TV. There, immediately in front of me on the screen at that very moment was a man opening a black box in the shape of a cube to reveal 99 inner cubes, each engraved with one of the 99 Names of God in Kufic script. Stunned, I looked in the paper to see what the programme was and it was one in a series called *Ramadan Journeys* about the work of creative British Muslims. It should have finished half an hour earlier, but a football match had gone into extra time. The man opening the box was Ahmed Moustafa, the British-Egyptian artist and scholar, and the artefact he had just opened was a visual representation he had created of the hadith of the Prophet that 'God has 99 Names, one hundred minus one; whoever enumerates them enters paradise'. The verb *ahsaaha* here has the sense not

only of enumeration, placing on record, or memorisation of the Names, but also of understanding them, being mindful of them and acting upon them. Just a word about the geometry here. A cube of 10 by 10 by 10, if opened along either of the two diagonals on any of the six faces, reveals 99 inner cubes. I say 99, and not 100, because the 100th cube in any opening is actually the apex of another opening along a different diagonal. This is the hundred minus one. Since there are two diagonals on each of the six faces, and each diagonal can open in either of two directions, there are therefore 24 possible openings of the cube. The symbolism is itself fascinating. The six faces of the cube and the 24 openings encompass the four cardinal directions together with height and depth, and the flow of time. The Qur'anic verse immediately comes to mind: wherever you look, there is the Face of God.

Immediately, I understood at some very deep and intuitive level the connection between the two cubes – the one in my dream, and the other in Ahmed's hands, the one empty and the other manifesting the divine attributes. The two cubes together represented the union of the inner and the outer, the hidden and the manifest, and the direction of the whole experience from the dream to the 99 Names was one of bringing the inner reality into form, embodying it in one's life. I also understood that the Attributes of Divine Perfection belonged to God Alone, and in order for the human being to embody any of them (as far as humanly possible of course because the human being can only embody a portion or fraction of them) one has to strive to empty oneself of the false self, the ego.

In a way, this was a rediscovery on an experiential level of my earlier academic research into the way learning and enlightenment are obstructed by the clutter of the conditioned mind and by the intrusion of the self. But I knew my dream of the empty box was more than a metaphor for the absence of mental conditioning or fixed ideas. It was for me a mystical experience, a glimpse of the foundation of spiritual life.

The next day, I told the dream to my wife Tania and to another mutual friend who tracked down Ahmed's contact details and called him at his studio in London. She told him what I had told her, and he immediately invited Tania and me to visit him the next day. To cut a long story short, within an hour of meeting him, he told me that he was holding an exhibition of his artworks in Rome the following year, the first exhibition

by a Muslim artist in the Vatican. The following year, the exhibition was to be installed in Sarajevo at the National Gallery and then in the Diocesan Museum of the Gothic Cathedral in Barcelona. The title of the exhibition, sponsored by the Altajir World of Islam Trust, was to be *Where the Two Oceans Meet* and Ahmed asked me if I would write the exhibition catalogue (including a major essay on his work) to be translated into Italian and Arabic, and later into Bosnian and Catalan. Astounded, I said: 'Ahmed, I am a teacher of English in rural Somerset; I know nothing about Islamic art, and very little about Islam. How could I undertake such a task?' He replied, 'That is precisely why I am asking you; you have no preconceptions and none of the conventional opinions of the art historian.'

So I wrote the text, and in so doing I explored Islam from the viewpoint of the art it had inspired. Within three months of starting to write it, Tania and I had both said our *shahada* and embraced Islam. I went to the Central Mosque in London to see the education officer to ask him his opinion on the quality of the Arabic I had learnt for the prayers, supplications and the recitation of surahs from the Qur'an. I recited the Fatiha and he was complimentary, asking me where I had become a Muslim. 'In Istanbul', I replied. He grimaced, and said: 'but there are no Muslims in Turkey; there are only Sufis'.

This was my first and rather shocking encounter with the tribal mentality which I thought that Islam had come to abolish. Sadly, I could give you many other examples of the same kind of thing in subsequent encounters in the years that followed, both from the Muslim and the non-Muslim side. But I don't want to dwell on the negative. Since my first metaphysical encounter with the cube, any difficult human encounters have been vastly counterbalanced by many deep friendships with Muslim friends, colleagues. and benefactors who have been an inspiration to me through the fineness of their character and their striving for *ihsan*, doing what is beautiful. The following year I founded the Book Foundation dedicated to the publication, translation, and distribution of *The Message of the Qur'an* by Muhammad Asad.

It might well be asked if I had encountered Islam in my life before I received the love letter from the Gulf in my dream of 1993. To answer that, I need to go back to my time at University College London in the late 1960s. I dropped out of my degree course in English after one year and did

not return to complete my degree until 1971. My four years away encompassed a period of intense inner searching and spiritual hunger which could find no sustenance or direction either through academic study or the pop culture of Swinging London that had captivated many of my peers, not to mention the new fad of tripping on LSD. During that period I assiduously explored the practice of many paths in various spiritual traditions. I studied and practised yoga, including its postures, meditation, and breathing practices and apply some of them to this day. I spent time at a Franciscan monastery in Dorset, having many conversations with the spiritual director, and an even longer stretch at the Ramakrishna Vedanta Centre in London, where I not only studied the great texts of the Advaita Vedanta tradition in Sanskrit but also learnt to meditate under the direction of the swami. I was invited to join both the Franciscan and Vedanta Orders. I was drawn more to the latter, but I knew that the monastic life was not my way. I confess that one evening at the Ramakrishna Vedanta Centre, where the diet was very austere and strictly vegetarian, I slipped out and walked to Holland Park to a Wimpy Bar for a large hamburger and chips.

I also studied astrology, and even made my living for a while drawing up and interpreting horoscopes. I studied depth psychology, explored the symbolism of dreams, and I sought out and found friends, fellow travellers and mentors amongst some exceptional people trying to live what can best be described as a conscious life. These included former pupils of the Armenian spiritual teacher Georges Gurdjieff, whose methodology of self-observation and work on oneself influenced me profoundly at the time. One of Gurdjieff's grandsons had been my best friend at school and I stayed with his family in London for a while, working at the Russian bistro of one of Gurdjieff's daughters. I can still make a great borscht (beet soup with meat stock, cabbage, and sour cream).

Then in 1971, aged twenty-three, I met Idries Shah, the Afghan writer and teacher, at his home in Langton, Kent, after volunteering to work in his garden. Shah was doing so much at that time to introduce the West to Sufism, not only the history of the numerous ways in which Sufism in some form had penetrated Western civilisation, but also (and this interested me more) the actual methodology of seeing through the conditioning and mechanical thinking which prevents the development of consciousness.

Later I was to take this up again, though in a more academic context, in my Ph.D. research in psycholinguistics in Papua New Guinea in the mid 1980's, where I explored the cognitive processes involved in learning, and especially the problem of fixed mindsets which generate stereotypical expectations that are resistant or even impervious to new ideas. These top-down cognitive structures include frames and scripts, dominant narratives, and even whole paradigms of thought. Binary thinking and a preference for intractable dichotomies are also often ingrained in this mode of thinking. To this day one of my abiding interests in the field of practical spirituality is the way in which such structures can be bypassed, including some of the radical methods in various spiritual traditions. These include koan-training in Zen Buddhism, by which a paradox or conundrum is meditated upon so as to loosen dependence on reason and dualistic thinking and provoke an intuitive leap, a flash of enlightenment. There is also the corpus of humorous tales about Mulla Nasrudin known throughout the Middle East. These stories may be understood at any one of many depths, not only as joke and moral, but also, like the koan, as a means of shifting habits of thought that impede more subtle states of consciousness.

My interest in Idries Shah's work in the early 1970's opened up for me the world of Sufism, and for the next twenty years I guess I was one of those Western followers of Sufi mysticism, though with no necessary grounding of that in Islam or Islamic spirituality. It's common for some Muslims to dismiss or even deride this brand of Westernised Sufism, detached from its roots, but I see it differently. Many of those Westerners are spiritually hungry; they are seeking the essence of religion, a universal path divested of culture, and they are drawn to the Sufi masters and poets because of the notes of love, humanity, and beauty which they sound and the promise they give of personal transformation. They are starting from an inner dimension. Sometimes, as in my own journey, they discover the tradition that underlies it, the formal religion, and that meeting of the inner and the outer, of essence and form, can be profoundly illuminating, transformational. The movement, though, is from the inner to the outer, and through that meeting, an infusion of substance, orientation, and direction which strengthens and deepens the inner quest.

For heritage Muslims, the journey can be very different, because they often start with the outer, the formal elements, often within a cultural

mindset, and their task may be to discover the inner and universal meaning of the forms they inherit. Their task may even be to liberate themselves from formalisms, just as one of the tasks of the new adherent to a religious path may be to encompass some degree of formal discipline. The outer without the inner is a husk without a kernel, and conversely the inner without the outer though full of potential is mute, having no form, no vehicle, no sphere of action, no coherent language in which to express itself, at risk of navel-gazing.

So I was drawn to connect the inner and the outer, to align myself with Islam, to embrace a tradition and a discipline and explore a civilisation, to become a Muslim when I was fifty years old. I deliberately avoid the labels 'convert' or 'revert' because I don't actually see myself as either. It's not that I don't see myself as on the Path of Return if that's what reversion means; it's just that I see that path, and the path of conversion, as a cumulative process of inner transformation, a continuing spiritual journey, a path of integration, not an identity crisis or a Road to Damascus experience, neither is it a sudden rupture with the past, a wholesale abandonment of one culture for another, nor the embrace of some new and exotic tribal affiliation. Least of all is it the embrace of a clash of civilisations.

But at the same time, there is clear commitment involved, a decision to follow a definite path as the prime means of transformation. I'd use a musical analogy, because music means a lot to me. To become a musician, to enter into the world of music, you need to learn a musical instrument (and that includes of course the human voice), otherwise you can only be someone who knows about music, or appreciates it. You cannot learn every instrument, but in learning just one you learn musicianship. In an orchestra there are many instruments, and each player has mastered one of them. Playing in an orchestra, each one learns to improve his or her musicianship by playing in ensemble with others, by listening to the other. The violinist does not play the 'cello at the same time, nor does the clarinettist play the flute, but each one of them is a musician. The same goes for other kinds of creative artists and craftsmen, and to scholars and practitioners in so many fields. They have chosen to strive to master something, and by so doing to realise and embody as far as humanly possible the beauty and majesty of an attribute of Divine Perfection. As the Qur'an tells us, does not every

creature on the face of the earth worship God in its own way, even if we have no knowledge of it?

Science tells us that sleep and dreaming are necessary both for the body to cope with the day's trauma and reset itself for the next. My dreams thus allow me, from time to time, to deal not only with life's events, but to also reset my own spiritual journey. So dream a little dream of me.

THE WELL IN CARRIACOU

Shani Alexander

I remembered the well in Carriacou. I had to wake up early, take a bucket, and walk half a mile to fill it up with water before school. I see myself on the trips back and forth, under the baking heat of the sun.

Carriacou is one part of Grenada, a tri-island state which includes the main island, Grenada, and Petite Martinique, in the southeastern Caribbean Sea. It has crystal clear waters, pristine coral reefs and long stretches of white sandy beaches. There are two seasons. In the dry season the sun beats relentlessly down on the 'Kayaks', the name for the inhabitants, doling out punishment for some unknown wrongdoing. The wet season brings relief via its rain, if only for a little while. The island has no year-round streams and limited groundwater.

I was born on this verdant thirteen square mile speck of land and spent the first twelve years of my life there. When I was eight, my mother moved to England leaving my sister, brothers, and me with my grandmother – 'Mama'. She had twelve children and at one time or another, most left their own sons and daughters with her as they went to Trinidad, St Maarten, England, or America. There was little work on the island.

We lived in a three-bedroom house in L'Esterre, with no piped water. It had a cistern which collected rainwater from the spouting that surrounded the roof. That precious liquid which fell from the sky was used to cook and drink. To wash our clothes and bathe, we had to go to the well – a hole dug by men hundreds of years before, stretching way down to the aquifer. The well gave us water; the well gave us life.

The family would rise at cockcrow. We – the grandchildren of various ages, limb lengths, and complexions – brushed our teeth, washed our faces and changed our clothes. The house was a hive of activity early in the morning. Then, when all that was done, our diminutive army would take our buckets, in varied sizes, shapes, and colours, and head off to get the water.

Along the way we would meet other children from the village. Sometimes we trudged along without speaking – one foot in front the other, in silent companionship, trying to bury our frustration at having no choice but to drag our bodies to the well so early. But other times we would skip, tell stories, share gossip, and laugh. Those were the times when the trees hang heavy with certain fruits. We would smell them and start to salivate. The Chinup tree that hung over Miss Clara's fence was too high for us to reach. There were plum trees though, on the side of the road, and we would have our fill. There were also oranges, which hung over the fence from Mr Joe's garden. The wiry old, brown-skinned man would often chase us with a cutlass when he caught us trying to grab one that was hanging low. He was never to catch us as our sprightly young legs allowed us to make a quick getaway.

When we arrived at the well, which had concrete surrounding the hole, one of the older kids would lower a bucket tied to a rope into the water below. There were no railings, no protection to prevent anyone from falling in. But I remember how the kids would always stand so confidently over the borehole, the bucket always sent down without hesitation, without fear that they might fall. Just dogged determination on their face, as their slim arms pulled the container up and poured it into one of the other buckets which lined the edges of the well. They performed those movements again and again and again, as natural as walking.

Then we would put a cloth, a 'carter', on our head, someone would lift the bucket onto it and like a trail of ants carrying food, we would walk home being careful not to move our heads too much. On most trips, by the time I arrived, my bucket would be half full and I would be soaked. The water would be poured into the drums placed at the side of the house. We would go back and forth like worker bees until they were filled.

We would not just fetch water for the family but sometimes the animals, too – the goats and cows that grazed in nearby fields, especially in the dry season. Again, the trail that led to them was peppered with an assortment of fruit trees. I remember that my fingers would sink into the flesh of the sugar apple if I squeezed it too tight to check if the luscious fruit was ripe. There were berries hanging from high up in the branches and we had to find a long stick to try to knock down a few. Sometimes one of the boys would climb the tamarind tree and pick a few and come down and share them.

For most people I know now, journeying daily to the well would be thought of as childhood hardship. But I often wonder if it was really so bad, as it was filled with these experiences. Of laughing with other kids, of eating those sweet, delicious fruits along the way, of being useful by providing the water we so desperately needed. When you live on an island and the rain does not fall, how else can you get water? My mother went to the well, her mother went to the well, her mother too. These life-giving trips connected us.

But it was relentless, and I rankled at the harsh duty imposed on me. There were days when we went twice before school if we woke early and walked fast enough. On the weekends, we had to make four, five, or sometimes six trips back and forth. And even though we started early, the hot sun would meet us soon enough.

One Saturday, I think I was about eleven years old, my cousins and I had already done several trips, and the heat was starting to punish us. But Mama told us to go back for another bucket of water. The drums could hold more. I told her it was getting too hot, but it was to no end, we had to go.

I stomped along the way complaining to my cousins. When we got to the well, I slammed the bucket on the concrete base and watched in horror as it bounced and fell in. My heart stopped. I looked at my cousins. They were wide-eyed. What did I do? We all stared down into the hole at the white bucket floating on top of the water. What would I do now? I knew what would happen if I went back without the bucket. Mama would send one of us out to get a whip, a small branch from a tree, or she would use a belt.

We rummaged around in the nearby bushes trying to find a long stick we could send down and somehow grab the handle of the bucket. I remember the sun was climbing higher and higher and the heat was merciless. After a while, we sat under a tree, bereft. I was feeling sick, already feeling the sting from the imminent beating on my skin. Eventually, a man came by, called in on a neighbour and emerged with a long stick with a nail on one end. The bucket was fished out.

Of course Mama asked what took us so long. I told her my bucket fell into the well and it took us a while to get it out. She just looked at me.

My head was full of relief, yes, but also frustration at my helplessness and lack of choice. Inwardly, I was pleading with her to see me, to see us. Not only were we weary from carrying the buckets full all morning but we

were being whipped by the heat. I was calling out to her to let us come up for air, we were drowning and she was not reaching out a hand to save us. Some sort of rebellion was brewing in my head, and now I think back to those times with a verse from Bob Marley's 'I Shot the Sheriff' ringing in my ears:

Every day the bucket a-go a-well.
One day the bottom a-go drop out.

In the dry season, we used so much water, we were always filling up those drums. With at least ten of us in the house at any one time, we had to bathe, we had to wash our clothes, we had to be clean. The sun, it seemed, also soaked up its share. One of the few beneficial things about the remorseless heat was that if we wanted to bathe with warm water, we needed only to leave a bucket outside. Most often, the sun overwhelmed us. I would get tired just walking under the sheer force of its rays. I remember the quick trips to the shop to buy Back-N-Neck 'chicken' for Mama or an eighths-ah-rum for my uncle, the tar melting on the road.

I also remember sucking on snow-ice, biting the plastic tip off the bag and letting the sweet, flavoured frozen liquid inside hit my taste buds and bring me much needed relief. We would also drink lime juice, 'gospo' juice and Kool Aid to quench our thirst and satisfy our sweet tooth.

As the dry season wore on, to save the water in the drums, sometimes my sister and I would take our laundry to the well. Armed with buckets, a wash board and a scrubbing brush, we would find a tree with lots of branches for shade and set out our patch. She took control of the washboard and handled the bigger pieces of clothing. I remember watching her movements, the white school-shirt spread out on the board, the soap passed along the collar, the scrubbing brush being moved up and down as the dirt melted away. I also remember the feeling of the soft material of the vest between my fingers as I rubbed my hands together, hearing the squishing sound of the water as it sluiced through my fingers. Then we would rinse the clothes and spread them on the nearby bushes to dry.

For many years after moving to England, being a child who went to the well was a source of secret shame. On TV, it was what poor people in Africa did, many walking much further than I did, and many being unable to go to school because of it. Like us, they needed to fetch water to drink,

cook, clean, and feed the animals. And from the television I learned that they were pitiable, they needed my help.

How was I going to tell my new friends that I too went to the well? That when I moved to England, it was the first time I lived in a house with running water? Or in a house where you could flush the toilet? Or at my astonishment of turning on the tap and all the water I could drink gushing out? So, I never talked about going to the well.

The only day we didn't go to the well was Sunday, when we had to go to church. This, too, was an essential, non-negotiable, part of our lives. Like everyone else, I was baptised and confirmed. To survive and live in Carriacou we had to have faith. Despite the abuse we got from the sun, we remained resolute. That strength of spirit, I believe, was fed and fostered in the constant church services. The scarcity of water and the heat were not going to break us.

My grandmother had unshakeable belief in God and prayed all the time, sometimes long into the night then waking early to pray. To ask and thank God for what, I cannot remember. Maybe it was for the strength and patience to look after all the grandchildren, or for rain during the dry season, or for plentiful crops in the rainy season.

We greeted the rain like a gift from heaven. Our house had a galvanised roof and I loved the nights when the sky opened. The melodic patter of the rain hitting the steel roof would soothe me to sleep. I loved that rhythmic sound, that I rarely hear nowadays.

The men would fork and prepare the land surrounding the house during the dry season for when the season changed. Then the grandchildren, whatever our age or size, would all have to go planting. First though, we had to put the chickens in their coop, and we would spend hours chasing them around the yard. Then we would take a hoe, fork, and bowls of seeds, and we would head out to lay the seeds.

We took turns digging small holes with the hoe. These had to be equal distances apart. Then four or five corn and pea seeds would be thrown into each one and covered with soil. Some days, we went in the garden for about an hour before and after school. We would spend longer on the weekends, until the land was planted. We would carry out this job with care, patience, and a dose of frustration because, again, it was hard work.

Then the water would fall from the sky, feeding and nourishing the seeds. Before long, the green shoots would poke out of the soil.

Weeks later, we would be in the garden again. Digging the moist soil to get rid of the weeds around the corn and peas and 'moulding' the young seedlings. Then we would plant other crops, in the spaces between – okra, casava, pumpkin. Soon, they too would bloom and grow, watered, we hoped, by the rain.

But it might not rain for several days or weeks, the water in the drums and barrels would run low, and, we would have to go to the well for water to bathe.

Our lives revolved around the water in the well and the rains, and also the sea, where we would also go to bathe. From time to time, we would go to the beach in L'Esterre, and on other occasions further up to Paradise Beach, with its turquoise waters, long stretch of white sand, and grape trees crawling along the borders. A few small boats would be bobbing idly in the ocean. Decades later, Paradise would be voted one of the best beaches in the Caribbean. In one sense, I felt pride. I knew this beach; it was ours. But in another, there was a twinge of disappointment because there again, my experience of it was filled with restrictions.

Mama would warn us not to venture too far into the deep waters. We girls were given a further caution, the salt in the seawater would damage our thick afro curls, so we shouldn't get them wet. We would wrap our heads with a cloth, sometimes with a plastic bag over it for added protection. On the beach, the girls passed the time laughing, playing in the sand and in the shallow waters, only venturing as far as our feet could touch the bottom. I did not learn to swim until years later, when I was no longer concerned that the water, now filled with chlorine, in a swimming pool in Highbury, would damage my hair. As for the boys, they were free to swim without fear of any consequences. They would often debate whether they could wade out to Sandy Island, a sandbank with trees about a mile offshore, but aware of Mama's warning, they did not dare. After hours on the beach, we would force our limbs to carry us to the well to rinse the salt water from our bodies, then drag ourselves home, exhausted.

I left Carriacou and moved to England in 1997. In the years that followed, the island and its inhabitants' relationship to water, changed. To address the water scarcity, in the early 2000s a Catholic organisation called

St Vincent de Paul helped build cisterns for most houses. Black water tanks also began to appear, installed on the side of houses. These large cylindrical, plastic containers, holding up to 10,000 gallons of water, brought respite to many people. Some with cisterns also now use the tanks to store additional water for when the seasons change. Others converted the tanks to work as cisterns, connected to the roof of the house to collect the water from the guttering.

On a trip back in 2013, I noticed that these made a difference. No one was going to the well anymore. I stayed in my aunt's house which had a cistern from which water was pumped into the house. People born in Carriacou, or with family connections to the island have been coming and going for as long as I can remember. Those who left for England, America, or Canada would visit family during the holidays, and many would build houses to enjoy the island when they retired. These homes would have cisterns and be empty for lengthy periods so they became another source of water for the locals.

In 2016, a desalination plant, powered by solar panels, was opened on the island. Carriacou, after all, has unlimited access to seawater and abundant sunshine. Kayaks can now buy water in the dry season. Even so, the National Water and Sewerage Authority of Grenada often run campaigns reminding the islanders that water is precious and should not be wasted. Those of us who grew up going to the well hardly need telling, but many others do. My aunt tells me she often has to remind her young daughter to turn off the tap while brushing her teeth.

Although access to water has improved, the heat has worsened. A 2022 report from the World Meteorological Organization noted that temperatures in the region have risen by an average of 0.2° Celsius per decade over the last thirty years. This may not sound like a lot, but it's the highest rate since records began and my brother and aunt tell me they can feel it.

To cool their homes people have fans and leave their doors and windows open. Aircon has not yet arrived for the many, only the affluent few. The electricity bills, for now, make it too pricey to run. But I think that widespread aircon on Carriacou is not far off. The International Energy Agency (IEA) expects that over the next three decades, the use of aircons in the tropics will soar as the temperature rises and incomes grow. Aircon

and electric fans, the IEA also tells us, already account for nearly twenty percent of the total electricity used in buildings globally.

I know the cooling units will ease, and maybe even save, lives, but Kayaks should be aware they will put stress on the power grid, whilst also exacerbating the very global warming that has made them necessary. This is true even if they are powered by solar energy. The hydrofluorocarbon refrigerants used in aircons are powerful greenhouse gases and often escape into the atmosphere. Furthermore, aircon pushes heat outdoors, raising temperatures nearby. It is only a 'solution' to rising temperatures in an exceptionally individualistic, short-term sense.

But climate change is bringing another threat to Carriacou: the island is drowning. This is something I could never have imagined back when I was making my endless trips to the well. Melting ice-sheets and glaciers have led to the sea levels creeping ever higher, eroding the land, and causing subsidence into the sea.

In her young days, my grandmother would gather sand on the beach in Harvey Vale, located in the southern part of the island, to sell. Today the place on the beach where she stored the sand, before it was picked up by trucks of those who bought it, is underwater. That place on the beach where people tied goats, sheep, or cows, while waiting for the boat to arrive to send them to Grenada, is underwater. The paths near the beach, where my brother once walked as a child, have disappeared. Most of the beach has disappeared under the surf. Seawater in Harvey Vale is almost up to the road. The government has brought in big boulders to try to protect the land from erosion, but the water keeps rising. In Tibeau, in the north, one of the oldest cemeteries on the island is slowly being claimed by the sea, with tombstones fully or partially covered at high tide. The locals began burying the dead here in the 1700s, now erosion and rising water levels are desecrating the graves.

According to a UN Climate Change report, in the past twenty-five years, Sandy Island, that dreamt-of swimming destination for my brothers and cousins, has lost about sixty percent of its area, while the small sandbanks that existed for hundreds of years between Carriacou and Petite Martinique have disappeared completely.

'Carriacou done.' Those were the first words my brother said to my mother and I when he finally got through to us on the phone. 'Houses,

shops, telephone poles, everything is on the ground. It is like a warzone,' he said.

There were a few storms during my time on Carriacou, when we would gather downstairs in the house, waiting for it to pass. But there was never any great destruction. My grandmother told us about the 1955 Hurricane Janet, the deadliest hurricane to hit Carriacou until then. But in the past twenty years Carriacou has been hit by three hurricanes: Ivan in 2004, Emily, the following year, and on 1 July 2024, hurricane Beryl made landfall. A category four hurricane, briefly reaching category five, the winds of up to 150 miles per hour devastated the island. Hurricane Beryl was the strongest hurricane in the history of the island. Nearly every structure on the island was hit. Schools, the police station, the hospital. The yachts, boats, oyster beds, trees, mangroves, forests – were all destroyed.

My mother and I spent that day by the phone, sometimes dialling my brother's number which would ring and ring, sometimes just staring at it and praying for him to call. Scraps of news filtering through via phone calls and social media – most communications systems were down, buildings were damaged, and a family friend had died.

It was my brother's first hurricane. He said he expected heavy rain, thunder, and lightning. But although it rained, it was not heavy. There was no thunder, no lightning. The wind, though, overpowered everything, and everyone. As the hurricane's eye passed over, my brother went outside to look at the sky. The usually brilliant sun, although it was there, had lost its punishing force. Instead, he said, it seemed to stare down silently, waiting uncertainly for what would follow.

When the eye passed, the wind returned with vengeance. My brother was with my aunt, downstairs at her house. They were warned earlier and had prepared as well as they could, filling two large barrels with water. When the wind threatened to rip the door off, they moved those barrels behind it to secure it. 'I was scared,' he said. 'I prayed silently for hours.'

My brother and aunt survived but the roof of my aunt's house was gone and the house we grew up in in L'Esterre was flattened. This was not bad luck: ninety-five percent of houses were either destroyed or damaged. With most roofs gone, there would be no way to collect the rainwater which fell later. But aid came, and quickly. Organisations like the

Samaritan's Purse arrived, bringing supplies and more than anything, helping the Kayaks, access water. They set up stations close to the sea and established a temporary filtration and desalination system. People brought bottles and carried as much away as they needed.

A blip in the 24-hour news cycle, many people did not hear about hurricane Beryl nor the destruction it left in its wake. Many more have never even heard of Carriacou. And those few who have, and who know what happened on 1 July, will mostly not care – it is just another of a litany of tragedies and catastrophes that happen elsewhere, to other people. But this will not always be the case. The world is getting warmer, the climate is destabilising. We have passed the 1.5° Celsius guardrail of post-industrial global heating that scientists warned we should not cross if we wanted to ensure a stable climate. We are on track to blast through the 2° Celsius guardrail beyond which human civilisation as a whole is imperilled. Soon, nowhere will be safe.

Carriacou is used to bad weather. Across the West Indies, people are accustomed to the hurricane season. But not on this scale. The locals thank God that only a few lives were lost given the scale of the destruction. But the Kayaks who worked abroad and saved for years to build their homes on the island, lost what they had built in an instant. They are unlikely to rebuild. Many have returned to England, America, or Canada. These retirees will not return to Carriacou.

For years after moving to England, I was glad to have left the heat of Carriacou behind me. I was glad to no longer have to go to the well for water, or go to the garden to plant. Yet I always thought that I could go back. Home would always be there. But will it? And for how much longer?

The building of cisterns, the desalination plant and the water tanks have helped remedy water scarcity on Carriacou. People can now access sufficient water so that when the rains do not come, it is no longer a concern, as it was for my grandmother. But that same water from the sea, which is being treated so people can drink it, is damaging, eroding, and drowning the island.

It is a physical impossibility that we will ever take back what has already been lost, and extremely unlikely that the island will be saved from the rising sea. Like me begging my grandmother to treat her grandchildren with some degree of humanity or compassion when she sent us back out

under the punishing sun for another bucket of water, Carriacou is begging the world to acknowledge the destruction that lies in wait from climate dysregulation, from unbearably hot dry and rainy seasons that arrive later and later, making agriculture more difficult.

Kayaks can make more use of solar panels and reduce fossil fuel use but those actions are utterly insignificant compared with those of much bigger nations. To save islands like Carriacou, a radical shift in the way people in richer and 'developing' nations live must take place. But I for one do not believe that this will happen. Yes, there will be gestures, and promises of billions to help smaller nations 'fight climate change' but rich nations' own energy consumption, and their extraction and exploitation of the world's resources, will continue. The fact that the last UN COP meeting, held in Azerbaijan, was the second in a row to be held in a petrostate, in a conference hall teeming with fossil fuel lobbyists, should be enough to show that international power brokers have little interest in mitigating climate change.

Even though the emissions contribution of small islands like Carriacou is vanishingly small, they are the ones who will be punished for the western world's addiction to comfort. At the international level, Carriacou and other small islands have no power of self-determination when it comes to global warming. The island will get hotter. The sea water will keep rising. Stronger and more powerful hurricanes will batter us. This they cannot stop.

As a young girl, I hated going to the well in Carriacou, and I wondered when it would end. But it did. Now, I hate watching the sea water slowly rise around Carriacou but I know it will not end. Kayaks may continue to pray and hold fast to their faith, but no saviour will come to rescue their land being devoured by the sea. In my heart, Carriacou is still my home and it breaks as I watch its destruction.

WATER AS METAPHOR

Naomi Foyle

The very term metaphor – from the Greek for 'to carry across' – suggests water, evoking a sense of words as vessels, pouring meaning from concept to image, energising and oxygenating our understanding of ideas and the world. The strength of a metaphor depends on its credibility and scope. For the figure of speech to be convincing, there must be a clear likeness between the referent (sometimes called the tenor) and the image chosen to describe it (the vehicle). To reward contemplation, resemblance must be complex, allowing not only for the pleasure of interpretation but also – especially in poetry – for the kind of fruitful ambiguity that reflects the inherently paradoxical nature of the human condition. Water, a shapeshifting element present on earth in strikingly diverse forms, from a drop to a snowflake to a deathly tsunami, holds immense metaphorical power and range. An archetypal poetic device, water is a universal yet highly mutable vehicle for tenors as varied as life, time, motherhood, emotion, purification, the unconscious, and life's very opposite, death. Often categorised as a 'feminine' element, water, although associated in Taoism with great virtue, is less often in the West considered as a metaphor for wisdom or activism. At a time when, across the globe, the flames of hatred are increasingly fuelled by the dead wood of ignorance and the toxic air of fake news, I have found it helpful to draw on poetry, spiritual texts, and the work of political thinkers to redress this oversight, considering the Taoist notion of 'the way of water' in relation to my own work using poetry to promote dialogue, peace, and justice in Palestine and Israel.

But first to dive into water's metaphorical expanse. Covering seventy-one percent of the Earth's surface, constantly in circulation in the atmosphere, present in every human cell and forming up to sixty percent of our bodies, water is essential to life. As such, it has long been considered

a resource beyond commerce, whether from God or Nature, a gift to
humanity that literally falls from the sky. As the Holy Qur'an puts it:

> And We send the winds fertilising, then cause water to descend from the sky,
> and give it to you to drink. It is not you who are the holders of the store of it.
> (15:22)

Elsewhere the Qur'an reminds us that a she-camel has as much right to
drink as we do (26:155). Even under global capitalism, in which water
companies pollute the sea and waterways, valuing shareholders over
customers, and bottled water literally costs the earth in plastic waste,
vestiges of this ancient belief in water as a common good and human right
persist in laws such as those in the UK requiring schools, workplaces, and
licensed premises to provide free potable water. This primal sense of water
as the 'gift of life' enables deeper readings of the image in poetry and
fiction. In Frank Herbert's *Dune* series, the effort to survive on a desert
planet generates the technological innovation of the 'still suit', that recycles
human fluids; but the centrality of water scarcity to this modern classic
science fiction text also invokes the preciousness of life and the cycles of
the generations, as the indigenous Fremen work together to achieve their
goal of greening the planet in a distant future none of them will see.

For as the Fremen's epic task reminds us, as much as life is a biological
reality, it is also fundamentally a temporal experience. Here too, water,
carries poetic resonance, its ceaseless cycle through evaporation,
condensation, precipitation and return to the sea, evoking a liquid
ouroboros, in its end its beginning, while the flow of rivers and streams
suggests the apparent linearity of time. At the same time water imagery
can help us understand that these two states – cycle and flow, eternity and
ephemerality – are not mutually exclusive. In Ancient Greece, Heraclitus
supposedly declared that we cannot step twice into the same river,
presumably because the waters are different each time. But the famous
quote is in fact a paraphrase. The misreading has been attributed to both
Plutarch and Plato.   Contemporary scholars, as American philosopher
Daniel W. Graham explains, have now identified the original text:
'*potamoisi toisin autoisin embainousin hetera kai hetera hudata epirrei* / On
those stepping into rivers staying the same other and other waters flow'
– and many interpret it rather differently. Heraclitus, Graham argues, is

observing that the essence of a river is to change: 'if it didn't, it would be a lake or a dry streambed'. The point the ancient philosopher is making then, is:

> not that all things are changing so that we cannot encounter them twice, but something much more subtle and profound. It is that some things stay the same only by changing. One kind of long-lasting material reality exists by virtue of constant turnover in its constituent matter. Here constancy and change are not opposed but inextricably connected. [...] On this reading, Heraclitus believes in flux, but not as destructive of constancy; rather it is, paradoxically, a necessary condition of constancy, at least in some cases (and arguably in all).

One is reminded of William Blake's nineteenth-century invitation to 'Hold ... eternity in an hour'. Accepting such overtures invites us into sacred or mythic time and may entice us to trace the entwined concepts of the eternal and ephemeral back to the watery image of 'the source' – the mysterious and even miraculous origins of both our fleeting individual lives and the universe itself. For believers of Abrahamic faiths, that source is, of course, God. In the Book of Genesis, God's first act was to 'create the heaven and the earth', at the time, dark, 'without form, and void', but also an oceanic chaos, for 'the spirit of God moved upon the face of the waters'. In Islam, where the creation story is dispersed throughout the Qur'an, much of the early action takes place in Paradise, until Adam and Eve are banished to Earth, but for Muslims too it is clear that 'He it is who created the heavens and the earth in six days – and His Throne was upon the water' (11:7). The Abrahamic story shares its liquidity with many world creation myths, in which order emerging from a primeval ocean is a common motif – holders to myths of linear progress might pause to consider that our distant ancestors had an instinctive, or perhaps deductive, sense that life emerged from the sea.

Once land is established in early cosmologies, rivers feature also, bearing already their connotations of the remorseless onrush of time. In the ancient Sumerian creation myth 'The *Huluppu*-Tree', translated from cuneiform tablets by the American folklorist Diane Wolkstein, unnamed forces at the dawn of time plant a single tree 'by the banks of the Euphrates' where, nurtured by those waters, it thrived until the 'whirling South Wind arose, pulling at its roots / And ripping at its branches' and

the river carried it away. The goddess Inanna, then a young and powerless woman, rescues the *Huluppu*-tree (possibly a form of willow), and plants it in her sacred garden in Uruk, where eventually – after being invaded by a serpent and the dark maiden Lilith – it is hewn down by Gilgamesh to become Inanna's throne and bed, and the source of two symbols of kingship she fashions for her brother and for Gilgamesh, her mortal protector. Whereas the wind here is a clearly destructive force, the river is a subtle element in the myth, suggesting the flow of time that both nurtures growth and transports the dead from the world. In plucking the tree from the Euphrates, Inanna demonstrates her divine nature, rescuing life from the torrent of time and transplanting it in the realm of the sacred where it becomes a vehicle (Wolkstein gives a Jungian analysis of the metaphorical significance of the myth) for her own psychological growth.

In relation to rivers, 'the source' is a small, tender, magical place, where a mighty spate is born from a delicate trickle, where something hidden is revealed and the unknown becomes knowable, springing to the surface from deep underground, or even, miraculously, cosmologically, from nothing, or its own death. In 'Fluvial', from *river / run: an ecopoetic trilogy,* a collection which traces the life cycle of the Atlantic Salmon as it heads back upstream to its spawning grounds to die, Helen Moore celebrates the teeming waters of British rivers and, rejecting a singular conception of 'the' or 'a' river, asks 'where does 'river' begin / end? / what does 'river' include?'. It's a question that provokes wonder. In *The Poetics of Reverie,* Gaston Bachelard speaks of 'the reverie which looks to go back up to the springs (*sources*) of the being', a meditation he associates with poetry, memory, origins and childhood. Through 'reimagining the lost childhood' – or inventing it – poets, he suggests, can remind us of our shared origins in 'the intimacy of the world'. It's a beautiful phrase, more resonant than ever in our age of digital isolation and political polarisation. As contemporary attachment theory explores on a psychological level, this primal intimacy – the experience, lack or loss of which profoundly shapes our ability to form healthy bonds with others – is inseparable from our relationship with our parents. Both mothers and fathers are historically associated with water – the ancient Sumerian word for 'water' was the same as for 'semen', and in the Qur'an human genesis is ascribed to 'a gushing fluid, ejected // that issued between / the loins and the ribs' (86:

6-7) – but for multiple reasons water is most widely connected with mothers. Its oceanic rhythms controlled by a celestial body whose phases reflect the human menstrual cycle; surrounding mammals in the womb and released in a rush when we are born; it is little wonder that water is a universal symbol for motherhood.

In French, of course, the word for ocean – *la mer* – is a homonym for mother – *la mère* – and in poetry the association inheres in images of oceans, tides, the moon, deltas, clouds and floods.

In 'A River Dies of Thirst', by the beloved Palestinian poet Mahmoud Darwish, the central figure of the mother is a heavenly being who nurses a 'small' and 'laughing' river on 'milk from the clouds'. When the mother is kidnapped by unidentified assailants referred to only as 'they', the river 'ran short of water / and died, slowly, of thirst.' This slender, folkloric poem is quietly remarkable both for elevating a divine woman to the position of sky god, and for its subtle critique of male violence. Although an obvious allegorical reading might be that 'they' are invaders of the land, in fact the only people mentioned in the poem are locals: 'nocturnal revelers' the river playfully urges to travel 'to Jerusalem and Damascus'. Hostage-takers being largely a male class of person, the poem might imply that women – and nature – can also be the victims of men in their own communities. Whoever has committed the crime, one interpretation of the poem, in light of the ancient symbolism of the river-as-time, strongly suggests that, without respect for the universal principle of mothering, without tenderness and selflessness, a stream of innocence in a people's history might evaporate.

While water's association with women is most apparent in its connections with motherhood, in Western spheres of thought including alchemy, the Tarot, astrology and Jungian psychology, the element is also traditionally considered 'feminine' due to its association with emotion – as opposed to the 'masculine' quality of reason. As tears, water represents grief. Dancing raindrops, gushing rivers, babbling brooks can all suggest happiness. Snow and ice evoke numbness or a cold heart; frost disapproval; steam anger. Alinah Azadeh, in her Substack post 'Gold in the Water', an account of her family pilgrimage to Thailand to mark the twentieth anniversary of the tsunami, which claimed the life of her mother, writes of

an encounter with a giant carp in a lake by a temple, prompting thoughts
of how water reflects her emotional voyage:

> As we follow the golden carp in the waters, I realise this is my first experience
> since we arrived, of stillness, of a moment of peace. Calm now the water
> which once rose up and engulfed this entire area, calmer the emotional turbu-
> lence that took hold of me for weeks – and I am sure of so many others across
> the entire coastlines hit by the wave – in the lead up to this day. A restlessness,
> a sleeplessness, an anticipatory anxiety mixed with a quiet excitement to
> finally be here with my grown daughter, son and husband.
>
> I sense now that we are not just a family of four following the flash of gold in
> the water, but that we stand here with so many unseen others; past pilgrims
> and ancestors. And for half an hour we remain in silence by the water's edge.
> Recording sound, image, or just seeking out the mother-fish moving below
> and around us.

For Azadeh, being offered blessings by the waters of Thailand is a healing
experience. Water in her story is very much the water of the heart. But
viewed through a patriarchal lens, the changeability of water makes it, like
women, fickle, untrustworthy, destructive. Thus although gods of the sea
are generally depicted as powerful older men, violent women are also
often associated with oceans. Although in 'The Drowned Ship' by
Palestinian poet Mourid Barghouti, many people are killed in a shipwreck,
both the tempest – compared to a busy seamstress – and one of its victims,
a widow whose bed is now half-piled with 'white snow', are female.
Water, though, inevitably a genderfluid element, slips through the
shackles of binarism, as does a powerful poem. At the heart of Barghouti's
short lyric poem, which could have been written in response to the
genocide in Gaza, the anonymous speaker observes that no one diving
down to investigate or ransack the ship is 'looking for the last gasps of
mariners and passengers / their last apprehensions'.

Water is also a symbol of cleansing, purification, the unconscious,
dreams, sleep, and death. While these concepts are traditionally overly
associated with women – as the virginal, irrational, and passive – they are,
like all emotions, inherent aspects of being human. This list can be rather
long. But let me then focus on water and wisdom. Water, as in 'the mists
of time', can represent forgetfulness, but as clear lakes, sparkling

fountains, calm seas, and old wells, it is a metaphor for serenity, lucidity, optimism, and depth, all qualities of a sage mind. We have so much to learn from water, and yet, as a species, we are obsessed with firearms, materialism, and airy talk. In her poem 'Saint of the Source', Kurdish Alevi poet Bejan Matur conjures the guardian of a spring, an old man who first 'summons words' and then says, 'We've lost heaven'. The speaker of the poem concurs, responding:

> It is we who lost heaven
> and understood nothing from the waters
> nothing at all.

And yet, water still shimmers and flows, giving freely of beauty and abundance, offering us reflections of our turbulence, its solution of emotional, mental, and spiritual peace. Where can we drink more of this precious elixir? And how might it help us navigate the social and political storms oligarchs and fascists are furiously brewing? Given the Western bias toward categorising water as feminine and therefore not to be trusted, it is perhaps not surprising that the most perceptive and persuasive argument for water as wisdom comes from an Eastern tradition, Taoism, the Chinese religious and philosophical tradition in which male and female are considered complementary opposites in a dynamic whole. In Chapter Eight of the classic Taoist text the *Tao Te Ching*, traditionally thought to have been composed by the semi-legendary sixth century sage Lao Tzu, water is appointed the highest of virtues. This is no whimsical honour. As contemporary Tao author Derek Lin summarises, water has seven specific virtues we should learn to emulate. First, water always seeks the lowest ground, reminding us to be humble. It is also an element with hidden depths, and depth is a quality to be prized in a person's character. Water is kind, as well, giving unconditionally as it travels, with no expectations. When calm, it reflects its surrounding with 'perfect fidelity', inspiring us to speak the truth with 'peace and integrity'. In administering itself to all things equally, water is courteous and just. Perhaps its greatest capability is its versatility – water is flexible, can change both direction and form. And finally, water has a 'heavenly sense of timing'. As rain, snow, delta flood, or low tide, its appearance varies according to seasonal and cosmological rhythms, reminding us of the vital importance of balance and appropriate action.

But though our personal lives might be happier if we learned the lessons of water, how powerful are its virtues in the face of war? We now live in a world the rich won, the major global powers increasingly governed by fascists, billionaires, and genocidaires clearly intent on starting World War III and destroying the planet we live on. How effective is it to be flexible, courteous, and kind in the face of rapacious greed and hatred and the threat of mass annihilation? In 'The Election, Lao Tzu, A Cup of Water', a blog post written in response to the first inauguration of Donald Trump as US President, the late American writer Ursula K. Le Guin, long a follower of the Tao, insisted that the 'way of water' was the only way to effectively resist structural violence. Calls to 'fight' injustice, she argues, lock people into a reactionary cycle of violence. She acknowledges that self-defence is morally defensible, but nevertheless still identifies it as a reaction. Standing firm, on the other hand, like the protesters at Selma or Standing Rock, holding one's ground while refusing to take up arms, breaks the cycle; non-violence is not a negative, but a positive action, one that 'takes control'. Rejecting the glamourisation of the 'warrior' archetype, Le Guin advocates for Lao Tzu's veneration of water, in thoughts worth quoting at length:

> The weakest, most yielding thing in the world, as he calls it, water chooses the lowest path, not the high road. It gives way to anything harder than itself, offers no resistance, flows around obstacles, accepts whatever comes to it, lets itself be used and divided and defiled, yet continues to be itself and to go always in the direction it must go. The tides of the oceans obey the moon while the great currents of the open sea keep on their ways beneath. Water deeply at rest is yet always in motion; the stillest lake is constantly, invisibly transformed into vapour, rising in the air. A river can be dammed and diverted, yet its water is incompressible: it will not go where there is not room for it. A river can be so drained for human uses that it never reaches the sea, yet in all those bypaths and usages its water remains itself and pursues its course, flowing down and on, above ground or underground, breathing itself out into the air in evaporation, rising in mist, fog, cloud, returning to earth as rain, refilling the sea. Water doesn't have only one way. It has infinite ways, it takes whatever way it can, it is utterly opportunistic, and all life on earth depends on this passive, yielding, uncertain, adaptable, changeable element.

The death way or the life way? The high road of the warrior, or the river road?

I know what I want. I want to live with courage, with compassion, in patience, in peace.

The way of the warrior fully admits only the first of these, and wholly denies the last.

The way of the water admits them all.

A provocative and persuasive meditation on pacifism, Le Guin's post is well worth reading today. She is not denying the scale of the problem of American fascism, nor the need to organise against it, and neither is she denouncing necessary violence in self-defence. She is, however, identifying the dangers of impulsive reactions and vengeful retaliations that only play into the hands of those in power. Tragically, such a dynamic has destroyed Gaza over the last sixteen months. That is not to blame Palestinians for their own genocide: both sets of leaders are responsible for their own decisions, and Gazan civilians are certainly not accountable for the actions of Hamas, who drove out their political opponents after coming to power. The point I think Le Guin would have made, and I agree with, is that the archetype of the warrior has not served Palestine well. The atrocities committed by Hamas and other Palestinian militants on 7 October 2023 gave Israel the pretext it needed to unleash fanatical hatred and cruelty on the captive Gazans with the active support of Western governments, who have also taken the opportunity to repress anti-Zionist protest in their own countries. If a just peace is at last achieved in the aftermath of the genocide, Palestinian liberation will have come at the harrowing price of hundreds of thousands of martyrs, over two million bereaved, traumatised, disabled, and impoverished Palestinians, and over twelve hundred Israeli lives, including old people, children, and terrified hostages, not to mention the demolishment of Gaza and toxification of its land. The historical context of the Nakba does not make military resistance the only or best method of resistance to Zionism. As the Palestinian scientist and writer Mazin Qumsiyeh has extensively documented in his book *Popular Resistance in Palestine: A History of Hope and Empowerment*, Palestinians have a long and impressive history of civil disobedience. We

will never now know if such a path to freedom could have been more effective and less costly.

Should national and world leaders begin to follow 'the way of water' that would truly be a sea change. Until then, it is up to ordinary people to strive to broaden this path. I cannot, of course, speak for Palestinians or Israelis; I can only speak for myself. As a Pisces, my star sign being the two fish swimming in opposite directions, I have long understood water as a metaphor for emotion, compassion, and flux, while Le Guin's pacifism resonates with my own Quaker values. In recent years, I have put my love of poetry in service of peace and justice in Palestine-Israel. I am drawn to this mode of activism because I believe that poetry, in its capacity to hold ambiguity and evoke empathy, honours truth in its deepest senses. At times my activities in this area have seemed barely significant, but I have come to see them as small steps in the way of water, that may yet create greater ripples and waves.

Water, Lao Tzu identified, is truthful, and poetry has a profound relationship to truth. The truth is not reducible to 'the facts'. Facts can, and must, be checked. But the most accurate data can never tell the whole of any human story. Beneath surface reflections of events, there are always deeper understandings about ourselves and the world to discover as we grow and change, and as we do the truth grows and changes too. This is why a poem can speak to us down the centuries and still seem charged with relevance: partly because 'beauty is truth, truth, beauty' as John Keats intuited in the early nineteenth century, and beauty can be timeless. But also because new generations bring new experiences to bear on a poem's complex images and formal choices. Poetry's truth lies as well in very ugly experiences. Poetry, Palestinian literary scholar Atef Alshaer, has eloquently said, 'has a duty to register pain and communion with the oppressed, with those whose very lives are under severe risk'. When the war on Palestine is also a narrative war, in which Zionists claim there is no such place as Palestine, and no such people, it is doubly crucial to hear Palestinians speak of their own histories and lived experience. As Poetry and Fiction editor at *Critical Muslim* and editor of the bilingual anthology *A Blade of Grass: New Palestinian Poetry*, and as an educator and academic, I have sought to platform Palestinian voices in print, on campus, at poetry workshops and events in the UK and abroad.

As well as being mutable, though, truth, like Heraclitus's river, is also paradoxical. We love and hate the same person. We fear and desire death. We believe in and doubt the existence of God. Truth itself, one might argue, is simultaneously relative and absolute. For paradox, in essence, is the human condition — from the time we are capable of abstract thought we are required to hold together in our minds irreconcilable contradictions — life and death, presence and absence, body and soul, good and evil, ends and means, the visible and invisible, the mundane and the sacred, and many more. Keats called the ability to entertain such contradictions 'negative capability', which he defined as being 'capable of being in uncertainties, Mysteries, doubts, without any irritable reaching after fact and reason.' Activism, of course, relies on data and analysis, but changing 'facts on the ground' ultimately requires changing people's hearts and minds, and to do this requires a synergetic and — here is water again — fluid process of overcoming polarisation by negotiating difference. Easier said than done when faced with people defending or denying the monumental evils of fascism, genocide, apartheid, and climate crisis, but binational groups in Palestine-Israel are committed to the process. Combatants for Peace, former fighters engaged in non-violent resistance to the occupation; the Parents Circle Family Forum, bereaved members of both communities who promote truth, dialogue, and reconciliation; Standing Together, a group who, while criticised for some poor political choices, organised regular demonstrations calling for ceasefire throughout the genocide and protected aid trucks from settler violence: all these groups, and others, demonstrate that, without denying the imbalance of power between them, Palestinians and Israelis can find common ground and work together for a just peace. The fact that Mazin Qumsiyeh, Founder and Director of the Palestine Museum of Natural History and the Palestine Institute for Biodiversity and Sustainability, and also the binational groups Women Wage Peace (Israel) and Women of the Sun (Palestine) have all been nominated for the Nobel Peace Prize this year is also a cause for hope. It must be terribly hard at times to bridge the gulf of experience that lies between the occupier and the occupied, but such peacebuilders aim to cultivate a faith in our shared humanity that can overcome even very difficult differences. As it says in the Qur'an:

And the two seas [ie, the two kinds of water in the earth] are not alike: this fresh, sweet, good to drink, this bitter, salt. And from them both you eat fresh meat [fish], and derive the ornaments that you wear. And you see the ships cleaving them with its prow that you may seek of His Bounty, and that perhaps you may give thanks. (35:12)

Truly, freedom lies between the river and the sea.

Poetry can also do political work because poetry invites empathy. The ability to feel another person's emotion fuses two of water's great virtues: truth and depth. Empathy, like water, can also be transformative. Feeling empathy for other people's suffering can motivate a person to move from inertia to effective action. 'One person's freedom fighter is another person's terrorist' is a self-evident paradox that gets us not very far. Accepting it simply resigns us to a cycle of violence. To read a poem, on the other hand, that makes one deeply feel the loss of a child, a parent, a homeland, might make one wish to take a stand with those who are seeking an end to the occupation, trying to stop the cycle of killing. On 7 October 2023, that cycle began to spin into a tornado of fire. Just as water changes with the seasons, I adapted my activism in response to the violence. I still go on marches, am still committed to the boycott of Israel and the promotion of Palestinian poetry, but I have made a new effort to support dialogue between Palestinian and Israeli poets and empathic readings of their work. Supported with a grant from the University of Chichester, I co-facilitated a workshop on Israeli and Palestinian poetry at the Anglo-Portuguese poetry festival *A Casa dos Poetas* last year. I have also published Jewish, Israeli, and Palestinian poets in *Critical Muslim*, and organised an event with Palestinian and Israeli poets at the Muslim Institute's last Winter Gathering.

As a genocide raged, I sometimes felt doubtful about this new direction, and though I have persisted in it and learned a lot from doing so, I certainly do not believe it is the path for everyone. I was encouraged at the start of this process by my co-facilitator in Portugal, Hugo Filipe Lopes, who has published an online journal of Israeli and Palestinian poetry and strongly believes in hearing what everyone had to say. But I know it is much easier for outsiders to take this position than for Palestinians and Israelis. I was also heartened, therefore, by the discovery of the anthology *With an Iron Pen: Twenty Years of Hebrew Protest Poetry*, edited by Tal Nitzan and Rachel Tzvia Back, containing poems that denounce the Israeli occupation of

Palestinian territories as 'the sin of Judah', which 'is written with a pen of iron and with the point of a diamond: it is engraved upon the table of their heart' (Jeremiah 17:1). Throughout the collection, Israelis express both their awareness of Palestinian rights, and their anguish over the many lives sacrificed to the Zionist pursuit of total dominion over the land. In an early image, 'The Horizon's Clenched Mouth' by Liat Kaplan evokes the fructifying and soul-cleansing power of water:

> A sudden rain pours down. Yellow bursts forth
> from the land of Palestine: chrysanthemums, oxalis,
>
> mustard, sunflowers, fennel, marigolds, groundsel, and sun.

But the treasure trove of flowers, gold on stolen land, is soon 'summer's stubble', forgotten in news of another army incursion into a refugee camp, and the poem ends:

> A beloved land, enraged, devours us. Day by day
> the darkness is fresh, as certain as sunset.
>
> One cannot bathe in the same blood twice. The body dims, only it
> exists now. Like the sea, like the sea. And there's no lifeguard
>
> Did she cry herself utterly away?

Surely, given the previous lines, that despairing cry against endless violence is an appeal to Israel to acknowledge Palestine? Yet I have had it on good authority from an anti-Zionist Israeli poet of long standing that Palestinian poets often find it overwhelming to be asked to deal with Israeli grief, even if that grief is prompted by guilt. I completely understand and respect Palestinians who do not want to participate in such initiatives. I have always asked Palestinians if they consent for their work to be used in workshops, or events that also feature Israeli poets, and while most have agreed, two have said a firm no, saying they considered such activities 'normalisation', or not 'centring Palestine'. Those who said yes include Naomi Shihab Nye, enthusiastically, and with a great willingness for me to quote her email to me:

> This tragedy continues so horribly, but you give me hope this morning. I
> agree with you! Share the land! Dialogue!

So much unnecessary disaster to renovate now!
So much grief!

I support all the humans who just want to live!

What might all this admittedly modest activity accomplish? Well, at the very least perhaps it might encourage people to believe that peace is possible. If we can't even model or envision peace, how can we ever achieve it? At the best, many such tiny streams might start to come together into a river, a small one at first, like Darwish's 'a river with two banks', nurtured by 'the milk of the clouds', but unlike his, not orphaned and parched: able instead to grow, singing 'sometimes ... heroically / at others passionately' in a rushing, unstoppable momentum toward an end to the occupation and the start of sharing the land. Perhaps that sounds utterly idealistic – yet even drops of water have force. Whatever our particular focus in this dire era of polycrisis, if those of us on the way of water remain resolute, perhaps we might slowly wear down both the rock and the hard place.

CHARGED WITH ENCHANTMENT

John Liechty

1.

My mother often used to reminisce over Deer Creek, a slice of her home state Iowa and of Eden from the sound of it, where she splashed as a girl in the clear stream winding through the family farm. A place of fish, frogs, crawdads, water-skaters, dragonflies, and sometimes a kingfisher or a great blue heron... of gentle breezes and glorious smells, of sunlight filtered down through the leafy arms of the cottonwoods, dappling the water's surface.

My father had his own slice of Eden to reminisce over. Following America's entry into World War II he was the very first youngster drafted in Fulton County, Ohio, but as a conscientious objector was allowed an exemption from military service on religious grounds. He spent the war years working under a programme called Civilian Public Service. His jobs included cutting hair on a psychiatric ward in a state hospital near Cleveland and digging ditches in an arid corner of northeast Colorado as part of a soil conservation project. Dad's favourite assignment saw him planting saplings at a nursery in Marietta, a town on the Ohio River. He was there only a few months, but the waterside sojourn marked him for life. And so, my siblings and I grew up listening to our mother's rhapsodies on Deer Creek and to our father's on the Ohio River.

Whether we are consciously aware of it or not, water is a major part of us – literally, given the fact that a human being is more than fifty per cent made up of water – but also in harder to gauge emotional, cultural, civilisational, religious, instinctive, or intuitive terms. Water shapes us and the worlds we inhabit sculpting livelihoods, identities, landscapes, both physical and spiritual. Water makes us who we are. Try to imagine Mark

Twain without the Mississippi, on whose westward bank he was born and bred, on whose waters he apprenticed to become a riverboat pilot. Imagine Charles Dickens or William Blake without the Thames, Walt Whitman or Winslow Homer or Dorothy Day without the Atlantic shore, Henry David Thoreau without Walden Pond, pilgrims at Varanasi without the Ganges. It is like imagining my parents without Deer Creek or the Ohio River. They would exist, but they would not be the same people, would seem diminished. Water shaped and sustained them, body and soul, as it shapes and sustains each life.

The intimate personal Edens we turn to for sanctuary and renewal are often as not associated with water. Among the finest descriptions of nature Mark Twain ever made are those in *Huckleberry Finn* covering the retreat of Huck and Tom Sawyer from the town of Hannibal to their special place, a wild uninhabited island downriver where the boys are at leisure to fish, camp, swim, smoke, air their grievances, and recover their equilibrium. Blissful bowers occur regularly in literature. In *A Midsummer Night's Dream*, Oberon has a hunch where he will find the estranged fairy queen, telling Puck:

I know a bank whereon the wild thyme blows;
Where oxlips and the nodding violet grows,
Quite over-canopied with luscious woodbine,
With sweet musk-roses, and with eglantine...

The bank in question may refer to a sloping patch of field or wood, but my mind's eye insists on a stream or brook close-by. A place so charged with enchantment calls for water.

Most everyone holds within some special place or experience connected to water. A particular moment has stayed with my wife like the sound of water lapping in 'The Lake Isle of Innisfree', to become lodged in what William Butler Yeats called 'the deep heart's core'. She grew up in Casablanca, a relentless expanse of concrete and noise... People do not, contrary to Humphrey Bogart's claim in the famous film, go there 'for the waters'. What my wife remembers is leaving Casablanca for the waters – therapeutic encampments along a remote beach, or lengthy stays in rural areas. She especially remembers visits to a spring where an aunt would sing out invitations to the turtles who lived there. Whether they came owing to the song or to the offerings of food they were about to receive, they came,

necks craning from the surface of the pool, bestowing a lifelong image on a watching child.

Our slices of Eden are prone to tarnish in what passes for the real world, subject to the decay brought on by time and chance and accelerated by human greed, short-sightedness, negligence, and indifference. The remote pristine beach where my wife camped as a girl is no longer remote or pristine – it is just another stretch of seaside development. The Moroccan countryside, depleted by decades of drought and flight to the cities and by a general eagerness to supplant agriculture with agribusiness, is not what it was. The singing aunt is long-gone, along with the farmhouse she inhabited and the fields and hedgerows she spent a lifetime helping to maintain. The spring is dry. As TS Eliot's *The Waste Land,* the twentieth Century's great between-wars litany of desiccation laments, 'the nymphs are departed' (not to mention the turtles).

As a boy I often visited the farm where my mother spent her opening decades of life, though by then one could scarcely recognise the Deer Creek we'd heard so much about. There too, the nymphs were departed. A few cottonwoods held out along collapsing erosion-eaten banks; but many had succumbed to increasingly routine floods that ripped down the channel after heavy rain. When it wasn't raining, the limpid stream pulsing on through my mother's memory amounted to scarcely more than a limp trickle in the real world – a sludge of manure, chemical fertilisers, pesticides and squandered topsoil. Deer Creek had been reduced to a drainage ditch where little beyond pathogens and the odd carp survived. When my mother was growing up in the 1930s, farmers in her part of Iowa were producing around 45 bushels of corn per acre. Half a century later they were averaging 120 per acre. Today the average yield tops 200 bushels per acre. Remarkable progress, on the face of it. But the toxic stew percolating down what's left of Deer Creek gives some indication of the toll. In the last 150 years Midwestern states like Iowa have lost over half their topsoil to erosion stemming largely from agricultural practice, or malpractice more precisely. The despairing images and tones of *The Waste Land* echo through the American heartland, and on to the ends of the earth:

A rat crept softly through the vegetation
Dragging its slimy belly on the bank
While I was fishing in the dull canal...

The lines trigger memories of my first trip to Hannibal, Missouri, with my parents. After visiting Mark Twain's boyhood home we went for a stroll, drawing up at a concrete pier down by the river where a man was stationed within a ring of onlookers. It was a fisherman in shorts and flip-flops, shirtless, fat, and slightly drunk. He had just landed an enormous catfish whose bulk I doubt I could have reached my ten-year-old arms around. It was a phenomenal fish that struck awe into the audience, along with disquiet. One did not need an ichthyologist to confirm that something wasn't right. The fish's skin was marbled with lesions the size of small saucers, pink as the inner flesh of a lip. Everything about the creature suggested deformity. 'What are you going to do with it?' someone asked.

The man punctured a can of Falstaff with a triangle-pronged opener. Pull-rings, a recent innovation, were far from universal; beer cans of the era were sturdy as steel oil-drums. He tilted the can to his lips, and with a wry foam-lined smile gave a shrug in the direction of the current. The message was unmistakable. He was throwing the dead fish back to the half-dead Mississippi. No one blamed him, or volunteered to take the meat off his hands – it didn't look fit to toss a famished dog. America was in the thick of the Vietnam War at the time. Waste, poison, and complicity were in the air, and in the water too. Mark Twain's glorious free-flowing river seemed to be going the way of Deer Creek.

The Ohio River was faring no better. Dad took us to Marietta, where he hunted in vain for the old haunts still vibrant in his imagination. The nursery no longer existed, the town looked unfamiliar, the trails where he'd walked the riverbank seemed to have vanished into thin air. The rest of us glanced at the water with scant interest. What was so special about the old man's fabled river? But then, this was the early seventies – an era in which Ohio's rivers were largely ignored save when a newsworthy number of fish went belly-up, or their chemical-rich surfaces caught fire. We looked at our father, cruelly accusing as children sometimes are, not saying it but plainly thinking as much: why did you bring us here?

Why have we brought ourselves here as a civilisation? To a place where water may still run clear and fresh in the imagination, even as it runs polluted, foul, or dry altogether in our wells, rivers, lakes, and seas? To a place where headlines such as 'Why is the UK Facing Water Shortages Despite Record Rainfall?' or 'How Salty Water is Putting Bangladesh's

Pregnant Women at Risk' or 'It is now Well-Established that 97% of
Gaza's Water has been Contaminated' have become commonplace ... To
a world where water or the withholding of water is a standard feature of
torture, intimidation, and domination; where water, or the withholding
of water, or the poisoning of water are used as tactics of war. Where
water is routinely squandered, splashed on the altars of Progress and
Profit, the duo of false gods our age has been so keen to venerate. Where
a careless conspicuous consumption of water often figures as a token of
prestige. Why have we brought ourselves here?

'If there were water...' a fragment hesitantly ventures toward the end
of *The Waste Land*:

And no rock
If there were rock
And also water
And water
A spring
A pool among the rock
If there were the sound of water only
Not the cicada
And dry grass singing
But sound of water over a rock
Where the hermit-thrush sings in the pine trees
Drip drop drip drop drop drop drop
But there is no water

Water diminished to a taunt, where the mere echo of a sound so crucial to
the spirit has more of the Chinese torture about it than of the restorative
music splashing through the Alhambra's fountains or 'dropping from the
veils of the morning' on Yeats's lake isle.

Still generally regarded as the definitive poem of the twentieth century,
The Waste Land may indeed be what we have termed a litany of desiccation,
yet before settling into the Slough of Despond, readers must decide what
to make of *The Waste Land's* parting line: *shantih shantih shantih*, close in
meaning one of Eliot's end notes tells us to 'the Peace which passeth
understanding'. Perhaps it is only a mirage, but the three Sanskrit words
fall on some ears like a curtain of rain, intimating that despair is not the
last word unless we make it or let it be so. The line and consequently the
entire poem may be read as a call to redemption – an eleventh hour shift

in tone, but an invitation none the less to clean out neglected wells, clear choked irrigation channels, rehydrate the human spirit, and set flowing a floundered civilisation.

Is it possible to set a shipwreck of a world flowing again? The *Tao Te Ching* suggests that it is, with energy drawn from the heart of life itself:

> ...When a man is in turmoil how shall he find peace
> Save by staying patient till the stream clears?
> How can a man's life keep its course
> If he will not let it flow?
> Those who flow as life flows know
> They need no other force. (15)

That deep force is natural, constant, and essentially simple. The process of letting it flow may be more involved, but at least the task is clear. In order to hear, we have to listen. In order to listen, we have to keep still. Water is at the heart of it all, at the core of existence, which, according to Lao Tzu:

> Might be likened to the course
> Of many rivers reaching the one sea. (32)

And again:

> Man at his best, like water,
> Serves as he goes along:
> Like water he seeks his own level,
> The common level of life,
> Loves living close to the earth,
> Living clear down in his heart...
> Loves kinship with his neighbours,
> The pick of words that tell the truth,
> The even tenor of a well-run state...(8)

The health of all we rely on – culture, agriculture, sewage works, politics, food, family, community, faith, progress, prosperity – relies on clean free-flowing water. Gandhi is said to have judged a nation's greatness and moral progress by the way its animals are treated – a useful and excellent gauge, but the gauge of the age as to a nation's greatness or moral progress will be read by its treatment of water. Is it treated with

reverence, gratitude, practicality, intelligence, foresight, humility? Or is it desecrated and abused?

2.

A friend of my father's was said to have the gift of dowsing, or water-witching as it was known. Clutching a willow fork with two hands, he could sense the potency of underground sources tugging the rod downwards like some unseen fish. The late Irish poet Seamus Heaney recalls this gift in his poem 'The Diviner':

Cut from the green hedge a forked hazel stick
That he held tight by the arms of the V:
Circling the terrain, hunting the pluck
Of water, nervous, but professionally

Unfussed. The pluck came sharp as a sting.
The rod jerked with precise convulsions,
Spring water suddenly broadcasting
Through a green hazel its secret stations.

The bystanders would ask to have a try
He handed them the rod without a word.
It lay dead in their grasp till, nonchalantly,
He gripped expectant wrists. The hazel stirred.

The power and pluck of water are everywhere. The Bible was an early source for me starting with Genesis, where by sentence two the 'Spirit of God was moving over the face of the waters.' Plants, fish, animals, birds, and human beings turned up. Adam and Eve seemed set for eternity in the lush Garden of Eden. As a child I could not figure out how anyone could have been so thick as to have gotten kicked out of those incomparable digs. Six decades on, I've got a better inkling. In any case, the human race smacked of disappointment from the very outset. Eden was an earthly paradise. You didn't work, thistles and thorns didn't exist (a detail I verified by asking my mother), death wasn't in the lexicon, the lion lay down with the lamb, and there weren't any rules apart from a handful of no-brainers – don't eat the fruit of the Tree of Knowledge, and steer clear of snakes. Our line screwed up; the rest is history.

Like Paradise in the Qur'an, the Garden of Eden was 'graced with flowing streams'. It was watered by a river that divided into four: Pishon, Gihon, Tigris, and Euphrates. Life was sweet. But it didn't take long before *Homo* (not-so-) *sapiens* was given the boot. Worse lay ahead. By Genesis Chapter Six, the human element of Creation had blundered to a degree that the Creator was having second thoughts. In short, people were wicked and God 'was sorry that he had made man on the earth, and it grieved Him to His heart'. The human race had become 'corrupt and full of violence'. (Sound familiar?) At which point water turns from a blessing and a mainstay to a medium of erasure. At the end of His rope, God opts for a Great Flood to 'blot out' the stain on Creation. Enter Noah, an upstanding enough sort that God relents, extending a second chance. Noah, his family, and a pair of every species at risk of drowning board the Ark in hopes of surviving the subsequent forty days and forty nights of rain.

'Often it does seem such a pity that Noah and his party did not miss the boat,' noted a congenitally acerbic Mark Twain; but our race survived. To commemorate its disembarkation on Mount Ararat, God sent a Rainbow as a sign that He would never again flood the earth. One of the first things Noah did on the heels of that ceremony was plant a vineyard and ferment a vat of wine, ending up three sheets to the wind and buck naked. Forty days and forty nights is a long time after all to be cooped up aboard a wooden vessel with spouse, kids, in-laws, and history's largest menagerie.

The Book of Exodus records the birth of Moses, a 'fine boy' and future champion to the oppressed tribe of Israel. The tyrannical Pharaoh of Egypt had decreed that every newborn Israelite male be tossed into the Nile. Thanks to a capable mother, sister, and a pair of complicit midwives, Moses escapes that harsh fate. The infant is hidden for three months among reeds at river's edge in a papyrus basket lined with bitumen and pitch. A miniature Ark, in effect, another water-borne prospect of redemption. Pharaoh's daughter discovers the basket as she enters the Nile to bathe. She adopts the infant inside as her own, naming him Moses, meaning: 'I drew him out of the water.' Moses' sister witnesses this twist of fate and astutely approaches the Princess with an offer to find the child a wet nurse. When the proposal is accepted, the girl arranges for her and the baby's mother to fill the position.

Stories of a blessed child drawn from water held universal appeal. As with the Flood account, variants sprang up worldwide. Well before Moses' time, Sargon, first ruler of the Akkadian Empire, was said to have been cast adrift at birth in a reed basket caulked with bitumen, to be rescued from the Euphrates by a humble drawer of water downstream. In the *Mahabharata*, Karna is born of a god and a princess, thrown into the Ganges by his desperate mother, and fished from the river by a couple who raise the young demigod as their own. Various folktales involve a king who upon hearing it prophesied that a newborn would one day take over the throne, has the child locked in a box and cast into the river. The box floats, eventually to be drawn to shore. And yes, the child inside grows up to occupy the throne for which it was destined.

Water plays a lead role in more than a few such archetypal stories. In 'The Water of Life', a king's three sons set off after the elixir that can save their dying father. Each encounters a peculiar dwarf who bids him stop. The oldest brother, then the second oldest dismiss the little man with an insult, galloping off only to end up wedged in a thorny ravine. When his turn comes, the youngest brother respectfully acknowledges the dwarf, is granted vital information concerning the water of life along with tools for its recovery, and succeeds in his mission. On his way home to the ailing king the hero goes out of the way to assist his foundered brothers, who repay kindness with treachery and betrayal. By story's end though, the third brother recovers the water of life, restores his father to health, and marries a princess to boot.

Wells frequent such stories, serving as places of danger and menace or of redemption and regeneration. In 'The Water Nixie', a brother and sister fall down a well only to be enslaved by a nixie and forced into lives of drudgery. The children run off, making good their escape despite the angry sprite's pursuit. The message seems to be essentially a cautionary one that has resonated throughout human history – best to avoid falling down a well. On the other hand, even such a catastrophe may culminate in rebirth as wellheads were potent symbols of promise and of life. 'Mother Holle' is a tale involving two sisters. One is sweet-natured and kind, the other selfish and ill-tempered. The girls' mother coddles the ugly child, her own flesh and blood ('A monkey', notes an Arabic proverb, 'is a gazelle in the eyes of its mother'). Meanwhile, she forces her

stepdaughter to sit by the side of a well spinning wool until her fingers bleed. One day in an effort to rinse off the bloody spindle the girl drops it into the well. On hearing of this mishap her stepmother chides without mercy, demanding the spindle's immediate retrieval. In despair, the maligned stepdaughter jumps into the well, losing consciousness.

Once the girl regains her senses, she discovers herself in a lovely sunny meadow full of flowers. There she performs a series of tasks, graciously coming to the aid of an oven full of baking loaves, and a tree loaded with ripe apples. She is eventually given shelter under the roof of a mysterious old woman called Mother Holle, whom she serves to the best of her ability. Having done her work well, the girl is sent home showered in gold. Consumed by envy and greed, the ill-natured sister insists on trying her luck too, jumps in the well, fails her tasks in the meadow by arrogantly refusing to help, and fails as well in service to Mother Holle. She is sent home covered in sticky pitch.

In 'The Frog-King', a young princess loses the golden ball she is playing with when it rolls down a well. A frog agrees to retrieve it if the girl promises to treat him with kindness and respect. She agrees but once the ball is restored, runs back to the palace and promptly forgets her promise. One day at dinnertime the frog turns up proposing to dine with the princess and even to spend the night in her bed. The girl finds these notions repulsive and pretends not to know the frog, but after demanding a full account, her royal father insists that she keep her word. The frog turns out to be a prince under enchantment, and the princess becomes his bride.

The well in the Old Testament story of Joseph is at once a place of peril and of deliverance. Tending their flocks far from home, Joseph's jealous brothers conspire to kill their father's favorite outright until Reuben persuades them to put Joseph down a dry well. Reuben later returns intending to help the lad escape only to discover that he has been sold to a caravan bound for Egypt, where he will in time fulfill a grand destiny. A wellhead, incidentally, furnished the setting for the courtship of Joseph's grandfather Isaac, whose wife Rebekah was chosen for her willingness to offer water to a stranger, and for offering to water his camels on top of that. A generation later Isaac and Rebekah's son Jacob (Joseph's father) first lays eyes on his future wife Rachel as she is bringing her flocks in to be

watered. He rolls away the stone covering the well and tends to her thirsty animals. Jacob and Rachel thus become an item, water sealing the deal.

Never is the preciousness of water more apparent than in desert places where its relative absence is so achingly conspicuous. When Abraham reluctantly turns his concubine Hagar and their son Ishmael out into the wilderness of Beer-sheba with nothing save a little bread and water, mother and child, victims of callous jealousy on the part of Abraham's first wife Sarah, expect only death. The water-skin depleted, Hagar lays her child in the shade of a bush, moving far enough away that her eyes may be spared what's next though she must still endure the boy's cries. God hears them too, whereupon Hagar 'saw a well of water; and she went and filled the skin with water, and gave the lad a drink.' Ishmael survives, going on to be traditionally revered as the father of the Bedouin peoples. In Islam the well revealed to Hagar is held to be the Well of Zamzam, a vital fixture in the hajj experience.

Psalm 104 extols the Creator for the gift of water:

You set springs gushing in ravines
running down between the mountains,
supplying water for wild animals,
attracting the thirsty wild donkeys:
near these the birds of the air make their nests
and sing among the branches.

3.

Life in the desert! I carry sweet memories of walks among the rhino-hide mountains of Oman, where one might chance upon a pool of water tucked in some *wadi*. On dipping a half-broiled head under the surface and sitting to rest in the shade of an acacia, you might then witness a series of visitations – a hatch of butterflies funnelling down through rock walls. Sand partridges, a chittering iridescent flock of bee-eaters, a fox. A creature bounding up a near-perpendicular precipice, at first assumed to be a goat given that we were so close to human settlement, but on second glance decidedly a gazelle. Dragonflies. A foot-long whip-tailed lizard, turquoise shifting to gold. Donkeys that had started wild, been domesticated across centuries, and reverted back to wild. Nibbling

minnows bent on regarding the dried skin of your submerged toes as haute cuisine. A trumpeter finch. Doves. A male wheatear flashing his attributes atop a boulder. Once I chanced on a wheatear nest tucked in a low horizontal cleft – a revelation of grass, twigs, and delicate fragments of rock. Architecture sublime as the Taj Mahal or Chartres Cathedral.

Sweet memories of Oman are apt to feature *fallaj* – rock and earth conduits channelling water to pomegranate groves or date palms or patches of alfalfa in terraced pockets of soil near habitations appearing from a distance to be mortared like swallow nests to precipitous walls of rock. Despite temperatures that could reach 120° Fahrenheit, fallaj water ran all summer swirling down channels, sustaining villages that had clung to life across centuries. It bears repeating that the preciousness of water is rarely more apparent than in desert places where its scarcity or inaccessibility is so achingly conspicuous. Sadly, it can as well be noted that a callous disregard for water is rarely more apparent than in desert places. The psalmist's praise for the Creator's gift to the desert is joined a few verses on by a warning:

> Sometimes He turned rivers into desert,
> springs of water into arid ground,
> or a fertile country into salt-flats,
> because the people living there were wicked.

A bitter memory of Oman involves the insolence that befell Yiti Beach. Yiti was a quiet little village along a tidal mud-flat where herons or flamingos might be spotted. Up the beach was a singular rock formation, a flying buttress of lunaresque scoria linking land and sea. Down the beach protruded a rocky shoulder round which you might make your way at low tide to a crescent of white, where ghost crabs erected mysterious sand-towers and gloried in freedom. The sea was warm as bathwater even in winter. We walked at Yiti, swam, and spent nights with the crabs. We grilled sardines. We tracked the moon and constellations, marinating in a kind of silence that is impossible to describe save to those who have come under its spell.

Then one year a slender three-story guesthouse arrived on the beach, a concrete nod to Tourism, regarded by many as key to the Sultanate's future. The new structure made an incongruous intrusion next to a cluster of fishermen's huts, but one got used to it in time. Maybe the owner was

from the village? Maybe profits from the place were helping the local economy? Agreeable surmises that helped dispel dark premonitions. A year slipped by, then another. Until one day we reached the beach to discover freshly planted at the edge of the mudflat a giant billboard that read: Welcome to Salaam Village. The billboard featured a sprawling modern complex bearing a scatter of computer-generated figures with computer-generated smiles at their lips. They appeared to be reclaiming a piece of Eden. They had arrived. In exchange for the requisite sum of money, anyone who cared to might follow in their computer-generated footsteps. The elect of Salaam Village would be housed in a trouble-free zone where there were no thistles or thorns, where death itself might be dismissed on the grounds that it seemed inconvenient.

The billboard coaxed one to ignore the rotten politics of the September 11-Global War on Terror era, the acidifying oceans, the unravelling atmosphere. One forgot the herons and other waders out stalking the mudflat in search of a square meal, the ghost crabs, the small-beer fishermen drawing their weathered fleet up the sand, the villagers, assuming such existed, who may have preferred their place on earth undisturbed, having learned to thrive on its rhythms of silence. None of the forgotten had been consulted when the decision was made that an Emirati company should be granted the 'right' to put up a place called Salaam Village. But then, intoned devotees to the cults of Progress and Profit, popular gods of a heedless age, what did a few crabs or birds matter? The forgotten could find somewhere else to live. And if for some reason they proved too backward to pull that off, perhaps they didn't deserve to be remembered in the first place. As for a handful of villagers averse to seeing their world turned to a clone of Dubai or Abu Dhabi or Everywhere Else ... Well, they could find somewhere new to live too.

At Salaam Village there would be prestige apartments and a marina. There would be spacious garages to accommodate the cars of the elect, and swimming pools to entertain their offspring. Maybe even a golf course – the billboard intimated as much. For of course there would be water, plenty of water. There would have to be to support 'Our Way of Life', a thing once aspired to by an exclusively prodigal set, now open to all thanks to Profit and Progress. How could there not be water? There would be cars to wash, toilets to flush, dishwashers to run, taps to turn, baths and

showers to take, laundry to do, patches of grass to irrigate, patio tiles to hose down. One had, did one not, a right, a duty even to participate in that cult of consumption billed as 'Our Way of Life'?

The billboard at Yiti Beach was mesmerising, but could not quite erase the memories or misgivings of all who saw it. Some recalled propaganda posters printed during the Chinese Cultural Revolution – bright-coloured caricatures of smiling peasants gathered round tables groaning under the fat of the land thanks to the benevolent vision of Chairman Mao and the Communist Party. The posters were as appealing as anything from Disney, though their charm was dampened somewhat by the thought that at least a million people had died in the Cultural Revolution, many of starvation owing to ill-conceived government policies. Other doubters remembered the Aral Sea and its pivotal place in the irrigation schemes of Josef Stalin, who had slated the area to become the cotton-producing wonder of the age. A 'Five-Year Plan' had decreed it. The Aral Sea had supported fishermen and fish, farmers and farms, culture and crabs. All that's left today is a puddle, a spent testament to Stalin's wet dreams. Some who looked past the billboard at Yiti Beach were reminded of Colonel Qaddafi's Great Man-Made River in Libya, a massive irrigation project, the biggest in history, drawing fossil water from a desert aquifer. Making the Desert Bloom was after all a rallying cry of the age, a pursuit regarded as entirely laudable. Israel had done it to what seemed universal approbation. Never mind that the Jordan River had all but disappeared in the process; never mind the suffering downstream. Never mind that in Ben Ehrenreich's words: 'what once was water, holy water, is now toxic sludge'. The architects of the gamblers' oasis of Las Vegas had Made the Desert Bloom in Nevada. The Saudis too, exporting wheat, giant circles of green in the sand made possible by an expensive (and some thought unconscionable) state appropriation of water...

The preceding paragraph was scarcely dry when the Guardian carried a story called 'Greening the Desert: Is Sisi's Grand Plan Using up all of Egypt's Water?' Stalin took down the Aral Sea. Sisi risks taking down an entire nation with a pet agribusiness scheme dubbed, with unintended irony, 'The Future of Egypt'. The preceding sentence was scarcely dry when a story appeared called 'Pantanal Waterway Project would Destroy a Paradise on Earth'. In the interest of transporting soybeans more

cheaply, the Brazilian government proposes compromising one of the last great wetlands on the planet by turning the Paraguay River into a canal. According to its many critics, the project would signify the 'end of an entire biome' unique for its quality and diversity, shrink the size of an already diminished floodplain, altar the natural flood cycle, trigger an explosion of industrial farming, fuel the devastating wildfires already plaguing the region, threaten the lives and livelihoods of indigenous peoples, and in sum, culminate in yet another 'senseless tragedy' – but apart from that! The assault on water makes for a relentless bombardment of 'news' in 2024. With nation states like these, who needs enemies? With leadership like this, who needs terrorists? A quip frequently attributed to George Bernard Shaw doesn't seem far off mark: 'the only thing we learn from experience is that we learn nothing from experience'.

Trying to look beyond that billboard at Yiti Beach I remembered a book called *Desert Solitaire*, which saw print in the late 1960s but was conceived in the fifties. Edward Abbey's reflection on his time spent working in a remote part of Utah at a national monument (before its upgrade to a national park) serves as a free-flowing hymn to water and a prayer for common sense. The author attends the starkly magnificent country he's stationed in as one might attend a venerable university, and from his education there concludes that letting the desert be is a more valid and practical art than the technocrats' much trumpeted 'Making the Desert Bloom'. Abbey bridled against the impulse of the age to genuflect to Progress and Profit; meanwhile his employer, the US National Park Service, was promoting easier access to wilderness for masses of people. This would mean paving roads, building visitor centres, accommodating recreational vehicles, turning camping into a high-end recreation consumers might be drawn to. Abbey argued that people yearning for closer contact to the land and drawn to the beauty of wild places would get to them without the convenience of campsites equipped with showers, air-conditioned shops selling bumper stickers and t-shirts, and all the rest of it. He was convinced that wilderness was a matter of utmost individual, national, and spiritual importance. Keeping it wild seemed the least its official guardians might feel called upon to do. Yet wilderness, Abbey saw, had been put up for sale like most everything else in a consumer society.

The last straw was the decision to build the Glen Canyon Dam on the Colorado River, which was already dammed to the point of damnation, sucked dry well before reaching its mouth at the Gulf of California. The rationale for building a dam many deemed unnecessary included the standard arguments for building whatever: it would create jobs, it would be good for the economy, it would encourage tourism, it would provide recreation, it would generate electricity, it would be a further feather in modernity's cap, it would please the gods. Progress and profit smiled on the project, which was completed in 1966. Abbey's heart all but broke. He had rafted the river long before such activities rated as tourist attractions. He had visited the remote confluence of the tributaries forming the Colorado River, the Green River, and the Grand River. He had explored Glen Canyon, spent reverent days and nights there, been awed by petroglyphs and pictographs on its rock walls, and by ancient cliff dwellings once home to the canyon's human inhabitants. He had imbibed the journals of John Wesley Powell, the one-armed Civil War veteran who'd led a team of explorers through the Colorado River's canyons in the nineteenth century.

The dam went up, Lake Powell was formed, Glen Canyon was submerged. Tourists arrived in lumbering recreational vehicles, houseboats in tow, having driven many hundreds of miles over tarmacked road where only a short time before there had been ... nothing! One could now water-ski in a place that until only recently had rated as the middle of nowhere! Many saw it as an incontestable boon. Nothing had been transformed into something. Nowhere had become somewhere. Progress and profit smiled on a cult following whose growth, like the economy's, showed little sign of letting up. People spent money. People made money. What wasn't to love? Voices like Abbey's for one thing, crying in the wilderness and on its behalf. For taking a stand against the new dam, the author of *Desert Solitaire* was tarred with the standard brushes, labelled a technophobe, extremist, apostate, contrarian, anachronism, anarchist, crank, lunatic, and elitist.

Half a century later *Desert Solitaire* remains in print, doing rather well in a world where reading books has been largely supplanted by a viral gaping into screens. Abbey's book is in fact holding up better than Lake Powell, shrunk to a shade of its former self after decades of drought. Glen Canyon

Dam no longer strikes many folks as a great idea. Even former true believers are keen to change the subject. Yet, the old gods die hard. A new generation of true believers professes faith in projects like The Line, a plan to bring Eden to the Saudi desert in the form of a futuristic city. Will there be enough water? Of course there will assures MBS, as the project's princeling mastermind is styled. Or if there isn't, the Red Sea can be desalinated until there is. The Line will be a mile and a half long (down from the initially proposed 110 miles) and ostentatiously high, and will feature waterfalls, lakes, gardens, and flying cars. It will house 300,000 people (down from the initially proposed nine million). The desert will be made to bloom and the elect will flock to live there, paying handsomely for the privilege. The bolder among the elect may opt to go further afield, chasing another billionaire's dream of exporting 'Our Way of Life' into outer space. Once Elon Musk gets Mars terraformed, its icecaps melted, and its colonists implanted with the happy chips necessary to save humanity from itself, life on the Red Planet may prove even grander than life in the Line.

Back to Salaam Village for those wondering how that story ends. Earth movers turned up; the project got underway. For months machines gouged and gnawed, pushed and pulled at the sand and muck, intent on bringing Yiti Beach into line. The ghost crabs did not find somewhere else to live. They merely expired. So too before long did the project, its sponsors and investors running out of money or ideas, or both. The machines fell silent, to be hauled away on long-bed trailers. The billboard came down. Prospective residents were no longer solicited. Salaam Village had become a ghost project, another scar on the landscape that would take centuries to heal.

The Chairman Maos, the Stalins, the Colonels Qaddafi and Sisi, the brash billionaires and brazen Zionists committed to 'Making the Desert Bloom', the Silicon Valley demigods keen on shaping and controlling the future, the money-drunk corporations, the venal governments – it is tempting and even consoling to put the war on the natural world down to their collusion. The public is open to the sorts of persuasion suggesting that 'we' are not involved in what might (despite its billing as Project Profit & Progress) be called Project Extinction, that while we may be gullible, we are at bottom innocent. But of course we are all complicit, embroiled to varying degrees in perpetuating 'Our Way of Life', indicative though it may be of something more on the order of a way of death. The

grandiose plans of the high and mighty are destined to fail, but Lao Tzu's
remark applies to schemers at every level:

> Those who would take over the earth
> And shape it to their will
> Never, I notice, succeed.
> The earth is like a vessel so sacred
> That at the mere approach of the profane
> It is marred
> And when they reach out their fingers it is gone. (29)

Lake Powell, the Aral Sea, Salaam Village, the glacial ice, 'The Future
of Egypt', the Jordan River... One could carry on tallying what's gone or
diminished, wallowing in loss, our cup, as the old cliché has it, half empty.
Homo sapiens's chances of coming to its senses, of doing the right thing, of
letting life flow? The odds seem slim at best. Our very survival as a species
is up in the air, 'Our Way of Life' become our way of death, an
evolutionary dead end. But I fear that my personal cup has a tendency to
go half empty, and suspect readers are growing weary of it. Let's try
again. Off we go, willow wands in hand, divining a way through to some
kind of ending we can live with.

4.

In *The Swimmer*, that strange and wonderful 1968 movie chanced upon a
few months ago, we go from pool to pool. The film, based on a John
Cheever story, stars Burt Lancaster as middle-aged Ned Merrill. Ned is
beset by a range of what Americans refer to as 'issues,' revealed to be
increasingly tragic and complex as his journey develops. At the outset we
find Ned sharing a drink with a well-heeled suburban couple by their
swimming pool. They urge him to stay on, but Ned has devised a plan to
swim home by following a 'river' of friends' or acquaintances' swimming
pools located between where he is and where he aims to end up. With
that, he dives in, swims the length of the pool, climbs out, and trots off
dripping across fields and back lanes that will take him to his next
destination. Ned swims that pool too, and the rest that lie ahead until the
'river' has carried him home. *The Swimmer* is one of the most curious films
you will ever see. I'd be hard-pressed to say exactly what it means, but

there is never a doubt that it is something profound, that it succeeds in channelling its mystery. That life is a river? That we follow it home? Something deep and powerful is going on in a story that at first glance appears to involve nothing beyond the superficial surfaces of a suburban enclave in New England. The early European explorers of North America dreamed of a Northwest Passage, a series of waterways bridging East and West, a shortcut to Asia, what a Walt Whitman poem extols as a Passage to India. In *The Swimmer*, Ned seems to chart such a passage, opening up a mystical connection (which is not to suggest that his enterprise or his fate is a happy one).

Another movie, 1991's *The Inland Sea* features a boat slipping quietly through a backwater world, a sublime fold of Japan tucked under the radar. The film intimates how water may convey us, body and soul. to places we've never been save perhaps in dreams and visions. Andrei Tarkovsky's 1983 film *Nostalghia* put some critics to sleep but struck others as a lush tone poem set to water. I recommend it to the parched in spirit. The list of water movies is long but I mention just four more: 1993's *The Piano*, for the remarkable image late in the picture of a grand piano sinking in the waves, tethered to a distraught woman who choosing to live, struggles free and regains the surface. Set in medieval Sweden, Ingmar Bergman's 1960 classic *The Virgin Spring* chronicles the violation and murder of a young girl and the revenge exacted on her killers – scenes of savage brutality muted when the child's body is at last retrieved for burial and a spring bubbles up from the spot where her head had rested. Water as a symbol of purification, atonement, resurrection. Alas and inevitably, there are films where water serves as a symbol of depravity. In Roman Polanski's 1974 masterpiece *Chinatown*, the race to control a desert city's water supply becomes a driver for graft, blackmail, manipulation, and murder. Clint Eastwood's 1985 film *Pale Rider* contrasts the gentle stream burbling through a camp of independent gold-panners with the deafening blast of the hydraulic pressure hoses used by company miners a few miles away, and with the gutted wasteland left behind. A symbol of purity twisted into a symbol of greed and violation.

The taste of water in all its glory grows increasingly unfamiliar, as does that of wild trout, of tomatoes ripe off the vine, of a crisp country apple. Such flavours linger more commonly in one's memory than on one's

tongue. We seem to be heading for a day when everything from a floret of cauliflower to a grape to a cucumber to a salmon steak to a cup of water will taste more or less the same, like some generic common denominator. The stuff we chew and swallow passes as food but tends to serve as little more than a vehicle for varying doses of salt, sugar, starch, and grease – the four staples, chemically enhanced, which account for contemporary spins on flavour and taste. Some may contend that water even at its best has always tasted and should taste like nothing – that it has no flavour. I doubt that this is the case. We simply find it increasingly hard to recall what true water is like. The inability to express water's flavour may also be a reflection of a general incapacity to articulate what we can't rightly grasp. We can readily say that a lime tastes like a lemon but seem tongue-tied when it comes to water, scarcely able to go beyond the obvious – that it tastes like water.

As I was growing up on the family farm we had access to well water, superior to the chemically treated 'city water' that ran from the taps of people in town. But I do not recall our water being regarded as anything extra-special in terms of flavour. And in terms of purity, who knew? By the time I arrived on the scene, in 1958, the widespread use of pesticides, herbicides, and chemical fertilisers in American agriculture had already made it probable that the water rural people were using was as bad as city water, maybe worse. We liked the water bubbling from a pipe driven down along a hedgerow bordering one of our more remote fields. Dad said it was artesian well water, and we agreed that it was cooler, cleaner, finer than what we were used to. An abundance of cattails and frogs enhanced the appeal. I'd be curious to know what 'branch water' might taste like, ladled from a cedar bucket. Its praises are sung by some character in a William Faulkner novel.

While branch water has eluded me, I am grateful for the occasions I've had to drink straight from springs and mountain streams. Wonderful. Yet the drinks best remembered are not down to the beauty or purity of their source, rather to the fact that one was memorably thirsty at the time. Everyone, I suspect, recalls specific drinks of water. One of my most vivid recollections stems from my boyhood, a fair share of which was spent driving a tractor up and down the fields under the summer sun – hot, dusty, droning, tiresome work. 'Where is she?' I used to think impatiently. But at some point I'd catch sight of my mother making her way along the

edge of the field, bringing a Mason jar of water. I idled the motor, put the machine in park, and jumped down to tip jar to mouth. 'Not too fast,' she cautioned. It was just tap water with half-melted ice-cubes clinking the glass, but I can never forget it. Nor can I forget the water from tilted Thermos jugs or the end of a garden hose splashing my face, some finding its way in. After stacking hay in a baking mow on a July afternoon, after catching chickens in a reeking broiler house on a muggy evening. Water!

The American poet and environmentalist Gary Snyder's poem 'The Spring' opens with a depiction of a road crew filling potholes – grind of heavy equipment, smell of soft asphalt, a relentlessly hot day… when the routine is gloriously broken:

> the foreman said let's get a drink
> & drove through woods and flower fields
>   shovels clattering in back
> into a black grove by a cliff
>   a rocked in pool
>   feeding a fern ravine
>   tin can to drink
> numbing the hand and cramping the gut
> surging through the fingers from below
>   & *dark here*—
> let's get back to the truck
> get back on the job.

Back to work. The closing lines serve to remind that while a human being may be afforded glimpses of Eden, permanent residence there remains off the cards. Man is still obliged to earn his bread through sweat of the brow, assuming he has not wormed his way into politics.

In 'Mid-August at Sourdough Mountain Lookout' the poet recalls an interlude during time stationed near the summit of a peak in the North Cascades of the Pacific Northwest. Again, a drink of water complements a visionary state:

> …I cannot remember things I once read
> A few friends, but they are in cities.
> Drinking cold snow-water from a tin cup
> Looking down for miles
> Through high still air.

Occasions of clarity, vision... clairvoyance, linked to water. In old Norse religion the great sacred ash Yggdrasil connected the underworld, the worlds in between and the heavens. Two of the tree's roots drew from wells, the third from a spring. The water from Mimisbrunrr, meaning the Well of Mimir, was said to grant vision to those who drank of it. Odin himself went to Mimisbrunrr in quest of clarity, but Mimir was not inclined to share the well's water for nothing. 'What would you give for a drink?' he asked, eventually proposing one of the god's eyes as a fitting exchange. Odin paid his dues, drank from the horn of water Mimir dipped for him, and though short an eye, saw as he had never seen before. The plucked-out eye is said to be lying still at the bottom of Mimisbrunrr.

It is hard to think of a symbol more potent than water in religious ritual and belief. Sacred springs, fountains, wells, rivers, streams, pools. Water sprites, nymphs, deities, spirits. Miracle water – Moses striking bare rock with his staff, a spring gushing forth in the wilderness... Naaman the leper cured upon bathing seven times in the Jordan. Water for ablution, cleansing, blessing, baptism, divination, healing, pilgrimage, offering, revelation, instruction. The sending of rain is a Sign, says the Qur'an (16:11), 'for those who think.' Rain and the life springing up in its wake are Signs (6:99) 'for people who believe.' Water to bless and clean the newborn coming into the world, water to bless and clean the cadaver departing it. Prayers for rain in countless manners and forms. The masked gods of the Hopi emerging from underground kivas to dance, lightning crackling over the mesas in response. A procession of villagers carrying the Virgin on their shoulders in drought-chastened Andalusia. Across the Straits, Friday prayers for rain in the mosques of Morocco. Water as the catalyst of Creation. Water as a promise of regeneration and spiritual vitality.

Weary and thirsty after a hard day's travel, Jesus rested at what was said to be Jacob's well in Samaria. There he asked a local woman to draw water. She was hesitant, startled that a Jewish stranger would request a Samaritan woman for a drink, as Samaritans were looked down upon and in any event, men of that time and place did not make a habit of conversing with women. Jesus went on to speak of 'living water,' telling the woman he could have given, had she asked for it, water from 'a spring ... welling up to eternal life' with a power to quench thirst once and for all. The woman was intrigued but baffled, taking the words literally at first, only

gradually coming to realise that the living water on offer was understanding, and the thirst a spiritual one.

To relieve someone's thirst is among the most fundamental gifts a person can bestow. Asked to recommend the best form of charity, the Prophet responded: 'to give water to the thirsty'. Jesus tells the story in Matthew 25 of a King who cites a number of kindnesses he has been shown, among them: '...I was thirsty and you gave me drink' – an act of consideration serving to illustrate the sorts of behaviour that might profit a soul on Judgment Day. In contrast, the damned will hear: 'I was thirsty and you gave me no drink'. Somewhat confused, those who'd passed the test asked the King to remind them when they had ever had occasion to give him a drink and relieve his thirst. 'As you did it to one of the least of these my brethren,' he explained, 'you did it to me.' To relieve the suffering of a fellow living thing – there is no greater endeavour. The Bhutanese term *yonchap* refers to a ritual offering of water to the Buddha, meant to be made with mindfulness and concern, a 'meditative spiritual practice' where one can visualise and think simple thoughts such as, 'when I offer the water, may all sentient beings be free from thirst, may everyone be quenched and let no one suffer from thirst'. A lovely gesture elevating the spirit to a recognition of duty to others, a willingness to serve, a readiness to act. The ritual offering of water is meant to foster a state of mind and spirit, a consciousness akin to prayer without ceasing.

5.

I do not doubt the past, present, and future existence of people who have mastered the art of prayer without ceasing, though the best I can claim personally is to have botched things to a relatively acceptable level on a handful of occasions. My early twenties afforded one such occasion; at the time I was crossing a serendipitous patch of existence. Things seemed to fall into place naturally, not because of any steps one was consciously taking but in spite of them. You weren't making things happen so much as letting them, and the system, if that's what it was, seemed to be working. Everything that passed my way felt charged with meaning, gifts intended for edification, including a job on a Colorado ranch that all but fell into my lap. One of my daily duties as a ranch hand was to provide hay and silage

to a bunch of cattle confined to a pasture on the far side of the railroad tracks, a mainline used by the Santa Fe, Burlington Northern, and Denver & Rio Grande railways. As many as thirty trains a day went through, generally at a brisk clip. One morning I set off to feed the cows as usual only to find the crossing blocked by a freight train stopped on the line. As I drew closer, a man appeared at the open door of a boxcar, signaling. I stopped the sputtering old John Deere I was driving, and went over to see what he wanted. He produced an empty plastic gallon container. I ran back to the ranch house, filled the container at the pump, and returned, relieved to find that the train hadn't moved. The man (he was about my age) nodded his thanks and drank. He'd started the current leg of his journey in El Paso. The jug had run dry in Walsenburg. He wasn't sure how far he was headed – Denver, maybe Greeley. A little tremor ran the length of the train followed by a lurch, and the boxcar edged away, gathering momentum. The encounter had taken less than ten minutes, yet it felt as if we had known each other a lifetime. I still think of the train-rider as a friend, though we did not so much as exchange names. I remounted the tractor, waited for the caboose to pass, and crossed over to feed the twenty or so cows stationed at the trough, all looking on quietly as if to inquire, 'What was that about?'

I didn't have an answer, or particularly care to. There had simply been a convergence of lives during a serendipitous spell of existence. A request for water, and a response. The right place, the right time. Whatever it was about, rarely had anything felt so right. Perhaps it was what a monk felt on offering water to the Buddha, to find himself thinking 'may all sentient beings be free from thirst, may everyone be quenched and let no one suffer from thirst'. An offering. Water as service. At church we used to wash each other's feet, kneeling, rinsing, then drying with a clean towel, the ritual based on something Jesus had done shortly before his crucifixion. Gathered with his disciples for a last shared meal, he had poured water in a basin and washed their feet. We took it to be an illustration of and an invitation to service. An occasion to humble oneself, to bend, to kneel, to cup hands in the basin, to offer water. To discover the exchange of joy that service entails. A nurse knows what it is to bring water to dry lips, to cool a feverish brow – a task, a duty, at times a drudgery – but at bottom a privilege, a joy. The patient knows it too. The gardener with her

sprinkling can, bringing water to sustain the plants. The sand grouse visiting a wadi pool, gathering water droplets in her belly feathers, flying for miles to deliver a drink to her clutch of thirsty chicks. A sign for those who think ... signs for people who believe.

Water resonates spiritually, and on the earthliest of material planes. We are products of a geography. Without water, what we experience as the real world would not exist, nor would we exist to perceive it. A glance at the map bears out water's essential place in things. The United States has given rise to a vast array of towns with names like Clearwater, Stillwater, Coldwater, Badwater, Yellow Water, Bitterwater, Drinkwater, Sweetwater, Mexican Water, Deepwater, Hardwater ... There's also Dry Lake, Lakeside, Storm Lake, Spirit Lake, Crater Lake, Heron Lake, Ambrosia Lake, Chippewa Lake, Salt Lake City. Walnut Creek, Gray Creek, Battlecreek, Mink Creek, Cripple Creek. Cheyenne Wells, Lathrop Wells, Ocotillo Wells. There's Baytown, Green Bay, Kootenay Bay, Bodega Bay. Detroit, Eau Claire, Portage, Fond du Lac, Delta, Watervliet, El Rio, Del Rio, Agua Fria, Agua Caliente. Cedar Rapids, Rapid City, Grand Rapids. Port Arthur, Port Huron, Port Aransas, Lockport, Bridgeport, Shreveport, Davenport... Manitou Springs, Cow Springs, Pagosa Springs, Eureka Springs, El Dorado Springs, Hot Sulphur Springs, Radium Springs, Old Horse Spring, Silver Spring, Springfield, Springdale... There's Oxbow and Shoals, Whitefish Point and Island Pond, Oak Harbor and Benton Harbor, Martins Ferry and Harper's Ferry, Powder Wash and Big Fork, Grand Fork and South Fork, Rocky Ford and Big Bend. There's Niagara Falls and Sioux Falls, Wichita Falls and Metaline Falls. There's Susquehanna on Pennsylvania's Susquehanna River — a Native-American name that struck Robert Louis Stevenson as enchantingly poetic on a rail journey west across the continent in 1879. Names like incantations. Is it any wonder Walt Whitman took such delight in rolling off his ecstatic inventories of place names?

Following rivers loaned me a sense of direction in the largely directionless drift of my late teens, along with an intoxicating sensation that I was, like the song said, 'going where I'd never been before'. I spent days on end driving small roads either side of the Ohio from Wheeling, West Virginia to Cairo, Illinois, touching down in between at Powhatan Point, the curiously named Fly, Martins Ferry, Marietta (where my father

had landed during the war – at last I was starting to comprehend the river's hold on him), Letart Falls, Coal Grove, Maysville, Cincinnati, Madison, Louisville, Cannelton, Evanston, Cave-In-Rock – my personal set of incantations. I drove slowly, stopped the car often, got out to walk around, read historical markers, drank many cups of the thin brownish liquid that passed for coffee whenever I ran across a cafe still open for business. One entered another reality along a river, an alternate world where the past spoke louder than the future. Things smelled different. People seemed different, as did the structures they inhabited. It felt as if something within you was being recalibrated, as if the tug of the passing current had an effect on your spiritual settings. How time eddied and purled, or at times stagnated, seemed different. A river town felt like a good place not to be in a hurry.

I dawdled down the Mississippi: Red Wing, La Crosse, Dubuque, Rock Island, Fort Madison, Nauvoo (where the Latter-day Saints had alighted for a time, where their founder Joseph Smith was killed in 1844), sleepy Hannibal, St Louis, Cape Girardeau, Vicksburg, Waterproof, Baton Rouge. I hitched rides along the Rio Grande and later drove it, headed for Colorado. Just getting out of Texas and across the New Mexico stateline required more than twenty-four hours, which tells you something about the vastness of the state, the roads I was choosing, and the car I was driving. From Boca Chica at the Rio Grande's mouth on the Gulf of Mexico, and on through Brownsville, Mission, Laredo, Eagle Pass, Del Rio, Esperanza, El Paso, Mesquite, Socorro, Belen, Albuquerque, San Felipe, Espanola (where DH Lawrence's ashes were incorporated in a curious block of memorial concrete), Alamosa, Del Norte, Creede.

Following rivers was an American standard, a pursuit that helped channel the nation's history, character, economy, and patterns of settlement. In the spring of 1804 Meriwether Lewis, William Clark, and a crew of thirty men set out poling a keelboat up the Missouri River. That endeavour is popularly referred to as the Lewis & Clark Expedition. Officially it was called the Corps of Discovery by the man who'd drawn it up, US President Thomas Jefferson. Lewis and Clark were charged with crossing the western half of a vast continent in order to gain a clearer picture of the new tract of land Jefferson's government had acquired. The Louisiana Purchase, as it was called, nearly doubled the size of the young

nation but few people apart from the Native Americans who lived there knew much about it. Lewis and Clark reached the Pacific Ocean late in 1805, christening creeks and rivers as they went – the Teapot, the Lolo, the Grindstone... the Milk, the Bighorn, the Marias, the Judith, to name a few. The Corps of Discovery had navigated the Missouri River north and west to its headwaters, mounted the Rockies, crossed the Continental Divide, and followed the Clearwater, Snake, and Columbia Rivers west to saltwater. A journey of over 4,000 miles! In 1806, the Expedition turned around and did it again in reverse. The native peoples encountered were at times a source of obstacle or hostility. More often they proved an invaluable source of assistance. The Lewis and Clark party received hospitality, advice, and support from the Mandan, Shoshone, Hidatsa, Nez Perce, Salish, Clatsop, and Chinook peoples. Great waterways made the Expedition feasible. Courage, competence, luck, resourcefulness, tenacity, horse sense, and diplomacy made it successful.

In 1869, John Wesley Powell led ten men in four wooden boats down the Green River to where it met the Grand, to become the Colorado. Some of the men and some of the boats made it beyond the Grand Canyon, making Powell's expedition the first to have run enough of the Colorado River to be called its entirety. Powell led a second expedition down the river in 1871. His entertaining account of these journeys was published in 1875 as *Exploration of the Colorado River and Its Canyons*. The boatmen met whitewater rapids galloping down channels etched through bedrock. They fought off a sense of foreboding and gloom in narrow canyon bottoms, where sheer walls of rock rose either side to a distant rim. As the Powell party made its way into Glen Canyon, which of its members could have foreseen that a century later pleasure boats would be riding the surface of an artificial body of water many fathoms overhead. What would they have made of such an inconceivable twist of history?

That change is inevitable and that change paves the way for progress remain stock truisms. But the rate and scale of change in its current form has left *Homo sapiens* and the natural environment we rely on reeling. What began as a trickle of human-induced changes to the environment some 10,000 years ago would build to a stream, until, by the Industrial Revolution, it had become a torrent prone to rage out of control. Edward Abbey reflected that as a kid growing up in rural Pennsylvania in the first

half of the twentieth century, it was still possible to find wild trout in the rivers and streams, and it was still possible to drink from a number of them without getting sick. It wasn't long before the trout were gone and not one stream remained from which it was safe to drink, not even the Susquehanna. At which point Pennsylvania, Abbey declared, had ceded the right to consider itself a great state. Furthermore, how could a union of states that consented to the desecration of its rivers and streams claim greatness? It was beyond chutzpah. If you could not drink its water, the nation you were living in amounted to a failed project, pure and simple. Many Americans were by and large sympathetic to Abbey's views even if they considered them somewhat extreme. Many others, converts to the nationalist cult of Progress and Profit, found such views not just extreme but irrational, offensive, even treasonous. Their nation-state's right to squander water was, they held, as God-given as its right to maintain a nuclear arsenal, or devastate southeast Asian villages in the interest of saving them.

Abbey's version of extremism now sounds sensible to more than a few people. Perhaps that is a good sign. The ghost of Edward Abbey, assuming it still haunts the homeland, must have pricked up its ears at the recent political slogan 'Make America Great Again'. Yes! it would have wailed in response. A place where rivers flow untrammelled and unpolluted to the sea. A place where wilderness is respected and upheld. A place where a child can kneel and drink from a stream and expect to find fish, trout included. That is a kind of nationalism worth the name. That is a kind of country worth having, one where you can drink the water, pure and simple. And where your neighbours downriver can drink it too. One day the nations might wake up to a world worth having, where prosperity and progress are real and attainable, where the impostor gods have slipped from their pedestals, where billboards depicting some Potemkin village future of fake grandeur are brought down to earth, where a delusional 'Our Way of Life' is supplanted by myriad expressions of a way of life any decent person would be proud to pursue, where water is treated with reverence and respect.

Might a revolution of reverence for water be declared in today's version of the real world, regenerating our politics, economies, cultures, and religions? Probably not this year. 'Make Nation X Great Again' sloganeers are not as a rule asking for clean or cleaner water, or a clean or cleaner way

of life. More typically they are asking for an extension of a bankrupt 'Our Way of Life', to the tune of: Tighter Borders! Lower Taxes! Smarter Phones! Cheaper Petrol! More Malls! Greater Military! Faster Internet! Growing Economy! Newer Technology! Bigger Profits! Unlimited Progress! Those running for office take up the list of demands and grievances, and pledge to do something. They tend to say little that actually matters, but then, there is little incentive – that is not the way elections are won. Bound by that version of self-interest termed the National Interest, they rarely propose to take on real need: 'May all sentient beings be free from thirst, may everyone be quenched and let no one suffer from thirst' is not held to be a vote-grabber.

As the rate of change appears to hurtle out of control, an old contradiction still applies: The more things change, the more they stay the same. Despite the upheaval and disruption associated with incessant change, it often feels as if nothing is in fact changing, save that the hole we're in sinks steadily deeper. Corporate and state interests salivate at the prospect of gaining tighter control over water – letting it flow is not a priority. Wars drag on and metastasise, often around issues of water. Water or the withholding of water is commandeered for malevolent ends. We grow numb to the suffering of others. We grow fearful for ourselves. Will we have enough? Entire populations are denied clean water, while a few meters off on the other side of a wall water is squandered. The interrogator holds this one's head under, the powerful begrudge so much as a drop to that one racked by thirst. Life out of balance. Too much or too little... inundation or drought. Water, scalding or frigid, to provoke pain or damage or fear. Shot through a high-pressure hose, released a drop at a time. Water as perversion. The Assad regime was conservatively estimated to have tortured 14,000 people to death during the Syrian Civil War, employing seventy-two kinds of torture, some reliant on water. Waterboarding, as one technique is known, forces victims at the brink of asphyxiation to feel as if they are drowning. Waterboarding was endorsed by former US Vice President Dick Cheney, though as he explained in the early days of the Global War on Terror, it was not in fact torture inasmuch as his government was above such barbarisms. On Judgment Day, how often will we be forced to endure the charge: 'I was thirsty, but you gave me no drink'? One supposes that those who have made a career of torment

do not lose sleep over the question. They have served the highest power they know. They are not as a rule people who believe. Nor are they people who think, unless the reptilian instincts necessary to political self-survival qualify as thought.

6.

The headlines maintain their relentless incursion. One from today reads: 'The Land is Becoming Desert: Drought Pushes Sicily's Farming Heritage to the Brink'. Another reads: 'The Bitter Battle to Protect New Zealand's Sea Floor Riches'. Yesterday there were others. Tomorrow there will be more. Following the news resembles some form of self-flagellation. Can it be good for us to 'stay informed' if staying informed amounts to witnessing endless loops of human suffering? Do we become more compassionate as a result? How many more headlines do we need before we may consider ourselves adequately apprised? How many more facts and statistics? A Palestinian in the West Bank on average consumes 50 litres of water per day. An Israeli 809, an Emirati 2,348, a US American 3,732, a Rwandan 50. More than one in ten people on Earth lack access to clean water. In the next five to ten years over two-thirds of the population will be affected by a shortage of water. More than 1,000 children under the age of five die each day from diseases tied to a lack of clean water – cholera, dysentery, diarrhoea, and malnutrition. Ninety-seven percent of the groundwater on our planet isn't safe to drink. In villages where water must be hauled in for daily use, women or girls find themselves walking longer and longer distances to wells or other sources, devoting greater and greater portions of their lives to the backbreaking demands of rock-bottom survival.

Assuming it took an hour of Internet use to cobble the preceding paragraph together, about five litres of water were expended. According to researchers at Imperial College London, downloading one gigabyte of data requires 200 litres of water. Cooling the massive data servers used by Amazon, Google, and others requires enormous quantities of water and electricity. Data centres in China use as much electricity as Hungary and Greece combined. 'Annual water usage by data centres in the US could support over 90 million peoples' basic requirements for one year.' And on it goes. The importance of such information is not in dispute, yet it is

difficult to feel 'empowered' by it though that is how we are told information is supposed to make us feel. For one thing, even a torrent of information is just a tiny drop in the virtual ocean. A person could go online for the rest of his life only to reach the grave no better off than when he started, vastly further informed yet no better informed. Our souls need something beyond information. Our spirits are sick to death, yearning for the water of life.

Little things happen, little by little, a trickle at a time. I notice that at the darts tournament I'm watching, the players drink water from glass cups refilled from a glass pitcher. A year ago they were using plastic bottles. A trivial thing, yet a part of how larger things develop. Distressed at the thought that data centres are being built in some of her country's driest corners, a Spanish writer notes that the opening of a Google data centre at El Cerillos, Chile has been suspended after an outcry from residents and local officials. Word that the centre would be tapping drought-stricken Santiago's diminishing aquifer for 7.6 million litres of potable water every day to refrigerate its servers was more than Chileans could bear. We can do here in Spain what they did there in Chile, the writer proposes. (Information, after all, is important – not so much the quantity as the quality, the timeliness, the ears it reaches, the decisions it inspires. 7.6 million gallons of drinking water per day? Why hadn't that detail been made more widely available before the construction of the data centre at El Cerillos went ahead?) Little things. Bigger things. A series of dams on the Klamath River has been removed, marking the first time in 100 years that salmon there can swim freely upstream. Quirky things... A London area barrister called to jury service insists on replacing the customary oath with one more personally binding, more spiritually satisfying: 'I swear by the River Roding from her source on Molehill Green to her confluence with the Thames that I will faithfully try the defendant and give a true verdict according to the evidence'. A drop in the bucket? Perhaps. But again, little things have a way of building.

The revolution sprung from a reverence for water is unlikely to prevail this year, but is on nonetheless. It's been on since the beginning, when the Spirit of God moved over the face of the waters. It has carried on through aeons of evolutionary history, feeding and sustaining the Tree of Life, flowing on through millennia of human history and civilisation,

distinguishing our dreams and visions: the river of the water of life, bright as crystal, flowing from the throne of God... flowing through the middle of the city, growing deeper, teeming with fish, banks either side lined by trees of life bearing fruit, their leaves useful for the healing of nations. It carries on through service, through the simple act of giving a drink to those who thirst. The revolution is on now, nurtured by the ongoing struggle and duty to live up to the gift of water, to let it flow. It will be on tomorrow, in a future that may include *Homo sapiens* if the species can live up to its name, divining paths to genuine progress and prosperity. The pluck of water, sharp as a sting, shows the way.

ARTS AND LETTERS

}

DROWNED WORLD

Alev Adil

I woke up early, with a start, suddenly evicted from a dream, as though compelled by a forgotten task or someone calling me. Villa Oneiro was situated on a small cliff just above the beach. My room had full length sliding doors and a clear view of the empty beach directly below. It was dark, the sun had not risen yet and the sea was a flickering expanse of pewter and mercury flecked with moon silver edged with an extravaganza of lace white foam. Only the wind, no one was calling. But then from a distance, I saw a figure rising out of the sea. I wrapped myself in a blanket against the early morning January chill and slid open the glass doors to the garden to take a closer look. A naked woman was rising out of the sea walking towards the shore. She was walking slowly, calm and determined,

her long dark hair plastered over her face and breasts. But she must be several kilometres away surely? Although my sense of distance and scale aren't particularly sharp, she seemed huge to me although faraway, not of a human scale at all. I watched as the sun rose behind her, a muted pearlescent light, until drizzle drove me back into my room.

I was the first guest in the breakfast room, half an hour before breakfast service began. A lone waiter was setting up heated chafing dishes of scrambled eggs and bacon. I'm sorry, it's too early, he informed me as he waved his hands to indicate that there were baskets of butter in tiny plastic pats and miniature jars of jam, bowls of olives and platters of halloumi and sliced tomatoes to be arranged in a suitable still life before the stage was set for breakfast. There's a woman on the beach, I said. Please can you look? There's something strange about her. Without even looking up he shook his head. I don't see anything, he said. Nothing. I went to the patio. She was advancing steadily towards the shore, her monumental thighs gleaming grey, white like wet marble. By the time I returned inside the waiter had gone to be replaced by a young woman whose painted eyebrows resembled acute accents, a diacritical decoration that gave her a permanently quizzical and cross expression, even when she smiled as I approached her. There's something outside, please come with me, I took her elaborately manicured hand and pulled her towards the patio. Her voice is high, calm, and sweet as we survey the empty beach under the faint drizzle. It is very beautiful, yes? Would you like coffee or tea? The woman on the beach had disappeared entirely. I drank my coffee and tried to forget her as I looked through the programme for the conference on literature and landscape which I was attending later that day.

My contribution to the conference was a paper called 'Plato's Atlantis: a Topography of Political Memory and Myth Making'. I'm not a classicist and dreaded being pulled into a discussion of the minutiae of Plato's text that would reveal lacunae in my knowledge. My paper was a rhetorical analysis of Plato's invention of a glorious history in order for a defeated regime to assert its present superiority. I was on a panel, 'Liquid Landscapes of the Classical World' with a Lithuanian literature professor from Vilnius University discussing the symbolism of the sea in the Odyssey and Dr Omar, a young Sudanese theologian based at a Dutch university, discussing the flood myth in the Epic of Gilgamesh, the Bible, and the Qur'an. Our session was scheduled in the afternoon, just before the coffee break.

The conference was running parallel panels and we were up against 'Landscapes of the Anthropocene' and 'Climate Fiction'. Perhaps these more contemporary themes were felt to be more pressing. Alternatively conference fatigue may have set in and inspired many to slip away from the proceedings to walk along the beach or take coffee at one of the cafes on the promenade. Our sparse and sleepy audience consisted of eight attendees, one of whom fled before the moderator had even finished introducing us. The weather had brightened and as I observed the sea from the presenters' platform I too wished that I was out there rather than in this over-heated, over-lit, and rather stuffy seminar room. Whilst Professor Šimkūnaitė speculated on whether the ancient Greeks were capable of apprehending the colour blue since they didn't have a word for it, I observed the sea sparkling in the sunlight and considered the many shades rippling in the waves and currents. I observed silver, steel, gold, azure, violet, cobalt, lavender, turquoise, ultramarine, indigo, teal, and cerulean. Doubtless an artist would have observed many more. I looked down at my pad and wrote 'does something exist if there is no word for it?' And as I wrote the words my body responded with an indescribable, eerie feeling that seemed to address the question and compelled me to glance up

towards the sea. I both saw her and didn't see her again, the monumental naked woman walking from the sea towards the shore. She had seemed indisputably real in the morning. This time she shimmered, something between a memory or a hallucination. On both occasions I was frightened to look her in the eye.

Distracted by the apparition my delivery was somewhat lacklustre, I read through my presentation dully, so I wasn't expecting the impassioned reaction it inspired in the rotund man in the front row. All the time I was speaking he was a tense flurry of movement, shaking his head, giggling silently, cleaning his spectacles and readjusting the hairband holding up his curly white man bun. As soon as the moderator invited questions from the audience he leapt to his feet. All three speakers have come from the field of literature, he was gesticulating wildly as he spoke, for them ancient histories are only stories, are only symbolic. I, Elias Zakaria am here to say, it is real, the flood. It is real. Atlantis is real. The moderator called a swift halt to proceedings. Let's have the post panel discussion informally over coffee, he suggested as everyone edged out of the room.

I decided to get some fresh air. As I left the conference centre to walk along the beach the white-haired Elias Zakaria was hot on my heels. Please, you must listen, it is surely a sign that you are here. It is no coincidence you

are here, none at all. You have misunderstood. You literary types you think stories are symbols, metaphors. Yes, but they are real too. As he spoke he took out a thick sheaf of papers out of his shoulder bag, a variety of dog-eared pages, some typed, photocopied, and even purple carbon copies. You must read my book. I have the evidence. Sheets of paper flew across the beach. As we gathered them I suggested we discuss this over coffee.

A garish mural, a cartoonish approximation of Botticelli's Venus, dominated the decor of the Aphrodite Cafe. The sea glittered seductively. A war jet from a nearby military base roared overhead. Miley Cyrus was singing loudly about writing her name in the sand. Elias Zakaria, manic and snaggle-toothed, was talking very fast and waving his chaotic manuscript in the air. Welcome to Cyprus, a waiter said. What can I get you? My pursuer waved him away. For many years I have been researching the location of Atlantis. It is here. Yes here. Cyprus is the highest point of what was once Atlantis. But there is more, and when I heard your paper I knew you were the messenger. I cut him off at that point. No, Mr Zakaria I'm not that at all. You have misunderstood me. My field is literature, not archaeology or geology. My paper is about how we create and imagine other societies and countries so that we can present ourselves as   superior and thus how these discourses are used as weapons to represent war as an ethical imperative rather than a moral crime. This is about how Plato talks

about Athens and Atlantis, how with his Atlantis story he creates a poetic prose based on philosophical values. These neither presuppose nor are they bound by historical precision, that is by facts. I'm familiar with the fact that there are many theories about whether or not Atlantis actually existed and that it might be in the Mediterranean, the Black Sea, the Atlantic, the Baltic, and even the Antarctic. All of these speculations are completely irrelevant to me, they're beyond my field of expertise.

Mr Zakaria appeared chastened but he continued. I think you are the chosen messenger, the Ἐκλεκτός. You understand that it is about the present, that Atlantis is not just about ancient history but about the wars in the region, the genocide going on across the water, about all that is happening now. You do not believe in the truth of these events. I must leave a document with you, please read it. Perhaps then you will understand. With that he left me to watch the sea and drink a flat white alone whilst I glanced at the article. It was about the recent discovery of an ancient Egyptian papyrus scroll sixteen metres long in the necropolis of Saqqara. The translation of the scroll revealed that it was the most complete and detailed version of the myth of Astarte and the insatiable sea. I was not familiar with the myth. Yam, was a sea god in the Syrian Ugaritic pantheon, possibly a forerunner of Poseidon in the Hellenic pantheon. In the Hebrew Bible, he was the enemy of Yahweh. In this papyrus, he demanded a series of tributes and challenges of the goddess Astarte, goddess of love and war, who was to become Aphrodite to the

Hellenes. Despite her success in meeting his demands he refused to be satisfied and demanded her wealth, her jewels, and her hand in marriage. The paper was long and full of erudite equivocation. I didn't read to the end.

That evening at the conference dinner I was able to clear my head of this brew of myth and mystery, although the conversation was hardly more cheerful. Dr Fortinbras and Professor Maronitis were experts in anti-immigration rhetoric and the militarisation of European borders. They were discussing a recent tragedy, a refugee boat that sank a few miles off the coast and coast guards who shot at the survivors as they swam to shore. This wine dark sea is a graveyard now, sighed Dr Fortinbras. On land there are camps, detention camps that the refugees can't leave, just a few kilometres from the tourist centres here. These are the genuine European values, mused the Professor as he scoffed a whipped feta hors d'oeuvre, the European values of institutionalised violence, Islamophobia and racism, despite all that the Lisbon treaty waffle about 'respect for human dignity, freedom, democracy, equality, the rule of law and respect for human rights including the rights of persons belonging to minorities'.

On my return to the hotel after dinner I decided to go for a midnight walk but the hotel beach below had been roped off with police tape. Several

officers were milling around shouting into walkie talkies. I retreated to the
desolate little bar behind reception where the surly waiter from breakfast
was wiping his glasses. He observed me with mournful eyes. I thought I saw
a tear slide down his cheek. Perhaps it was a trick of the light. Do you have
a cigarette? I asked him. I gave up a long time ago, but it has been a stressful
day. I can roll one for you, he offered. He rolled two and we went out onto
the patio and smoked in silence as we watched the cops. He rolled another
for us both and as the flame from his lighter flared I saw he really was
weeping. Another boat, he said. There is a terrible current in the bay. It is
not safe for swimming, although the tourists do. Every year a few drown.
He shrugged. That is their choice. But this was a boat of refugees. A child
was lost. Dead? I asked quietly. He inhaled a lungful of smoke and shrugged.
I don't know, I heard the mother wailing, she is still on the beach. The
others ran away. If they ask I tell them I see nothing. I was inside. I am a
refugee myself. They may detain me, if they think I am involved.

The mother is wailing down below, her ceaseless weeping ignored by the
police. Their search lights sweep the darkness. The wine-dark sea is a
graveyard now, the insatiable sea. I see her momentarily in the beams
penetrating the darkness. Her eyes are reflected black on black on the
water. Now I know her, the vision haunting me. She is Astarte. I am
Εκλεκτός, the chosen messenger between the goddess of war and the
insatiable sea. I head down to the beach, pushing past the police, to the
edge of the raging sea. The goddess is there she lifts me high over the waves
and then down deep deep fathoms beneath where the child shines like
moonlight. I grasp her in my arms, heavy and lifeless, hold her up to the
goddess' huge basalt black eyes. The child comes to life, begins to cry,
clings to me. Then we are on the beach again surrounded by police, the
mother running towards her child.

I make my way back to the hotel wrapped in a foil blanket where the
mournful barman is waiting for me. He rolls me another cigarette. How,
how did you save the child? You disappeared so suddenly. It doesn't make
sense. No, I agree, it doesn't make sense at all. You wouldn't believe me if
I told you. I would, he says, I am from across the sea. I was born in Tyre in
Lebanon, my parents were from Yafa in Palestine. All my life, none of it
makes sense, and no one believes you when you tell it.

A CONVERSATION AT SOUTHAMPTON DOCKS

Steve Noyes

1913

Marmaduke loved Southampton docks. It was something to do with the smell of salt water. He strode along past the lighters and fishing-craft, heading towards where he thought the P&O steamer was docked. It was foggy. Sloshing could be clearly heard against the pilings. Persons appeared suddenly from the fog, bang, and he swerved. The lascars, smelling sweaty in their loose-robed clothes, seemed to step from their dim anonymity, straight from their native lands, taking on corporeality ten yards away, as though the fog was a chemical agent that contracted the reach of Empire. It was that soupy. Marmaduke continued along the docks, striding through smells: wet rope, pitch, nose-itchy tea. Things kept looming up.

There it was. The P&O steamer. The building-high sides of it. The piles of coal in their iron wagonettes being winched up a rear gangway, the odd shiny lump hopscotching down the pile and leaping to the dock; the wagons of luggage being eased down another gangway, bookended by lascars. Coal in, baggage out. Thrilling. A knockety-knocketing somewhere off. The tarry ropes and inclining ramps. Gulls squawked and burst up to settle again, regally, on the precise tops of pilings.

Marmaduke was not to leave for hours yet, so he continued to walk, his luggage left at the P&O sheds, back there, left insouciantly with the clustered other passengers, who, out of their element, nervous, were sitting with their luggage, keeping their vigilant hands on it, sentencing themselves to hours of boredom. He was too excited to stay in one place. Within a few hours he would be headed where his curiosity led him, to Ottoman lands, to Istanbul, to the sudden steep stone stairs and coal smoke

and wooden houses of Üskadar, where one, having left the Europeanised city and crossed the Strait of Marmara, first became aware of Asia outfolding all the way to India, and beyond. He supposed that others, in an earlier age, had felt this brief flutter of romantic expectation when they crossed the Danube. The world was getting smaller, or the Ottoman Empire was: by being more familiar its exotic nature kept withdrawing, even as one neared it. (Marmaduke remembered that Arabic had a verb, *'as'asa*, that could mean both to withdraw and to advance.) Yet there was still such fuzziness, such misrepresentation. He'd had conversations with men who'd spent twenty years in India and knew little about the land. He chuckled at his much younger self and his Not So Grand Tour. His romantic thoughts of sunshine, palm trees and ancient civilisations.

Marmaduke considered himself everyone's friend, the emissary of frank decency; he did not see himself – in his urban finery, the jacket and vest, the waxed moustache – as a stereotypical Englishman, though he supposed he was. Somewhat. He was one of those educated liberals who was confident to get to the heart of the matter within hours of arriving in any port; consequently, he ruefully estimated, he gained something and missed something. *'As'asa* indeed! He knew that his sympathies were wide and, then again, he knew that he could afford wide sympathies.

Nevertheless, he had become incensed by the smug London talk about how the Turk was bound to get his comeuppance in the Balkans. Imagine – men who had never travelled in Muslim lands. The thought-patterns of opportunistic vultures circling in the upper draughts. He had decided to go, to find out what he could about the actual Turks. To root around. Away from the imperial prejudice and the weight of obvious ententes. Away from questions of naval tonnage. Already he could see the series of dispatches he would write for *The New Age* and, as he visualised the spread of his text, his stride quickened.

He passed another ship, spar and pulley creaking to lower bales of something – Cotton? Hemp? Coir? Then a jetty loomed up and he heard Cockney voices, saw a barring rope, a couple of customs-officers, at their feet a pile of sled-runners. He saw that the piles of sled-runners dwindled far down the jetty. They were yellowish, pointed. And then his mind caught up with his eyes. They weren't sled-runners. They were ivory tusks.

He stopped to ask where they were from but the lads didn't know and he let it drop. That yellowing seemed to stretch into an indentured world of pain. The thrashing of a humongous creature helpless on its side in the red dust. He wheeled around and headed back towards the P&O steamer. Presently he heard and then he came upon a circle of people in hats and bonnets, some sitting on steamer trunks. There were bursts of laughter. He sidled up and insinuated himself into the inner circle.

At their centre was a short and portly Indian man in a *dhoti* and sandals, gesticulating, speaking in some Indian language. Beside him was a box and some playing cards, suggesting he had been performing some card tricks. But now he was into a prolonged patter. He called the audience ''a'ies and gen's', suggesting imitation of Cockneys, until another darkish Indian man in a very British, and unseasonable, suit of heavy worsted, corrected him, filling in the consonants. The antic little performer revolved, making sure that his entreaties reached every single face, while his helper displayed a studious amusement at all this, the first tiny fractures of age around his eyes.

Marmaduke recognised the short performer as the gully-gully man, the Indian who had probably amused them all, port outbound, starboard home, with a variety of tricks, games, japes, monologues, soliloquys and songs. This must be his last attempt to wring emoluments out of his audience. The gully-gully man pointed at a large, conical basket. He said that he had often entertained the round heads of Europe – many chortles – while his helper corrected him.

'Pardon me, The Cowed Heads of Europe!'

'No, The *Crowned* Heads of Europe!'

Something familiar about this helpful gentleman. Overdressed. Like me, thought Marmaduke. Natty cravat. Rumpled suit. Pocket-watch. The gully-gully man held up his hand. 'Truly there are horrors everywhere, and there is one that never ceases to horrify good Christian people like yourselves. Even though you have lived in India many years, and heard many tales, I daresay there are some secrets that have escaped your notice. Now, here, I can reveal to you the most, the most, the most ...'

'Astonishing,' said the man in the rumpled suit.

'Astonishing! Yes, even such an experienced old 'India-hand' as I ...'

The crowd swelled into smug laughter at an Indian being an 'India-hand'. His counterpart, the suavely cooperative vocabulary-supplier,

frowned. For a moment his eyes met Marmaduke's. Could this man have been my guide in Egypt? thought Marmaduke. In Syria, much earlier? Rashid? No, it couldn't be. He would never dress like a Mayfair gent. Why was that word 'Mayfair' suggesting itself?

'My friends, my good, good friends, even *I* am scared of what might occur when I summon this being from its slumber. Will it be in a sunny mood, or will its counts, uh, its countints –'

'Countenance,' said the helper.

'More matter and less art,' said a member of the audience, which was beginning to dwindle.

'Now where was I?' said the gully-gully man.

'Countenance,' said the Indian gentleman. Was that a sliver of amusement that lingered, Marmaduke wondered, underneath the static majesty of his eyes?

'Countenance, yes,' said the gully-gully man. 'A most excellent word. Will its countenance darken? Will this creature, confined for so long, cut off from its fellow creatures, *strike?*' He jabbed his hands at them, and a couple of ladies shrieked.

The gully-gully man drew a flute – a *saz*, actually – from his clothing, assumed a lotus position behind the basket, and blew the first pentatonic notes of a strange air. Yunus? Qadi? Saad? Tunis? Mahdi? Hah! thought Marmaduke. Oh, for God's sakes, man, how do you even know that he's Muslim?

The bottom of the basket began to rock from its base, at first subtly and then, as the flute made variegated elaborations on the melody, more boisterously, one side lifting slightly, then the other. The woven lid also stirred. It seemed to be prying itself upwards by a crack. The *saz* achieved its most raucous timbre. People were gasping prematurely.

And then the man stopped playing and whispered in his colleague's ear.

'That high?' said the gentleman. 'Very well.' Turning to the crowd, he said, 'he has named his sum. For a total of five guineas, he will reveal the secret in the basket.'

The gully-gully man produced a flat-cap from his robes and passed it to the nearest audience member. It made its rounds. Marmaduke moved in until he was shoulder to shoulder with the gentleman, who smelled

slightly of coffee, and the man turned and fixed Marmaduke with a blank and patient look.

'It's a long way from London solicitor to shill for the itinerant gully-gully man, isn't it?' said Marmaduke.

He registered Marmaduke's question, but his expression did not change. He said to the crowd: 'There, there, make sure our mutual friend's time at dockside is profitable. Give what you like, but please give.' Then he turned back to Marmaduke and said, 'I don't know what you mean. Do I know you?'

'Good sir, we met maybe ten years ago.'

'A lot can happen in ten years. I am not a solicitor, as you claim. I am recently retired from the India Civil Service.'

'We talked. It was rainy. We had coffee. In a club. A large club. A gentleman's club.'

'I'm prepared to believe,' the man said, 'that I was in a gentleman's club, but I'm afraid the details of our acquaintance quite escape me.'

'We had a long talk. Before lunch was served and we had to vacate the place. Damn it. You were ... you were nervous because you had to argue with a Marquis – it's coming back to me – about some sort of lawsuit, and he was terribly rude. Don't you remember that?'

'Eager to argue, perhaps. Nervous, never. And if I counted everyone who was rude to me, and remembered them, I would be in a perpetual snit.'

The two men took the measure of each other. They were now a very large portion of the audience. The gully-gully man, satisfied by his take, resumed his blowing on the saz; with each strident note, a girl piped up, 'A snake! Cor, I bet it's a snake!', and a boy clutching his mother's skirts wept theatrically. The gully-gully man began to sway – the lid fell off the basket – a girl in a turban slowly rose – namaste-hands raised above her head – reared as though a cobra – spat out droplets of saliva. The kids laughed. The parents laughed. They coughed up more coins. And once the last donation had plopped in his cap, the gully-gully man strapped the basket on his back and he and the girl departed.

'Yusuf Ali, wasn't it?' said Marmaduke.

The man nodded. 'Yes, Abdullah Yusuf Ali. And you are?'

'Marmaduke Pickthall. How is it that you are allied with a gully-gully man?'

'One might say,' Yusuf Ali said, with a tolerant smile, 'that is, if one had better manners, that I have joined forces with an honest tradesman who plies his Wunderkammer prestidigitations in much the same manner as his father, and his father's father, plied them a century ago. Lucrative trade cannot just be confined to blacksmiths or jewellers, for fascination and amusement, too, are fungible goods and may, with some imagination, be conjured out of thin air. Why, one might say that my occasional partnership with him is evidence of my interest in a sort of trades-based adult education. It occupied a few hours and brought some needed levity into my journey.' He shook hands with Marmaduke.

This 'needed levity' gave Marmaduke pause. Why so solemn?

'The last time I was here was a trip to the Continent with my wife,' said Marmaduke. 'I'm sorry, I can't quite recall . . . were you, I mean, are you married?'

'Yes,' Yusuf said.

That all-too-immediate yes, the eyes evasive, told Marmaduke he had better move on. 'And are you still a barrister?'

'My good man, I've been the magistrate of a whole district in India.'

'That's impressive. Well, my good magistrate, it's going to be a few hours before my ship is ready to sail. Would you care to have a coffee or tea with me? There's a place near the departure hall.'

Yusuf agreed, and gave instructions to his manservant as to the handling of luggage.

The café was as gloomy as the fog. It smelled of rancid beer-stains and tobacco. Marmaduke ordered a pint, Yusuf tea. Yusuf is stiff, rigid, Marmaduke thought. He could afford to have a pint. He'd known many Muslims to drink in the Levant. 'How long have you been helping that gully-gully fellow?' said Marmaduke.

'Oh, this is the first time. He's an amusing chap. He thought that I might add a little something to his act. You know, I can't even remember his name.'

The drinks came and they raised and clinked glass and cup.

'You're going to Turkey,' said Yusuf. 'Might I ask why?'

'You might say that I'm trying to influence a careless English policy towards the Ottoman Empire.'

'Ambitious.'

'Yes, I rather doubt rather that I shall find sympathetic ears upon my return. The politicians have pretty much written off the Turks, unable to think beyond Germany and France – and Russia. Which is why they should think about Turkey's far eastern borders. But no, our elected representatives seem to have ruled out Turkey as an ally. But I think otherwise. So, I'm going to see what the condition of the country may be. The current crop of young leaders seems ready and able to reform the government. They made a good start.'

'I'm afraid, my dear man, that you are optimistic when it comes to the Turks. A few army officers in Istanbul have made a splash, that's all. There was a certain cautious wading into modernity some five years ago. That tide has receded.'

Marmaduke chortled. 'The watery metaphors have died. The tenor drowns out the vehicle. The vehicle wheezes to a halt in the puddle. The tenor falls into the orchestra pit.'

'Capital, my good man. I *was* straying into cliché. But the facts have to be faced. In Istanbul I'm sure you will find people *au courant* with the fashionable opinions of London and Paris. And yet the vast, Anatolian hinterland has never known progress.'

'It seems to me that you are condescending towards our Turkish friends. And on the other end of that wilderness, as you put it, lies Beirut, which is a pretty cosmopolitan city, where there are Arab newspapers full of the new stirrings of the century.'

Yusuf Ali took a long sip of his tea. 'What is it that you hope to find?' he said. 'Do you have any Turkish?'

'I did pick up some, years ago. But I'm sure, with a little more study, I can find like-minded Turks with which to discuss the evolving situation who want to keep their options open, despite their dealings with Germany, and keep up a cordial relationship with Britain.'

'How very apt that you have used the word *cordial*. For that is the relationship that really counts now, dear Pickthall. The *Entente Cordiale*. I'm sure you're aware that the Ottomans are unlikely to survive the decade. Like a tourniquet, the powers are restricting all lifeblood to the

West, and choking off the perimeter, which is surely the situation of the hapless Turks.'

'Well,' said Marmaduke, 'time will tell. Since you've come from India, might I ask what the general mood is there? Are Indian minds sufficiently allied with the Empire that they would come to England's aid, should war break out?'

'Unquestionably. Stalwartly.'

'Hasn't there been a certain amount of dissatisfaction?'

'It's easy to mistake the churn of trivial complaints for reality. We cannot and will not see another Mutiny. India will remain solidly British.'

'I should have inserted an inshallah in that sentence.'

'Inshallah,' said Yusuf. 'May Allah forgive me.'

'In any case, what disturbs me, and has motivated my little excursion, is the threat of a larger war that might leave the entire Levant up for grabs, once the dust has settled. After a great war, the bulk of it on the Continent, no one is going to spare a thought for the fate of the Ottoman Empire. And then who is going to hold sway from Istanbul to Damascus?'

Yusuf sighed. 'I can assure you —I have this at the highest levels —that there is little chance of this dreadnought competition flaring up into war. We have made alliances, and Germany is well aware of them. Rest your mind about that. There are power-brokers who would spring into diplomatic action if any of the parties brandished and rattled the keen edge of the sabre, inshallah. Oh, yes, there are certain politicians in Westminster who love bellicosity and take it as an insult that the Hun is capable of armament. But do you really think that the Kaiser would move against his cousin?'

'Just for the sake of argument ...' Marmaduke brought into play the saltshaker, the ashtray, the beer-bottle, and the tin teapot. Yusuf leaned over the table intently as Marmaduke manoeuvred these pieces like an expert gully-gully man. 'Germany expands a smidgeon into the northern lowlands. Soldiers on the move. Towns becoming garrisons. The Cabinet is recalled from a break, and hears of further incursions. France declares war on Germany. Austria is said to be preparing its troops. Mindful of its treaties and agreements, what do you think that the Cabinet would do? Ships within shot of each other in the Channel. Shots fired in Alsace-Lorraine. Diplomatic telegrams are sent posthaste by the Foreign Office

without reply. Key figures are vacationing, or on shooting weekends. The Cabinet is fractious, eager to act. Whether we like it or not, a limousine would find its way to the Palace. The sovereign would admit the Prime Minister into his presence. The King would have little choice but outright support.'

'A sad day indeed if we relied on the monarchy to decide,' said Yusuf Ali.

'I'm well aware that the approval of the monarch is ceremonial. Unfortunately, with the recent stuffing of the upper chamber, so is the approval of the Lords. What, then, would stop a headlong rush to war? The papers have been priming the prospect for years.'

'Fear not, good Marmaduke, the Cabinet would not find the prospect of war on the continent salubrious. Why, it might go on for years. All trade would stop. Stop on a dime. And there are other considerations. I found in Booth's admirable work – have you read it?'

'Booth? No, I'm afraid not.'

'*Life and Labours of the People of London*. You should read it. The papers may make their vainglorious announcements of bellicose readiness, and print the foolhardy statements by military officers, many of them retired and in any case used to a different kind of war, cavalry war. You see, for them war is a matter of hoisting an oriflamme and that is all there is to it. Two weeks of field-glasses from the rear, and back to their Kensington clubs. There is much more to it than that. I recently had the opportunity to peruse the latest edition of *Life and Labours*. It should give us pause. There is the question of whether the citizens are up to the task.'

Marmaduke shrugged. 'I don't see why they wouldn't be.'

'Are you aware, as Booth reminds us, that a good quarter to a third of the so-called working class are getting by on just enough nutrition? Should war break out, these sorry specimens, as Booth also reminds us, their legs crooked from rickets, wheezing, given to various types of indigestion, may not have the strength to fight for protracted periods. This is especially problematic because the supply of food, with which a fighting force fuels itself, is likely to be interrupted. Back in the agricultural homeland, children and women and the old will be doing the work of the absent soldiers. Forget the strident calls for rousing cannon-exchange in the Channel. That may be the least of it. Either the enemy would win those

exchanges and land their armies on our coast, a day's march from London, or – and this is perhaps the worst of it – the naval skirmishes shall be inconsequential, the moot result of the even-handed race for tonnage, and the war shall take place largely in France. That is the most likely scenario. A pitched battle with a 500-mile line to hold. Do you really think that the skinny and sickly lads of the shires are up to that?'

And Yusuf Ali, with the confidence of an undergraduate debater, spread his hands so as to gather agreement.

Marmaduke, as he listened, gripped his tankard. He wished that what Yusuf said were not so. He realised that what he wanted out of his trip was unlikely to occur. He wanted a way to insert the huge fact of Turkey into the jostling of Continental powers, to extend entente. There was no real chance of that. He knew that. However. He had met many people with opinions such as Ali's. Their preferences were, like great engines mired in bogs, heavily set for the status quo. Marmaduke swallowed some lager. He saw last week's letter from Enver Pasha, freshly arrived at his desk at Five Chimneys, inky and warm and welcoming, and looked forward to meeting him.

Yusuf produced a hankie, and began to wipe his throat distastefully.

'I happen to know,' Marmaduke said.

Yusuf waited, harvesting junk from his fingernails with his other fingernails, and considered whether his interlocutor's longish pause was in itself a concession.

'Yes? You know ...?' he prompted.

'I happen to know a splendid fellow the name of Enver, a military man, and one of the so-called Young Turks, who have taken matters in hand. He wrote to me recently. It's true, first things first, there are a lot of economic issues they must face. The debt is a heavy burden, and there is bound to be a shaking down of things once their new ideas make contact with the more reactionary and traditional elements of society, but why can't we just take a moment and envision what a renewed Ottoman stronghold would mean to the world, a bulwark against balkanisation, and the protector of many *millets* that might otherwise easily disappear? Picture it. A Turkish nation as a gateway and administrator of the entire Orient, its coreligionists spanning Syria, Iran, Afghanistan, a veritable arcing land

of Turan from the Bosporus to the Northwest of China.' He proceeded to detail his vision.

Yusuf patiently heard Marmaduke out, though he was bored with this fantasy of an Islamic Empire far exceeding the scope of the current one. On the man went, galumphing, Yusuf thought, silk roads, agriculture, culture, the phoenix-like rebirth of Samarkand, its styles echoing in the streets of Vienna, the parliaments of Europe sending diplomatic pouches to Nishapur, all of this romantic *Imperium Ottomanicum revixit* studded with palaces and gorgeous mosques, with its own currency. Yusuf realised he had stopped listening and was continuing the fantasy in his own head. Poppycock. And all because Marmaduke had received a letter from this Enver fellow. Well, let him dream. Yusuf doubted such vaunting constructions. In his view, in this age, bonds were likely to get weaker, not stronger.

A shadow lanced across Yusuf's mind: *a letter.* A letter from a solicitor. The letter that changed everything. Revealed the drama he had never once imagined. Theresa's demand for a divorce. No matter how many times he read the letter, he could not argue or bargain away its absolute, categorical nature, and he really ought to refocus, before he revealed, once this Marmaduke stopped talking, how little he had been paying attention.

Marmaduke was now describing some sort of world government, the turbaned representatives of this Turkish mastodon of an Empire filing down the ladders of a Zeppelin airship and shaking hands with the Europeans. Preposterous.

'I hardly think so,' said Yusuf. 'You might as well be talking about the Planet Turan. You are living in the past. If I were wont to wager, I would bet against it. And though I am loth to do so, I would bet against Britain holding Egypt in perpetuity. Regarding your mighty Ottoman Empire, have you given any thought to what this forward-thinking bunch are going to face when they meet the Wahhabis in Arabia? *Those* Muslims are not going to take kindly to any sort of rapprochement with people they regard as idolators.'

'A fair point,' said Marmaduke.

'With their steadfast and self-righteous hatred of anything that smacks of *bid'a* they will surely hinder your fond dreams of pan-Islamic progress,' said Yusuf.

'Be that as it may,' said Marmaduke, thinking, May it all turn on a merciful God, a God who wished to spare Creation a whole continent of blood. 'Why do you insist on the end of the Ottomans? You would never countenance the end of Empire in India.'

'The Raj has lasted more than two centuries. I daresay we can apply Newtonian mechanics to it. Objects at rest tend to remain so.'

'The Ottomans have held sway for *four* centuries.'

'It is not so much a question of longevity, it is more a question of adaptability,' said Yusuf.

Adaptability. How swiftly, Yusuf thought, everything could change. Teresa, solicitors, shame.

'Bang on,' said Marmaduke. 'To be honest, I'm not sure how well I'd adapt to some huge upheaval. I might run away instead! Put my head in the sand! But inshallah we'll do our best.'

'Yes, inshallah.'

Yusuf realised how much he liked Marmaduke, wrong though he was. The Ottomans would not continue to hold sway. Any love or bond – global, international, national, tribal, familial, could, like Ibn Khaldun's *asabiyya*, a centripetal brotherhood, any adhesive *raison d'être*, could, under the right conditions, grow so attenuated that it failed to hold. It would break. Bonds break. How ludicrous it had been of him to imagine his wife and his children as a beaming tribe grouped on the front steps of the house in St. Albans swearing a sort of photographic fealty to him. In the divorce pleadings a respondent had been named. An Obed Thorne. That hurt. Another man. The distant image of Theresa in her wedding-dress, in the little church in Brighton, came to him.

'Be that as it may,' said Marmaduke. 'Adaptability. You were saying.'

Yusuf shivered his attention back to Marmaduke. 'I've always thought that an interesting expression, "be that as it may". Prologue to your putting forth a countervailing vision ... ah, now it's returning to me, those hours we spent a-rhubarbing ten years ago. 'Be that as it may' has the unmistakeable ring of a vast concession you are about to make, no? A war may render our ideas about the future suppositional, nay, delusional, is that where you'll go next?'

'A countervailing vision sounds better than a vast concession.'

'Please, enlighten me,' said Yusuf.

'You know it's rare to get a chance to shuffle borders like playing cards to players the size of nations, but I'm afraid that is likely what we are going to get at the other end of a war: a land-grab. By us. And France. Assuming we win. And I think we will win. I haven't read your *Life and Labours*, but can it really be that bad? A brace of tars entered this watering-hole not twenty minutes ago, and guzzled their pints, and they looked right healthy.'

'Germany's population is much larger. The odds are with them.'

'It seems strange, but you're forgetting that Britain isn't just a group of islands; it is the brain of an Empire, and we can count on our colonies to supply us with men enough to make Germany regret their ambitions. Now, do you think that the average Indian—'

'I cannot conceptualise an average Indian. As you are probably aware, India is the home of discrete communities, and my own community is probably the smallest. That is, except for the Jains or some unhappily marooned Zoroastrians.'

'My point is, can Britain expect the support of Indian soldiers? Why should the Indian Muslim some four thousand miles away abscond to an antipodean battleground, simply because we asked? And why have you returned to British soil on the very brink of conflict? Surely your efforts could be better spent in India,' said Marmaduke.

A swift tribulation travelled from under Yusuf's right eye into his jowl where it died. Yusuf motioned to the boy for more tea, and took his time stirring sugar into it.

'That is, if you're willing to discuss it,' said Marmaduke.

'I am confident that we can expect an enthusiastic contribution to the war effort, not only in fighting men, but drivers, ditch-diggers, makers of supplies and material. I think you'll find the Indian heart is, above all else, loyal—and that loyalty extends from the lowliest peasant to the Nabobs and Nizams and Amirs and Akoonds, splendid fellows. India will fight for King and Empire. There was a tremendous outpouring of patriotic sentiment when the King showed his sacred face in India, and I have been trying to inflame the urgency of supporting Empire in various organs. I keep up a constant stream of insistence on this issue. I step up. Can you say you have concrete plans for how to use what you learn in Turkey?'

Marmaduke licked the froth from his pint off his moustache and sat back, fed up.

'Apart from my general optimism for Turkey's future,' he said, 'I rather like *lukuum*. And Iskender kebab.'

'At least you are now in the realm of the possible,' said Yusuf, and when he saw that defiant spark in Marmaduke's eyes, he put up his hand. 'Please don't be offended. I imagine that you want to see, because of our times and all the gravitational bodies jostling and nudging each other slightly out of their typical orbits, how *they* see their future.'

'*And* I hope to practise my Turkish,' said Marmaduke. 'The reason I want to practise my Turkish is that it's great fun, and apart from an agglutinative grammar that builds ideas out of pithy little additions, I daresay that my present mission will give me ample occasion to use that most helpful of particles. I refer to the evidential or hearsay *imish*. What a marvel this little fragment is! Just insert *imish* in the middle of the verb and you know right away that you have to take whatever action or happening with the proverbial grain, because it has come from another mouth. And if you use *imish* with a Turk, why, he will hit you with an equally suppositional *imishlik*. And you can bat these *it-is-saids* and *it-is-thoughts* back and forth like an *imish* Wimbledon match. Why, my friend, if we allowed *imish* in court proceedings we would never get anywhere near the truth. I would go so far as to say that the helpful little twister of the verb, *imish,* has changed my life.'

'And…?'

'Well, I would want to know what the constantly erupting wars in the Balkans were costing the Turks.'

'And?'

'Dear, dear Yusuf. Do you, in your normal course of things, before you do anything, have a fully worked-out program? If you do, how on earth do you cope with something new, and where would your curiosity be …oh … I see … you're having fun with me.'

'I have heard it said,' said Yusuf, 'that people reliably report that having fun with you is among the best types of fun. *Imish*.'

The sun had come out and was rubbing and flaring against the greasy windowpane. Both men became aware of their tawdry and humid

surroundings. They could see the streaks where the boy had dragged his rag across the table. They could feel their shirts stick to their chests.

'I'm not really mocking you,' said Yusuf. '*Au contraire*, I think you're brave. To think outside national boundaries – well, one can't deny, diplomatically speaking, that boundaries are the name of the game – but they can close off possibilities. I didn't expect a full itinerary. I was just indulging in some sparring. I hope you surprise yourself.'

'I wish you the same, my dear man.'

'Alas, perhaps not this time.'

'Ah?'

Yusuf rotated his cup and stared into his cooling tea. 'I expect that I will call on my usual cohorts. The National Liberal Club. Read the papers. Maybe speak at the Royal Asiatic Society. I don't know. If I'm fortunate, I may get invited to Lord Morley's in Oxfordshire, but I'm not really much one for shooting. And you know what those people are like. Their interests are in the main diversional, and their outlook has been formed in the last century.'

'You need to do something new ...' Marmaduke saw that the planks of the dock outside were steaming.

'In any case, there are other duties and tasks that I must perform.'

'Of course, you must,' said Marmaduke.

A long moment ensued, the sort of moment before which everything was frothy and light, like whipped-cream, and after which everything was stiffer, but easily shattered, like meringue. Amid this sensed delicacy, Marmaduke waited for Yusuf to continue or change the subject.

'You see ...' said Yusuf.

Was that a moistening in Yusuf's eye? No, surely not, thought Marmaduke.

'It's not your kids, is it? They're in good health, aren't they?'

Yusuf seemed to slump. Marmaduke began to tell a story to himself, because he didn't know what else he could do. Perhaps Yusuf had come home in order to help his wife with the children. He did hope that there wasn't some sort of medical emergency, because there wasn't very much one could do about that, it really was a case where you had to trust the doctors and Allah, well, mostly Allah, to make sure that the family member came out the other side all hale and hearty, able again to laugh

and take up their work, or their schooling – come to think of it, how old were Yusuf's children? – and after a few weeks, or maybe months, depending on what the doctors said and the relative speed of the recovery, then Yusuf could pack off again to India, maybe with the wife and kids in tow and maybe not, and maybe in a few years the son could dolphin over there and continue Yusuf's work, as so many families did, but the key thing was for Yusuf to take heart and steel himself for delivering the empathetic commiseration that lay ahead and was expected, for it was clear that he was needed. Do remember, good man, that Allah does not burden any soul beyond its— 'What's that? Water? Boy! Boy! Fetch this man some water.'

The boy brought a glass of water and Yusuf placed it against his forehead before he gulped it down. He then said, 'I'm most grateful for your sympathy, Mister Pickthall, but I'm afraid you haven't correctly described the situation. You have, though, divined that I am hard up against it these days. A man's life, as you probably know, is subject to inner storms far more devastating than those in the world around him.'

Marmaduke met this altogether lapidary statement with the receptive eyes of the confessor he imagined he could be. There was every possibility that Yusuf intended his distress to remain vague. Very well, Marmaduke thought, whatever it was, it was Yusuf's business, not his. Yusuf was making a circular, tracing motion with his fingertips on the tabletop, overture to a considered statement that he seemed in no hurry to make.

The café was completely empty. There was still time left before the southbound passengers started to trickle in to drink, just in case the *Southern Star's* bar was not immediately available upon embarking. The barman here had opted for a siesta with his forehead pressed against the zinc. His boy was idly swivelling a rag inside a glass. From far away, he heard the plangent, loud-hailing cry of the harbour master shouting about this or that other departure. Sometimes it was hard to know what to do, thought Marmaduke. You could press further into whatever was making Yusuf phlegmatic, or you could let it lie. Marmaduke chose a third option.

'I daresay that the Company should be glad to have you back, once you've taken care of business here in Blighty. Capable chap like you. Experienced. Savvy. Oh. Dammit. Sorry. What'd I say? God's sake, don't. Bear up, man.'

Yusuf rubbed his eyes and raised his voice to clear a tremble in it. 'I'm afraid I've ended my employment in the Company.'

'Why would you do that? Oh, I'm sure you had your reasons. But need such a move be permanent?'

'I'm afraid it is, and I have negotiated a pension.'

'That's good. Isn't it? Is it good?'

'You don't have any idea, Marmaduke, what it's like for someone like me in the midst of the so-called heaven-born. They are so set on getting their own offspring situated in the Company that they have no time for assessing the merits of people such as myself.'

'You're not saying. I mean, are you saying …?'

'Exactly. Every time I applied, there was just no opening above a sub-magistrate. I'm not going to have any dolphin sons *en route* to Bombay, I'm afraid. My superior Meston tiptoed around the issue, but there was no promotion in the cards for me. And you see …'

'I'm listening …'

'When I think of the time I spent in the extreme heat, oh, years ago, one of my first administrative assignments, following around some German or Swiss in their mulberry orchards, pretending to be interested in various types of Indian sericulture so I could write a monograph on silk production that has probably been read by some twenty people—the very people to whom I was going 'Yes, I see,' and 'Capital plan you have there' to—only to find out that that book, and my other one about Indian culture, had bought me precisely nothing in terms of promotion. And now, *this*!'

'Yes, this. I quite agree. Intolerable.'

Marmaduke had no idea what 'this' was, but it seemed best at this juncture to acknowledge the existence of this *this*, and hope for a smoother, expository patch.

'I don't want to pretend to know your story,' said Marmaduke. 'It is your story, and doubtless you know its inner depths. But you seem to be suggesting that your … your advancement was not possible due to racial prejudice. Am I right?'

'If only my superiors in the Company were honest about their prerogatives. Instead. they washed their hands of the whole problem once they established a few quotas for clerks. The quota came to represent their entire Christian duty and to go beyond it, madness.'

Marmaduke kept silent.

'One fumes to think of their polo games, their leisure in the gymkhanas, the frosted-glass and palm-treed clubs, knowing that there was a qualified darkie out there in the dusty plains, or the feverish jungle, hearing case upon case upon case, while they knocked off and languorously chit-chatted beneath the importunate efforts of a hand-wafted fan.'

'But surely … '

'Even my mentor could extend himself only so far as arguing for my pension.'

'Perhaps now you're better off. I mean, you can make a go of it in England. And your wife is no doubt looking forward to having you around. Is she already home?'

Now Yusuf was writhing, as though there were a potent mass, steadily enlarging in him, making him uncomfortable at his edges.

'Damn it, it's that my wife wants a divorce and the situation has gotten so, so shameful that I have to grant it. And the children have to be taken care of.'

'Oh.'

There, I've said it, thought Yusuf. Apart from Meston back in India, this was the only other person he'd told. Bound to come out sometime. But his relief at his utterance was quickly followed by disappointment in himself and a gulp. What must Marmaduke be thinking? He will probably change the subject, thought Yusuf.

Marmaduke put out a hand and touched Yusuf's elbow.

'*La yukallifu Allahu nafsan illa wus'ahaa*,' Marmaduke said. 'Allah doesn't burden anyone greater than their ability to bear it. And all pain is temporary.'

'*Sub specie aeternitatis*, true. But it doesn't give me very much succour in the here and now. If only I had seen where those dusty years were leading. I was blind. I know what loneliness feels like. My stays at home were short. She must have felt very alone,' said Yusuf.

'I think your employment as a magistrate, my dear fellow, has accustomed you overmuch to appreciating both petitions. There is no need to arraign yourself and weigh the charges against you. Why, it sounds like she is the one who sinned against you!'

'I should have married a Muslim,' said Yusuf.

Outside, the fog had returned.

The thought did not comfort Yusuf. He was sunk in a variety of tortures: the mingling of beauty and giddiness, the elixir of Teresa's exceptional, why, of *their* exceptional fates. She had just been a junior typist in the pool at Lincoln's Inn. Away they went. The cleric raised an eyebrow as he said 'or forever hold their peace.' Of course, neither Teresa nor he noticed that. For a while, good money obscured everything, as money often does. Then he was thousands of miles away, in England intermittently, and the kids kept coming. A picture of lonely Teresa was suggesting itself, she prodding a fledgling fire with a poker, sighing to the inglenook, but it didn't quite form. Fragments of shadows was all he had. Did I really know her? Yusuf thought. 'Look, Marmaduke,' he said. 'You seem to spend time away from your wife, don't you? I mean, here you are, venturing forth to Istanbul, with plans to stay a few months, true?'

'That's true.'

'And yet you're not worried about what Muriel might get up to in your absence?'

Marmaduke tried not to grin, but he grinned, and regretted it, though his thought had been so silly that the grin was irresistible. A swift steed charging into the courtyard at Five Chimneys; a dashing rake dismounted; girlish giggles from within the house; a longish period with chickens pecking in the foreyard dirt; and then the gallant rider, swinging up and riding off. His wife Muriel coming to the door, dewy-eyed, with a fond wave at the diminishing rider. Why, it was right out of *Madame Bovary*. Marmaduke let out a little laugh.

'No, I can't say I've ever worried about that. You have to understand, we've known each other since we were fifteen. And we don't have children. She has her interests and I have mine. Why, each of us is a free servant of Allah!'

'Do you not miss her? Does she not miss you?'

Marmaduke had rarely if ever considered this. He knew very well what Muriel was up to. She was gathering herbs with the neighbouring children. Singing around bonfires in the evenings. Taking surplus eggs to the market. Gathering petunias and larkspurs and foxgloves for her parents' graves. She was kneeling in the otherwise empty pews of the parish church.

'My children hate me,' said Yusuf. 'I don't know what I did. My eldest son especially.' Yusuf did not relish having to talk to the lad about the divorce. He knew his son's scornful looks and sarcastic comments too well. It was like looking at a younger version of himself rendering judgment on him, the pudgier, more fatigued combatant. 'He may not even talk to me.'

'Let's not get carried away. They're children. They hardly know you. Maybe this is an opportunity to get to know them.'

'Perhaps. Perhaps.'

But Marmaduke could see that Yusuf was no longer across the table. He was in the preoccupied place that suffering is.

'She took up with another man.'

'Ouch,' went Marmaduke. 'But look, that's all the more reason to get rid of her and focus on the children. She's certainly not going to get them, after having done that!'

Though Marmaduke had thought that this phrase would soothe Yusuf, why, the man scarcely seemed to appreciate that Marmaduke had spoken. Instead, Yusuf Ali stared out the window. He was thinking that the sea-routes that lay behind him, and the roads to St. Albans that lay ahead, seemed impossible to mentally traverse now. They had utterly changed their meaning and no doubt their appearance. No matter what he did, he would be lost for some time.

'You will get through this,' Marmaduke added.

'Do you happen to know of any good governesses?' said Yusuf.

Marmaduke didn't. He couldn't help him. Yusuf would have to climb out of this hole by himself. He checked his watch. 'I do say, it's high time I was off.'

This was not strictly true. It was only the first boarding, and his man would already have taken his baggage to his cabin. Still, their talk had reached an end. He arose, brushed off his front, and reached over and squeezed Yusuf's shoulder. 'Goodbye. *Allah yarhamuk.*'

'Goodbye. *Ma salaam,*' said Yusuf. 'It was good to see you again. You know, when we see each other, we talk and talk, and yet we never seem to reach a conclusion.'

'I'm sure that next time things will have improved. Markedly. Inshallah.'

'Inshallah.'

The café brightened marginally as the door swung open and dimmed as it swung shut. A Pacific and Orient tout was loud-hailing passengers in distant, dreamlike tones. Yusuf lay his cheek against the table. He felt woozy. He began to drift. The fog outside was punctured by a striding lascar, and he thought he could see in that brief aperture a magical gangway to another time and place. The rays of sun shot through the leaves and caught the silver edges of the cocoons. The farther trees had nimbuses of midges around their crowns. A mulberry orchard. The ground underfoot was uneven. He stumbled. He was not paying attention. He had just about filled up his notebook. His hosts had showed him practically everything and they were making their way back to the bungalow. He wiped his forehead. Beastly hot among the mulberries, and Yusuf's attention was faltering.

The boy came and discretely collected the glasses without disturbing Yusuf.

His hosts wandered away from him, speaking German. A labourer up a ladder was pruning dead leaves; his loincloth damp, his back slick. The cocoons were actually drab. Fantastic that from the plainest, common strands the loveliest and softest silks were span. When Adam delved and Eve span. Could it be, it could be that when he reached for and touched a cocoon, brushed that fine and subtle fuzz, his cuckolder reached out and caressed Teresa's hair for the first time?

THREE POEMS

Saadia Peerzada

In New England

I say salam to my neighbour, she smiles—
waalaikumsalam warahmatullahi wabarakatuh,
I feel ashamed of my shorter salam,
the baby in the pram is calm as water.

In this foreign, far-off country,
some faces are Muslim from a mile away—
something in us closed off…
Everyone is allowed tenderness
but our share never seems to reach us.

When we all walk into khutbah,
the first dua is for Palestine—
blessed was the day the land rooted itself
in the heart, as love,
Blessed is the day when freedom arrives
and decides to stay.

Being Muslim women on the Sonipat-Delhi Highway

In an auto with a saffron flag stashed under its roof,
the sun turns my friend's face into gold.
We say all the wrong words,
'In sha Allah' hyphenates each clause.
We call cities by their pre-bastardized names,
fear doesn't change the language we know the world in
but we need the fear to keep us safe.

At Jama Masjid, an uncle walks north for maghrib,
his keffiyeh worn with time.
Young boys in kufis cross the road recklessly.

4:48 am in Srinagar

Home is a loose pile of bricks,
nothing identifiable ties me to the outside.
Summer insects crawl on my walls,
magnified in the light–
the obituaries remain the same, the names change,
a void big enough to make a city of itself.

Everything looks the same in the dark
the silhouette of home,
light from the camps,
and the air – pregnant
with something that makes it hard to breathe.

I am a house at fajr,
only partly lit,
I pray to God to let the light in.

FOUR POEMS

Abigail George

I want a free Palestine

The child is not dead
   — Ingrid Jonker

I want Bibi Netanyahu not to be angry
I want him to stop this war
and this endless fighting
I want him to give Palestinian leaders
a seat at the negotiating table
I want a ceasefire
I want to take over the world
I want to be happy
Not this schizophrenic-mess
We're living on an artificial alarm clock
someone says in my Instagram feed
at two in the morning
Mandela speaks to me
He speaks to me from beyond the grave
inside a poem
When I read this poem
it feels like ice in my veins
it feels as if I'm eating an apricot
Mandela reads Ingrid Jonker's poem
in the silence
in the aftermath of my father's
eightieth birthday

As night turns into day
I want to take over the world
and stop the war
I want to stop the Israeli-Palestinian conflict
I want to bring the dead back to life
but you can't bring ghosts back to life
I want to see happy people
I want to not have limbs amputated
I want to hear the children's laughter
Not these bombs going off inside my head
I don't want to see this airstrike
in front of my eyes
I don't want to see this fibula
I don't want to see the dog buried in the rubble
I want a ceasefire today
I don't want a ceasefire tomorrow
Tomorrow might be too late
Tonight turns into daylight
and I find Rilke in Gaza, in Rafah

Mandela said so

Mandela loved children.
You've all seen the images.
Go to the internet. Be witness
at his birthday parties. My
heart takes flight on the
odour of death. I have
spoken about this before.
Question/s: in war, what
comes after the wildfire, what
happens to the children, to
the laughter. What happens
when the concrete jungle is
no more. When the river is
sticky, bloody and ancient, when

it turns to dust, to liquid, to
masala, to alien fluid and when
that is no more, what happens
to the surface, to the aorta, to the sea
When the wave is no more
silence descends, creeps into
the city, every terrain, the dark, the light
This morning as the dark turns
into light I listen to the milky sweetness
of the poetry of Ari Sitas on a
poetry show called The Red
Wheelbarrow. Poetry devours
the light in much the same
way an air strike in Gaza wipes
out entire families. Ari Sitas
says he went into a 'mad period'.
Oh, how I know all about
that. I think his poems are genius,
a tender slaughterhouse.

The sea

Does this sea have a
dendrite, is it made of
serotonin? Do endorphins
run through the tears
of children? Does this
sea only know of storms,
this planet aligning itself
with the dying, with cranial
pain? I think of the word,
'gland'. It is master. It is
cell. It holds me prisoner.
I think of two more words
in inverted commas, the
sweetness of honey and

milk found in 'blood spilled'
or is it 'spilled blood'?
What intimate knowledge
of rich veins and blood does
this sea have of war crimes,

what kind of birds fly over
this sea, do mental birds
live in mental cages? This
sea is as bold as Ari Sitas'
voice. Every poet has words
and even the complex design
of those words have the courage
of smoke that silences, the
power of bone and flesh
that grapples and crushes
the outsider. I am an outsider.
I turn into a wave in the
sea's embrace. The blood is
warm and rich. It flows. It
has never stopped flowing
for years and years and years.
Perhaps one day, after thousands
of years, perhaps trees will
grow out of this sea.

From the point of view of the lake of tears

Palestine bleeds
The Jungian moon
Gaping hole
where a heart should be
Kitty Hawk's maturity
Up in the air
Bomb
Air strike

The bomb falls
lands nowhere
lands everywhere
Blood inside
Now outside
Bloodstained clothes
The human stain
Wait for the darling emphasis
Controversy
in the brain's psychology
Limbs have instinct
The body has no head
No arms
No legs
They've turned into branches
The walking dead
War has become a television show
They want more violence
More death
More dead bodies
More screams
Watch them branch out
Belief has an axiom-will
I spent an afternoon reading
Ajise Vincent's poetry on the recommendation
of a friend. Rainclouds gather, hunger,
bell, this grape, wrath, this glass of pale
milk
These don't exist
in a ghost world
People marry
They get on
with their lives
which reminds me
I have poems to write
I too must get on
with the act of living.

REVIEWS

}

DOCUMENTS OF DISPOSSESSION

James Brooks

Where are you, I wonder, in the incessant flow of worse-than-horror-film imagery?

I just checked in on social media, and can tell you that I'm at a tangential scene – so no fathers with sunken cheeks and empty eyes climbing over rubble, carrying the remains of a son or daughter in a polythene bag like so much meat. Instead, the last video I saw featured a throng of a hundred Maccabi Tel Aviv football hooligans at Ben Gurion Airport, safely back home after wreaking havoc in Amsterdam, where their side was battered 5-0 by Ajax.

They're bouncing up and down, waving flags and singing a song in Hebrew. According to the text atop the short video, it goes:

Olé, olé, olé, olé!
Let the IDF [Israel Defence Forces] win and fuck the Arabs!
Olé, olé, olé, olé!
Why is school out in Gaza? There are no children left there!

'The world's first livestreamed genocide', they call it, and that's an accurate description of how this last year of Israeli mass murder has been experienced – dare I say 'consumed'? – by those of us fortunate enough to not be living it first-hand.

The direct relay of atrocity-to-smartphone is certainly novel, but, as Palestinian activists remind us, the 'history [of the Israel-Palestine conflict]

Under a Blue Sun, directed by Daniel Mann (La Bête/Laila Films, 2024).
Israel Palestine on Swedish TV 1958-1989, directed by Göran Hugo Olsson (Film i Väst/Story AB/Ström Pictures/Sveriges Television/Tekele Productions, 2024).
A Fidai Film, directed by Kamal Aljafari (Kamal Aljafari Studio, 2024).

did not begin on October 7' – and neither did its documentation and diffusion in moving images. Three films recently shown in London engaged with this filmic legacy, and to watch them in the order they were screened was to travel haltingly, painfully back in time to before Israel itself was 'created' ('stolen', if you prefer).

Under a Blue Sun opens in what most viewers would correctly assume as the present day – but also in 1987. Smoke rolls and eddies around a workshop bathed in red light; a laptop sits untended on a table, with images of a desert playing on its screen. A female voice recites a poem in Arabic – 'I'm going home / Where to? / Where I belong…' – and the desert imagery is interrupted first by a black-bearded man wearing a pakol, the woollen cap favoured by the Afghan mujahideen, and then by Sylvester Stallone in full eighties pomp – his sullen, thuggish face framed by an elaborate, cascading pompadour.

The scene is from *Rambo III*, inarguably one of the most poorly-aged artefacts of US imperial propaganda, its datedness less attributable to the hero's haircut than long-shifted geopolitical alignments. *Rambo III* saw Vietnam vet John Rambo (Stallone) lured away from the good life of monastic meditation, construction work and martial arts combat in Thailand to join the mujahideen in their fight against Soviet occupation.

What the film shows of 'Afghanistan' is in fact Arizona or, more often, as on the laptop, Israel's Negev / Naqab desert. The black-bearded mujahid onscreen is Mousa, played by Israeli actor Sasson Gabai, and his dialogue with Rambo there, replayed later in *Under a Blue Sun*, would backfire spectacularly on its American authors:

Mousa: Alexander the Great tried to conquer this country, then Genghis Khan, then the British, now Russia. But Afghan people fight hard. They never be defeated. Ancient enemy make prayer about these people – you wish to hear?

Rambo: Mm-hmm.

Mousa: Very good. It says, 'May God deliver us from the venom of the cobra, teeth of the tiger, and the vengeance of the Afghan.' Understand what this means?

Rambo: That you guys don't take any shit?

Mousa: Yes. Something like this.

The root of *Under a Blue Sun* lies in director Daniel Mann's discovery in the Israeli military archives of documents laying out the production deal for the shoot. Mann, an Israeli filmmaker, academic and writer, discovered that military personnel and hardware, including attack helicopters, were used in the film, and some of the arms and ammunition deployed were genuine. He did not manage to uncover how much the deal was worth to the IDF but it wouldn't have been cheap. At the time of its 1988 release, *Rambo III* was the most expensive film ever made, costing around $60 million ($160 million in today's terms).

Early scenes in *Under a Blue Sun* offer a meditation on the blurring of military and entertainment infrastructure deployed in *Rambo III*, and other films shot in the Negev / Naqab. But the film soon moves on to find its central thematic subject – the dispossession and disenfranchisement of the Naqab Bedouin – largely thanks to Bashir Abu-Rabia, a Bedouin painter and special effects artist who worked on *Rambo III*.

Abu-Rabia is in his early seventies, and looks ten years younger. He is a friendly, avuncular companion, mostly smiling and with a twinkle in his eye peeping out beneath a floppy fringe of white hair. Yet, as Mann noted during a post-screening Q&A at the Institute of Contemporary Arts, 'it's very clear that he is also angry, and justifiably so'. Despite taking great care and pride in his special effects work, Abu-Rabia has never watched *Rambo III*. 'For him it was a documentation of his own dispossession', Mann said.

In Abu-Rabia's retelling, so much was obvious at the time. Recalling a day when Stallone was on set with four of his stand-ins, Abu-Rabia says

Frankly, it was humiliating… Believe me, if these young men [the stand-ins] didn't need the money, they would have told you: 'This is a bad joke.' For the Arabs, the Muslims, it's as if Rambo was showing gratitude and glorifying a free Afghan nation. Half the people there knew it was hypocritical.

Abu-Rabia's tribe, the Jahalin, were largely driven off their ancestral lands during the Nakba. Now, Abu-Rabia bitterly recounts, his fellow tribespeople 'live like refugees on the outskirts of Jerusalem. They are squeezed into corners. They can hardly breathe'.

We join Lobna Sana, a Bedouin architect and activist, younger than Abu-Rabia and with her anger closer to the surface, for an exposition of

these suffocating conditions. Of the 90,000 Bedouin who lived in the Negev / Naqab prior to the creation of the Israel, only 13,000 remained, Sana recounts. Other survivors were pushed into the refugee camps of Gaza, the West Bank and Jordan, or into the Sinai.

For those who stayed in the desert, Israeli colonisation meant that the Bedouin's traditional, semi-nomadic, pastoral way of life was either severely curtailed or destroyed entirely. As Sana explains, the contemporary Naqab Bedouin exist in 'two different realities' according to whether their home is in a recognised or unrecognised area. Conditions for those in unrecognised dwellings are dismal and unsanitary, with homes – often makeshift shacks and tents – liable to summary destruction by the IDF.

Life is still grim within the recognised areas, which include dilapidated townships built by the Israelis between the late sixties and eighties. *Under a Blue Sun* gives viewers a taste of this when we accompany Abu-Rabia to his village, granted legal status in 2005 but still unconnected to the electricity grid. The children's hearing has been damaged, Abu-Rabia tells us sadly, by the constant thrumming of generators.

Mann gives his subjects time and space to tell their stories, and the film is at its best when they do so. It is on less sure footing during segments where Mann narrates emails he has supposedly written to Stallone, asking for the actor's participation and reflecting on *Rambo III*'s production. These sections seem out of place and contrived – a flubbed attempt to shoehorn a gonzo subplot, a half-hearted version of Michael Moore's *Roger & Me* into a film that has no need of it. Indeed, as we learnt at the Q&A, these emails were a contrivance. No such messages were ever sent.

Less showy, but more effective, are the shots of the desert itself. The Negev / Naqab features both as backdrop and also in standalone, static shots interspersed throughout. It is thus established as a constant, impassive presence, utterly impervious to the follies of humankind, unknowing of even the words they choose to name it by. With its countless immoveable rock formations, hills, and mountains, the desert seems possessed of an infinite resistance – and its metaphorical relationship to the Palestinian struggle is clear.

Towards the film's end, both Abu-Rabia and Sana turn to the Negev / Naqab's flora rather than its landscape for allegorical inspiration. 'Making the desert bloom' has been a central plank of Israeli policy and 'hasbara'

(propaganda) ever since the state's creation. Huge irrigation, afforestation and agricultural projects have been undertaken to make it happen, including the planting of northern European pine trees on ancestral Bedouin land. Such afforestation projects are vigorously resisted by the Bedouin, with protests predictably and violently quashed by the IDF. Following footage of one such protest, Sana says:

> These pines, I see them as an alien organism. On the hills, the plants are different. There is basil, rocks, and all the local flora that cannot grow under the pines. You can see their struggle with this soil. The pine is not adapted. It doesn't belong.

Abu-Rabia's insight comes on a visit to a house he once knew that was built by the Bedouin in the fifties or sixties. He arrives to find only rubble and crumbling foundations, but a tree planted for shade has survived. 'It holds on,' says Abu-Rabia. 'That's the tree's fate. And ours.'

'All these trees are a people's gift to its land and unity,' a voice intones (at least, according to the subtitles) during an early segment in *Israel Palestine on Swedish TV 1958–1989*, making the viewer question a title card at the start telling us that the channel responsible, STV, aimed to provide objectivity, in line with its public service remit. Half an hour later, we are treated to some more Swedish-language 'making the desert bloom' hasbara when naturalist Nils Linmann, ambling about in some recently irrigated desert copse, tells us that 'there is no place where the miracle of Israel is as obvious as it is here'.

Israel Palestine is the latest work by Göran Hugo Olsson, whose previous archival documentaries include the much lauded *The Black Power Mixtape 1967–1975*, from 2011, and *Concerning Violence*, from 2014, which draws upon Franz Fanon's essay of the same name to examine 'anti-imperialistic self-defence', as the film's tagline called it.

To make *Israel Palestine*, Olsson trawled through over five thousand hours (two hundred and eight days) of STV footage, ultimately selecting just under three and a half hours for inclusion. The footage is presented chronologically, with each report or excerpt given several minutes runtime and preceded by a title card detailing the context and authors. We are told, for example, that the segment on desert afforestation was taken from a five-part series by Lars-Eric Kjellgren called 'Israel – Land of

Wonders', broadcast in 1960. The viewer is given little further guidance other than that furnished in the reports. The end result is unexpectedly engrossing; despite the thematic and tonal disjointedness of consecutive sections, the viewer can trace undergirding narratives along the decades. Even so, the entire exercise is permeated with an air of immense tragedy. We know how the narratives culminate in our time, thirty-five years after the final clip was filmed – in genocide.

This knowledge both clouds and clarifies any viewing of *Israel Palestine*. For example, are the torchlit Zionist parades shown in the opening clip, from 1958's 'A Young State in Focus', really so shockingly redolent of those in Germany twenty years earlier, or does our foreknowledge make them so? Such matters are further complicated by the lexical register deployed in the reports, which is often bracingly different from that used today. The 1958 clip speaks approvingly of 'the Zionists' colonisation of Israel' as being at the state's origin, as 'colonisation' carried positive connotations in fifties and sixties Sweden. Its use therefore encodes both bias and honesty, a seemingly impossible combination.

Among other things, *Israel Palestine* is a study of media bias. Most of it, as you would expect, is pro-Israeli. But from the vantage point of the UK in 2024 – my vantage point – this seems almost desirable, because bias against Palestinian voices is surely better than their exclusion, and the bias has heightened anyway. What's more, the bias and exclusion now stand on solid legal footing. As we are reminded in every news report, Hamas is a proscribed terrorist organisation in the UK. As such, it is a criminal offense to express support for it. This renders unbiased reporting on the preeminent group pursuing armed struggle in Palestine impossible, because if any element of the reportage could be considered to show Hamas in a positive light, it would potentially break the law. Exclusion of Hamas's voice from discussion thus becomes inevitable. Meanwhile, even after more than a year of what the International Court of Justice has agreed is plausibly a genocide, support for the IDF is not subject to similar legal restrictions. British citizens can fly off to join the Israeli army, do a tour of service, and return home safely, no questions asked.

There are many knock-on effects in the UK media of this legally mandated exclusion. For one, an air of suspicion of terrorist sympathy and antisemitism now lurks over every Palestinian or pro-Palestinian person,

group or event that is featured. In the first months of the Gaza genocide, this suspicion would be immediately expressed in the question 'do you condemn Hamas?' aimed at any Palestine-supporting person in interviews, perhaps most cravenly by Kirsty Wark on the BBC's 'Newsnight' programme to Palestinian diplomat Husam Zomlot in October 2023, after several of his relatives had been killed in an Israeli airstrike. For another, the absence of voices supporting Palestinian armed struggle can only increase the suspicion that its partisans are all crazed terrorists, motivated purely by antisemitic bloodlust – a depiction that aligns neatly with Israel's justification for Palestinian slaughter.

For all their bias, the STV reports do still frequently feature the voices of partisans of armed struggle. Those selected for inclusion in *Israel Palestine* are marked by their clarity of purpose, which is unambiguously Palestinian liberation and not murderous vengeance. In a report from 1969, by which time the Popular Front for the Liberation of Palestine had adopted the goal of the one-state solution, we see Ghassan Khanafani, the PFLP's spokesperson, calmly answering the question of whether the PFLP would accept a Palestinian state according to the 1948 or 1968 borders: 'To us, it's one nation, one homeland… It's our land and we are fighting to liberate it.' A year later, we hear the equally erudite Mona Saudi, a Jordanian artist and friend of Khanafani, speak of left-wing groups like the PFLP wanting peace, but 'not the peace of governments. A peace between people. A socialist state where religion has no place, where ethnic origin has no place.'

More complicated feelings may be aroused by an expression of this ideal aired a few minutes before Saudi's. A hungry-looking, wide-eyed boy, barely a teenager, holding a Kalashnikov rifle, is asked what will become of the Jews once the revolution has conquered Israel. His answer is delivered immediately and unselfconsciously: 'The Jews who want to live with us can live with us.' But this is followed by his affirmation that he will 'fight until the last drop of [his] blood'. The segment is from a report on the Palestinian fedayeen in Jordan. 'What kind of mentality comes up with this?' asks the reporter as the training of child soldiers plays onscreen, conjuring an inherently murderous Palestinian psychopathology. But the viewer, seeing the squalid refugee-camp setting, may be spurred to give a different answer – one involving a grief-ridden mindset that settles within

a people held endlessly in exile, humiliated by a usurping state of much greater firepower, and driven by sheer desperation to enlist their own children in the fight for restitution.

Israel Palestine includes many such segments detailing phenomena that are inconvenient to the narrative of either side, and may have fallen from popular memory entirely, at least in the West. Not long after the report on the fedayeen there is one on Jews in Ramla who are subsisting in conditions as grim as those found in the Jordanian camps. These Oriental / Mizrahi Jews talk of having been 'lured' from their homes across the Muslim world by Israeli propaganda, only to find themselves stuck miserably at the bottom of Israel's racial hierarchy, which places the central and eastern European Ashkenazi on top. The report focuses on Israel's Black Panther Party, formed from the ranks of the Mizrahi discontents, and its tentative alliance with the Palestinian struggle.

Elsewhere, Olsson's film serves as a reminder of how implacably pro-Zionist mainstream Western politico-media discourse has become. It is almost impossible to imagine a contemporary Western leader condemning a Palestinian attack and then adding that 'there is always a reason behind such acts' which must be addressed for such attacks to cease, as Swedish prime minister Olof Palme did after the Munich Olympics massacre in 1972. Media broadcast of a voice like that of Israel Ishak, an attendee at an anti-government protest in 1973, is even more unlikely. Ishak's comparison of prime minister Golda Meir's rhetoric on Palestinian birth rates with Nazi discourse in the twenties, and his fears of Israel's corresponding descent into fascism, would obviously be adjudged as antisemitic. Such stridently critical voices are vanishingly rare in contemporary Israel and seem to have been expunged entirely from its public discourse – thanks, of course, to the very tendency Ishak warned against.

Many of us who came of age after the period the film covers – that is, anyone younger than about fifty-five years old – will mostly know of that era's major political players from reading. For this audience, of which I am a member, *Israel Palestine* is thus a rare opportunity to see those names on a page as living, breathing human beings, inhabiting personas often lost in print. Mostly, the impression they give is unfavourable. There's Meir, her Wisconsin accent constantly undercutting her animating political ideal – that several thousand square miles of ground in the Middle East that no-one

in her family had ever visited was somehow the homeland of *her* people. There's Anwar Sadat, his venal grin and immaculate suits revealing him as every inch the traitorous crook Palestinians would come to think of him as, after his betrayal of them at the Camp David Accords. And there's his co-negotiator, or co-conspirator, Menachem Begin, menacingly reciting his intransigent Zionist rhetoric to one journalist after another – 'We liberated Samaria and Judea... We didn't take away our country from anybody,' or, later, 'Who are the Palestinians, my friend? I am Palestinian.'

The only big beast of the era who emerges from *Israel Palestine* as more than a one-note character, with his own traceable story arc, is Yasser Arafat. We see him first (or rather, he first crops up in my notes) as the charismatic, improbably at-ease resistance leader giving his famous 'do not let the olive branch fall from my hand' speech at the UN in 1974, a revolver holster visible on his waist. A subsequent report buffs the romantic image of him as rock-star revolutionary – he 'never sleeps in the same place two nights running', we are breathlessly told – an image he largely lives up to in a 1976 interview. By then, though, we can feel desperation cracking through the charm as he recalls Swedish support for Vietnamese armed struggle and looks straight into the camera lens to tell viewers: 'I am sure you will do the same with the Palestinian people'. We see him again in the eighties, exiled in Tunis, struggling to keep a grip on the Palestinian Liberation Organisation he still leads and a Palestinian polity losing faith in the PLO. And he's right there at the film's end, in the clip from 1993 that serves as the epilogue. In it, Arafat is onstage in Oslo, still smiling, having just signed off on what his former friend Edward Said called 'an instrument of Palestinian surrender, a Palestinian Versailles' – the accord that ultimately delivered Arafat his satrapy, the Palestinian Authority. It is not a happy end.

The last film in this coincidental trilogy, Kamal Aljafari's *A Fidai Film*, exhibits a wholly different approach to the editing and presentation of archival footage to that in *Israel Palestine*. This is partly down to its director's aesthetic sensibilities – Aljafari's oeuvre sits comfortably within the 'art film' category – and partly down to the incomplete, corrupted nature of the footage involved.

Indeed, the source material for Aljafari's much more impressionistic film speaks directly to Palestinian dispossession, as it was stolen by the IDF

from the wrecked Palestine Research Centre in western Beirut in 1983. The centre, which was set up in 1965 by the PLO and accorded diplomatic protection by the Lebanese government, was hit by a car bomb planted by a proxy Israeli terrorist group, and then looted by the Israeli military. Thousands of films, books, newspapers, press clippings, and microfiches in the centre's archive were taken off to be pored over, annotated, and defaced – and ultimately enlisted as data in the service of further Palestinian dispossession and oppression. Aljafari recovered a fraction of the looted films from Israeli researchers who had gained access, and assembled them into *A Fidai Film* – part aleatory archival documentary, part ravaged mood piece.

Unlike in *Israel Palestine*, the footage is not presented chronologically, and only loosely thematically, and the viewer is given no information about the date, location, or wider context of each segment. Also unlike Olsson, whose directorial decisions appear to have been mostly curatorial, Aljafari has left his authorial marks all over his film. Aurally, he does so via deployment of music, abstract noise, disquieting passages of nonsynchronous sound, and readings from Khanafani's writings. Visually, he has digitally altered many of the clips so that flames occasionally appear somewhere in the frame, or bright red markings cover the film's surface. The red ink is sometimes scribbled over text printed on the film by its Israeli custodians, sometimes it obscures peoples' faces or figures so that they are blotted out as red silhouettes, and sometimes the ink fills hairline cracks running vertically down the celluloid, and we watch a deluge of oxygenated blood stream down the screen.

At other moments, Aljafari stands back and leaves us alone with some broken-off fragment of the Palestinian tragedy: on an arduous trudge through thick mud in a decaying refugee camp, with twenty or thirty smiling men on a beach posing behind a banner bearing the legend 'Eilat Massachusetts 1945', looking down from a roof on Israeli soldiers, probably sometime in the seventies, as they steal some Palestinian children's football. As a whole, the footage covers a time period of at least forty years. There is a UK news report on a bomb blast at the PLO headquarters, which must have occurred only months before the Palestine Research Centre was looted. And there is footage from the time of the British mandate – of Palestinian streets teeming with life, of some impenetrable but apparently

good-natured scuffle involving men and boys in thobes and tarbushes, and perhaps (I'm not sure of the date) of British soldiers harassing a veiled Palestinian woman. The gross, Nakba-denying Israeli lie of 'a land without a people for a people without a land' should hardly need debunking, but these tantalising and enigmatic fragments do so.

A Fidai Film is not just a jumble of rescued and treated footage. Guided by the soundtrack and its evolving visual motifs, the film advances according to an obscure and dreamlike logic appropriate for its journey through a living nightmare. For me, the film served as an excellent complement to *Israel Palestine*'s more objective historical treatment of Palestinian calamity. From scraps of stolen and recovered film, a few pages of Ghassan Khanafani's prose, and his own ingenuity, Aljafari has fashioned a lightning rod that channels the deep emotional pain of multigenerational dispossession and exile.

The screening I attended was bookended by an introduction and Q&A with Simon Fisher-Turner, who provided some of the film's music ('sound' may be more accurate). As it turned out, he had composed and recorded this remotely, without much contact from Aljafari, and with little knowledge of how his work would be used. He couldn't, therefore, provide much insight into the director's creative praxis or psychology. He did, however, read a poem by Harold Pinter before the film played that was almost impossibly apposite. Its central stanzas run:

The long dead look out towards
The new dead
Walking towards them

There is a soft heartbeat
As the dead embrace
Those who are long dead
And those of the new dead
Walking towards them

Again — where are you now in the flow of worse than horror-film imagery? Who are the new dead for you? When will this nightmare end?

MASAFER YATTA

Liam McKenna

Oscar-winning documentary *No Other Land* both opens and closes with shots of the West Bank at night. In the first, as the film starts, the energy is frantic; tight camera angles on a stressed phone call through shaky breaths, driving through the dark towards IDF activity. By the last, all this frantic energy has coalesced and dissipated. We're left instead with a resigned stillness, the camera motionless as families pack their lives into trucks and leave behind the place that has been their home for generations.

The film is produced by a collective of four Israeli and Palestinian activists. It documents Israeli efforts to displace the residents of Masafer Yatta, a collection of villages in the Hebron Governate of the West Bank, and the resistance efforts of the villagers and their Palestinian, Israeli, and international allies. The story is told by a combination of professional, filmic camerawork, and handheld footage captured by Basel Adra, a resident of Masafer Yatta and the film's narrator, co-writer, and co-director. Alongside Adra in front of the camera is Yuval Abraham, an Israeli journalist from Be'er-Shava, who reports on, and becomes involved with, the struggle of the people of Masafer Yatta. The remaining two documentarians are Rachel Szor, an Israeli who is the film's cinematographer, and Hamdan Ballal, a Palestinian activist and photographer, credited as editor. All four co-creators are credited as co-writers and co-directors.

The film begins in the summer of 2019, with footage of Israeli bulldozers tearing down homes. 'Don't fear, my dear, they will leave soon,' one woman tells a young girl, as they watch soldiers demolish their house. As the seasons move on, destruction of property escalates into violence against the person. In January 2021, a villager called Harun Abu Aram struggles to prevent IDF soldiers from confiscating his family's generator. Aram poses no threat to the soldiers themselves. But any resistance is

unacceptable; one soldier raises his gun and shoots Aram in the neck. We see Aram again throughout the film, paralysed from the neck down, living in a cave as his family's home has been demolished. When his mother remonstrates with Israeli soldiers, begging to be allowed to build somewhere for her son to live, they refuse to acknowledge her. By the summer of 2022, speaking with international journalists, she can only lament: 'I hope I could help him. I hope God takes him and relieves him from this life'.

No Other Land, directed by Basel Adra, Hamdan Ballal, Yuval Abraham and Rachel Szor (Yabayay Media/Antipode Films, 2024)

Time and again, pressed by angry villagers to justify themselves, Israeli soldiers fall back on the law. Asked how he can live with himself, one responds: 'That's the law, why should I be ashamed?' Soldiers pin written demolition notices under rocks, as if insisting on the trappings of legality dissolves the need to confront the reality of what they're doing. That there is not, of course, any real concern for law or justice becomes undeniable (if it were not already) when we see soldiers standing happily alongside civilian settlers, doing nothing as the settlers throw rocks and abuse at the villagers. It is in a way less infuriating when the pretence is dropped. Asked by Abraham how he would feel if someone destroyed his own home, the Israeli supervising the demolitions does not bother holding up the law as his shield, but says bluntly 'don't bother me in the morning'.

This is a study of 'might makes right'. But the film is not merely a passive record of Israeli brutality. It has things to say, or at least thoughts to raise, about the nature of power, of resistance, and change. In an early scene, Adra describes how the villagers joint together during his youth to build a school for the village children. The Israelis called this illegal construction, and issued an order for the school to be demolished. Then Tony Blair, at that time the Special Envoy of the Quartet on the Middle East, passed through Masafer Yatta. Adra, accompanying footage of Blair moving through one of the villagers, tells us how Blair stayed for a total of seven minutes.

When he left, Israel cancelled the school's demolition order. 'This is a story about power,' Adra says.

Jumping back to the present, we see the school still operating. A young girl insists to her father, who suggests they stay home after a night of IDF activity and stun grenades, that there cannot be any suggestion of taking a day off school. We see children learning to read the Arabic *abjad*, reciting *aleph, baa, ta*. Later on, as the film crescendos, we see the IDF bulldozers roll in, a class of children scrambling out of the window and then watching their school torn down. Tony Blair is not there this time. Another lesson about power.

Underlying all this is an anxiety about what the film's protagonists can do – about what anyone can do – to effect change. In early scenes, the Israeli journalist Abraham worries that his reporting on Masafer Yatta is not being seen by enough people. Adra chides him for his impatience for things to improve. 'You want to solve everything in ten days and go home,' he tells Abraham. There is a practicality about this, but equally a firm sense that change will come – it is only a matter of time. As time goes on, this optimistic realism evaporates. This is not because nobody pays attention. Far from it: in 2022, we see a montage of reports in the world media on what is going on in Masafer Yatta; Adra interviewed by the international press; Abraham arguing with chauvinists on Israeli TV. But, for the people who matter, nothing changes. IDF demolitions continue, if anything worsening in vindictive reprisal for the villagers' efforts to fight back; the villagers' school is destroyed; wells are filled in with concrete; IDF soldiers stand alongside masked settlers.

Despite all this, the film never becomes a counsel of despair. That is due in large part to the film's success in capturing the community shared by the people of Masafer Yatta. In the filmmakers' hands, the villagers are not treated as mere props, there to demonstrate Israeli injustice. Instead the audience is drawn into the villagers' community, watching as they share meals, smoke, and work together, as children play and learn and enjoy life even as things are torn down around them. All this is aided by the film's beautiful cinematography, and the subtle but often haunting score, provided by Julius Pollux Rothlaender in his second full-length film work.

Just as important to the film's emotional resonance are the moments of vulnerability shared between Adra and Abraham. The two men share an intense comradeship, but one which is tempered always by the knowledge of their fundamental difference, each on either side of an apartheid. Abraham works to expose what the Israeli authorities are doing to the people of Masafer Yatta, joins the villagers in their marches, even confronts IDF soldiers as they tear down the villagers' homes. But ultimately he has another home to go to, and the villagers do not. 'Running away again?' Adra sometimes asks him when he drives back to Be'er-Shava after a stay in the villages. The tone is light, but masks a real tension. Moreover, as one villager observes, even if Abraham repudiates it, everything the Israeli authorities do is done in his name. The film is not seeking to condemn Abraham, nor does it attempt to resolve the tension of his role in the villagers' community. All these things are complex, and the film's strength lies in showing us these complexities.

At the centre of everything is of course Masafer Yatta itself; the land and the community of people who live there. As the film tells us, these are a people, and this is a land, with a contested history. That contest played out in the Israeli Supreme Court, with a 2022 decision representing the culmination of the villagers' efforts to seek a resolution to their plight on Israel's own terms.

The villagers themselves trace their presence in Masafer Yatta to the early nineteenth century, when pastoralists moved into the area from the nearby towns of Yatta and Dura. Israeli efforts to take the land for themselves then began in earnest in 1980, when much of the territory occupied by the villages was designated a closed military zone. While in principle the residents can obtain permission from the Israeli authorities to build within the military zone, in practice permission is rarely if ever given. Given the comparative ease with which Israeli settlers are able to build on the land, the lie in Israel's excuse that military imperatives compel refusal of permission to build is obvious. But in this case, Israel's intent does not need to be inferred. In July 1981, then-Minister of Agriculture (and soon-to-be Minister of Defence) Ariel Sharon instructed the IDF to declare training zones in the area in order to restrict 'expansion of the Arab villagers from the hills towards the desert'.

That remark was made at a hearing of the Joint Government and World Zionist Organisation (WZO) Committee on Settlements. A transcript was unearthed by Akevot in the state archives while proceedings in the Supreme Court were ongoing, and put before the court. Yet it goes entirely unmentioned in the court's decision, notwithstanding that it contradicts the essential premise – that this land is needed for military purposes – of Israel's position. When the facts are inconvenient, find new ones. And that is exactly what the Court's decision does. Far beyond just ignoring the 1981 transcript, the Court denies the existence of any long-term settlement at all in the area before the military zone was established. As the Court, and the Israeli authorities in general, would have it, the community in Masafer Yatta arose only in response to, and in an attempt to frustrate, the legitimate Israeli military activity there. The villagers are not innocent pastoralists forced out by Israeli occupation, but are cynical invaders, playing pretend at suffering any injustice. That term, 'invaders', is not a paraphrase of the Court's decision, but appears directly in it, with the Court describing the villagers as 'invading the firing zone', and the Israeli authorities suffering through 'dealings with invaders'.

Set aside, for a moment, the suggestion that any Israeli occupation in the West Bank can be considered legitimate. As a straightforward exercise in the distortion of factual reality, the Court's judgment is an exemplar. The author of the very text cited by the Court as demonstrating the lack of significant settlement prior to 1980 – Life in the Caves of Mount Hebron, a 1985 work by Israeli anthropologist Yaakov Havakook – has rubbished the Court's conclusions as cherry-picked and divorced from the truth. In the book, based on Havakook's observations from living with Palestinians in the South Hebron Hills between 1977 and 1981, Havakook describes how some pastoralists would stay for six to eight months a year in caves in Masafer Yatta, while others, particularly the younger generation, would stay in the caves the year round. For the Court, this becomes evidence that any Palestinian presence in the area was purely transitory. But as Havakook explains,

> Not everything is defined according to the Western criteria of Tel Aviv or Ramat Gan, with property taxes and electricity and water and documents. The jurist, with all due respect, is sitting in a big neon room. He knows how to

read legal clauses and is good at phrasing things in convoluted language, but he doesn't live there. He has not inhaled the smell of campfire smoke inside the cave, he hasn't been butted by a goat... judging a lifestyle through the eyes of another culture seems strange, unintelligible, and from here that interpretation can be a false one.

The Court's decision was wrong, as multiple commentators on the decision – including Professor Eliav Lieblich of Tel-Aviv University – have convincingly set out. It was wrong on the facts, when rejecting the villagers' long continuity of residence in Masafer Yatta. It was wrong when, in an argument of stunning perversity, it said that the villagers were bad faith actors who came to the court with 'unclean hands', because they had not lain down and accepted their situation but had carried on trying to build on their own land. And it was wrong, even if it were right about everything else, to say that Israeli interests could justify abolishing Palestinian homes and schools, while permitting Israeli settler activity in the very same areas. The Court's decision goes beyond the 'everyday evil' of the Israeli occupation in the West Bank, as it has been described by the Israeli historian Ilan Pappé, and denies the villagers' basic reality. As Professor Lieblich has put it: 'as someone who follows closely the rulings by the Israeli Supreme Court concerning the occupation, I find myself frequently disagreeing with them. Yet, I do not recall a ruling in recent decades so lacking legal nuance, so unconcerned with international law, and so willingly blind to the context as this one'. The author of the judgment, Justice David Mintz, is himself a settler, living in Dolev, a settlement not far from Ramallah. This is yet another story about power.

No Other Land might be a dangerous film to appreciate. When shown at the Berlin International Film Festival, accusations of antisemitism immediately followed, in particular because Adra and Abraham (accepting the prize for best documentary) at the ceremony decried the 'slaughter and massacre' of Gazans, and the 'situation of apartheid' endured by Palestinians. The mayor of Berlin, Kai Wegner, described these remarks as 'intolerable relativisation'. The Minister of State for Culture, Claudia Roth, after the festival said that the filmmakers' speeches were 'characterised by a deep hatred of Israel', never mind that she was captured on film applauding after the speeches. In a defence of herself that would be comic if it were not so offensive, Roth clarified that she was only

clapping for the Israeli, Abraham, and not for the Palestinian Adra. This spinelessness is a stark contrast to the film itself, and the strength of character in adversity of the residents of Masafer Yatta. Roth might learn from Abraham, who has received verbal abuse as a 'traitor' to his country, and was forced to delay his return to Israel after the festival because of death threats and physical intimidation of his family members, but has never wavered in his commitment to his principles.

Despite this controversy, *No Other Land* has seen almost universal praise in reviews. It deserves that praise. This is an intelligent and beautifully told film, one which confronts the viewer with difficult questions rather than content itself with the easier, though still important, task of standing witness to the injustice of Israeli settlement in the West Bank. It might be futile to hope that any change for the better is coming to the people of Masafer Yatta, at least in the near future. But one thing *No Other Land* shows is that while we cannot control the world, we can control our part in it. If we reject, as we should, simply falling into apathy in the face of an unjust world, then all that is left is to act however we can in response to that injustice. *No Other Land* is itself a valuable act against a gross injustice. It is to be hoped that its audience follow its example.

SHAMELESS ETHICS

Iftikhar H. Malik

The rise and fall of the empires, all through human history, keeps historians and theorists busy in conjuring up multiple explanations, and the British Empire is no exception. Like its other European counterparts—with obvious variations—it has been the most far-reaching in terms of its holistic legacies causing most of its explanations often falling within a binary perspective of adulation and denunciation. The fact that the British Empire initially began as an English project at its inception, and at its zenith covered more area and people that any of its preceding and contemporary counterparts, is beyond dispute both for its apologists and detractors. Even its decriers, varying from the nationalists to the leftists or from post-colonialists to the antiracists, recognise its recurrent impact through multiple trajectories such as the language, literature, arts, monetary systems, educational structures, bureaucracy, military cartography, gender and class demarcations, and the very political systems that more than fifty states currently embody even after a formal dissolution of the entire overarching paradigm.

Colonialism: A Moral Reckoning by Nigel Bigger, William Collins, London, 2023.

Sailing for the Empire: Slavery, Piracy and Trade: The Life of Admiral Sir John Corbett in Letters and Paintings by David Peretz, EER Publishers, Brighton, 2024.

Historians like Linda Cooley, Princeton Professor and expert on British imperial history, writers such as Sathnam Sanghera, British journalist and author of noted works on British imperialism, and the Indian politician and diplomat, Shashi Tharoor, have exposed the exploitative nature of British imperialism. But the Empire has been vigorously defended by apologists

such as Niall Ferguson, the British–American conservative historian. Colley traces the origins of the British identity and shows that it is deeply embedded in its imperial past. Tharoor finds Britain blooming at the expense of India —reverberating some of the views reflected in works by political philosopher Franz Fanon, the left-wing British historian and television pundit David Olusoga, and Sanghera. Ferguson has been unremittingly censorious of the British and other critics of the British Empire by flagging what he sees as multiple and enduring contributions rendered by Britain to its colonies. Even the institutions such as the BBC, in their reverence for Gandhi and other anti-colonials, presumably underplayed. Hence, Ferguson's television series, accompanied by a volume, which appeared in the 1990s within a Fukuyamian 'end of history' context. They became a trend setter for celebratory commentaries on the Empire.

   But the debate came back with its full intensity following demands for reparation for slave trade, amidst movements such as Rhodes Must Fall, Black Lives Matter, and decolonisation of the entire academic spectrum, especially in the humanities. These movements triggered Nigel Biggar's entry into the fray. Bigger is a British Anglican priest and theologian, and a Professor of Moral and Pastoral Theology at the University of Oxford, where he runs a a project on the Empire and Ethics. He launched himself with a heated outburst against the critics of Empire by vocally defending a 2017 article, 'The Case for Colonialism, by Bruce Gilley, a Canadian American professor of political science, submitted to *Third World Quarterly*. Not trained as a historian, his opinion columns were seen by agitated Oxbridge dons as ill-timed and unconvincing. But support from like-minded colleagues and a prompt contract from Bloomsbury publishers set Biggar on a journey which even for an otherwise accomplished historian would prove acutely daunting. Amidst the furore, his publishers withdrew the contract in 2021 which only further motivated him to publish his manuscript. This rejection solidified his resolve to publish his strong defense of the Empire with William Collins. The end result: *Colonialism: A Moral Reckoning*.

   Often appearing a rather fledgling defence of the Empire and its discomfiting accompaniments, Niall Ferguson described *Colonialism: A Moral Reckoning* as a fearless defence against 'increasingly vitriolic detractors' of Empire; whereas another right-wing historian, Vernon

Bogdanor, found it 'scrupulous, fair-minded and scholarly analysis of the morality of colonialism.' Like his critics, Biggar's supporters are numerous including some historians from the former colonies. To Krishan Kuman, it is 'a work of exemplary clarity and fairness,' while the late Zareer Masani, former BBC producer and advacate for right wing causes, saw in it 'a hugely impressive ethical map of empire based on an encyclopaedic reading of events and literature around them.' Conservative historian, and a champion of the West, Andrew Roberts, agonises over book's cancellation by the first publisher whereas Indian economic historian, Tirthankar Roy, finds it 'scrupulously honest reassessment of a controversial episode in world history.'

Divided into eight topical chapters and two conclusions, the volume is essentially anchored on published works without any recourse to primary source material. It is essentially based on secondary Western sources, though Edward Said, Eric Williams, and Shashi Tharoor get a brief references along with some African writers, who found the Empire as a 'mixed bag'. Like the Empire itself, Biggar identifies Cecil Rhodes, the nineteenth century British mining magnate and politician in southern Africa, to be 'a moral mixture' and sees in him a 'colour blind' individual who initiated the first black African newspaper besides bequeathing a prestigious fellowship, whose beneficiaries include Africans. This kind of untenable premise, appearing in the introductory chapter, put our author on a rather weak wicket, though it set the tone for subsequent chapters—which are, collectively, in thrall of the Empire. He taunts his former colleagues at Oxford, including Elleke Boehmer for her eminence as one of the pioneers in post-colonial studies, and accuses her of being Vladimir Putin's 'ally' as well as of the Chinese Communist Party—an allegation that smacks of a rather superficial understanding of varying nature of academic disciplines. A few paragraphs further down, one can see where our author is coming from. He is worried about the break-up of the United Kingdom, owing to external threats and internal mainsprings such as the Scottish nationalists. Given his own limitations as a historian, and a vast academic terrain that he is coursing through, Biggar claims not to write a history of the British Empire. Instead, he purported to offer 'a moral evaluation' and here his *others* are a motley crowd of Indian princes, African kings, and indigenous chieftains across the colonised continents

who, to him, fall short of moral sobriety. It is ironic that while attempting a defence of the imperial rule, Biggar does not stop applying the long-forsaken tropes of ethical equivalence where indigenous elite were, en-masse, seen as oppressive, brutal, sexist, and capricious.

When citing the example of individuals like John Malcolm in India and Lord Cromer in Egypt, Biggar finds a wide variety of Britons working in the Empire, often for their own good but also in the larger interests of the colonised people. Quite a few of them are motivated by moral values and Christian ethics and not out of selfish reasons and here he offers the example of India where the colonials, even after several years of service, would not settle down in the country. Though in a subsequent section he rationalises the British emigration to North America, Australia, New Zealand, and the African highlands on the plea that previously the land of these regions and their resources did not belong to anyone! The argument falls flat since in a Eurocentric way he considers written documents to be the mainstay of proprietary rights which has not been the case in most of human history but that does not deny the ownership by the locals over their soil.

While acknowledging a strong interface between slavery and colonialism, Bigger tries to absolve the British on two counts: everyone had been practising slavery including the Africans themselves, and secondly, the British were often humane to slaves until they became abolitionists following 1807 thus saving millions of lives. Compensatory payment to the slave owners after the abolition of slavery in 1833, according to Bigger, was even then viewed as 'distasteful' but a 'necessary political compromise'. He is quite dismissive of the celebrated history Eric Williams and challenges his view of slave labour providing the foundational capital for industrial development, which rather falls on the side of trivialisation of the large-scale human contributions that the Africans made over the successive centuries. While discussing slavery during the imperial era, Biggar seems to seek redress in blaming the Africans and Arabs for running the ignoble pursuit with the British Empire being posited as a redeemer. To him, even the 1881-1889 Mahdist rebellion in Sudan was a product of a reaction to suppression of slave trade by Britain. An absurdly challenging claim. However, as the research by José Lingna Nafafé from Bristol University shows, it was not Britain or any other West European nation that pioneered abolitionism; instead, such efforts began in Africa where the

Angolan prince Lourenço da Silva Mendonça mounted a campaign against the Portuguese enslavement in the seventeenth century. He became a pivotal figure in championing the abolition of slavery after he was exiled in 1671, first to Brazil and then Portugal. More than a century before William Wilberforce and the rest, Mendonça approached Pope Innocent XI in 1681 petitioning the Vatican, Portugal, Italy, and Spain to stop enslaving Africans. He also demanded abolition for New Christians (that is, Iberians forcibly converted to Christianity) and the Native Americans.

Defying the accusation of cultural imperialism, Biggar has no qualms in asserting that British cultural superiority—in many realms—proved a beneficial factor in turning around non-European societies. He notes:

> Yet when I as a twenty-first-century Briton look back at my medieval forbears, it seems obvious that my culture is superior to theirs in a wide array of respects—scientific knowledge, medical practice, economic productivity, social equality, political freedom and public safety. And the common colloquial tendency to use the word 'medieval' as a synonym for 'barbaric' suggests that I am not alone in that perception.

The point well-taken. But does that still give a license to any society to venture and capture someone else's in the name of civilisational progress or moral unrighteousness? His quotes from David Livingstone or portraying such Percy Cox, the nineteenth/twentieth century colonial administer responsible for dividing the Middle East, and Gertrude Bell, the orientalist traveller and administrator, as 'do-gooders' cannot obfuscate the reality that colonialism was inherently an uneven relationship based on the use of power and force, often implying multiple forms of violence. Abolishing *sati* or banning female circumcision - despite all the kindly intentions - cannot hide the fact that like abolitionism they were arguably applied to justify physical control of people and their lands. In the same vein, by banking on a recent and equally ambivalent concept of sovereignty, dispossessing the Natives from their lands is unjustifiable. To Biggar, a lack of documentation, underutilisation of land and its subsequent use for 'developmental' purposes, makes a compelling case for settlers and colonialism. This coming from a professor of ethics and theology is unnerving, to say the least. Both Ferguson and Biggar, in their zealous support for capitalism, may consider primacy of private property a prerequisite for modernity and development,

yet it does not mean that premodern/precolonial societies lacked systemic ownership given the fact that we are talking about several millennia of human history having been land-based.

Biggar cannot escape the fact that the Empire is tainted by colossal human rights violations on a gigantic scale when one encounters enduring legacies of the Irish Famine (1845–1849), the Bengal Famine (1942–1943), the post-1857 revengeful tirade in India, the Amritsar Massacre of 1919 and the suppression of Mau Mau Rebellion (1952–1960) in Kenya. He takes a rather persuasive recourse to comparing these events to the proportion of violence that Hitler, Stalin, and Mao committed in the past century. The redeeming quality is that he does not deny the industrial scale violence yet finds British imperial structures conducive to native exigencies eliciting support from a wide variety of population groups. Here he relies on historians such as Margery Pelham, an Africanist, who claimed to have found wider support for colonial presence across the Sub-Saharan regions. This premise of collaborations remained quite popular in the 1960s where partisan advantages engendered a mutually convenient inter-dependence. Other than this dependency thesis, hypothesis about Britain—or for that matter other European imperial powers—sleepwalking into assuming colonial role do not amply explain the reasons behind such a significant historical reality. Denying the colonised any agency of resistance and autonomous strategies, understandably led to the evolution of several new areas in scholarship focusing on peasants, women, tribals and the rest who soon began to feature in the leftist, gender and subaltern genres of scholarship, foregrounding the discourse for decolonising the entire academic terrain. Biggar fails to differentiate between nationalist movements and more xenophobic forms of nationalism along with misperceiving resistance as inherently violent typology. This unilinear reading of recent history only exposing Biggar's own inadequacies as a historian. And, little can be said about is Christian ethics which is totally devoid of any ethical notion. This is not to belittle Biggar's extensive notes and bibliography covering 164 pages with a final warning for his readers, who may be mainly British: 'anticolonialism is not a reliable guide to Britain's colonial past, and it encourages us to draw wrong lessons for the future.'

David Peretz's biography of Admiral Sir John Corbett, one of his ancestors, tells a different story. John Corbett had a vast seafaring experience during the nineteenth century, especially after the British abolition of slavery. The book is based on meticulous research piecing together life of Corbett from his extensive letters and sketches. Without succumbing to uncritiqued adulation, Peretz—not a trained historian otherwise—has consulted personal collections along with other archival repositories dealing with the Royal Navy and the Empire. The result is a refreshing reconstruction of a life offering a close encounter with the monitoring of ships trafficking slaves across the Atlantic, rescue missions in the Caribbeans, and the Second Opium War. Peretz's biography of Corbett, provides an insider's view of coordination and strategisation of active warfare at a time when steam engines had been recently introduced though means of communications were still not as prompt as a generation later. Corbett's visit to India before the stormy events of 1857 offers a brief searchlight on the landscape, people, East India Company's expansive empire and the hunting expeditions. Corbett is aware of the goings-on in the Crimean War and despite his best desire, is unable to see the action but yearns for complete annihilation of the Russian navy in the Black Sea and even of the prized capital. He notes:

> I shall not be satisfied until I hear that the whole Russian army have been... forced to surrender... Next year if they hold out so long we ought to burn St. Petersburg... I am sure we can do it in a satisfactory manner if it is set about in earnest.

Corbett's active role in the Second Opium War, covered by the British press including *The Times*, and through his letters to his sister, Mildred received wide acclaim, back home. It lead to his promotion which he relished while vacationing at home in 1857. Just in his mid-thirties, he was promoted to captain a ship and deputed to continue anti-Chinese campaign that he records in his letters and sketches. Lord Elgin, helped by reinforcements from India and England and through timely material support from the French, first captured Canton and then proceeded towards Peking leading an armada. The imperial forces surrendered rather too quickly entering into a treaty with the British allowing extra-territoriality to the latter which ironically became a norm in a scramble for

China, followed by a similar colonial enterprise in Africa. Corbett, like many of his contemporaries, had a low opinion of the Chinese since, as 'the rascally tartars laid a trap' leading to another punitive campaign. In a letter sent back on 13 October 1860, he touches upon the European destruction of Peking:

we hear that our army is at Pekin and indeed beyond it having taken possession of the Emperor's summer palace about ten miles north of Pekin. The French were there first of course plundered the place getting we hear the most beautiful things ever seen. They afterwards burnt the palace. So much for our allies.

According to Peretz, Corbett 'did however get a small share of plunder from Peking.' Sadly, such views of the Chinese were symptomatic of racism pervasive across the various strata of British Empire and society. Following his command of a naval contingent to Japan, where he produces sketches of cities like Hiroshima, Corbett officiated a court martial

of two mariners of the *Pearl* who were tried on the charge of manslaughter, they having shot some defenseless wretched Chinamen [while looking for pirates]… One man I'm glad to say got imprisonment with hard labour and I wish both had. Our men think no more of shooting Chinese… than of shooting dogs.

Following his rather late marriage, Corbett stayed on in England to raise a family but then resumed his naval service in the late 1870s as an admiral. His official assignments took him back to Africa, Muscat, Karachi, Bombay, Singapore, and East Asia until he decided to retire in 1887 at the age of sixty-five choosing the life of a country squire by virtue of a comfortable pension and through inheriting valuable properties from his own family and that of Grace Corbett—his spouse.

Peretz's main purpose, unlike that of Biggar, is not to defend the empire. Instead, he aims at reconstructing the life story of one of his forbears, based on his correspondence, sketches, photos, and naval archives. Corbett's letters to his mother, sister, and wife represent Victorian ethos where, imbued with Christian sentiment and professional probity, working for empire was deemed a noble profession for self-discovery and personal enrichment besides seeing the world beyond the English shores. Here, views of the Africans, Indians, and the Chinese remain racialised with the colonials exhibiting a sense of invincibility—a kind of perspective which, to Biggar, may hold some nobler ethics instead of sheer racism and exploitation.

WHAT DO OCEANS SAY?

Khuda Bushq

Kuala Lumpur, along with all the bells and whistles that modernity demands of the contemporary megacity, is blessed with an abundance of *butiks* and *tamans*, hills and parks respectively. Many of the contemporary *tamans* find themselves on *butiks* as the common place of rain and floods results in much of the lasting beauty being found on the higher lands. One of these taman-butiks is undertaking a bit of an identity crisis. Today, it might be called Bukit Perdana, but some of the older denizens know it as Lake Gardens. Perdana literally translates from Malay into 'the first', and

is found in such titles as *Perdana Menteri*, Prime Minister, or *nombor perdana*, prime number, and even in *pertunjukan perdana*, or series premiere of a new show. Perdana also finds itself associated with items of federal importance in Malaysia. The official name of Bukit Perdana comes from the massive 91.6 hectares of the Perdana Botanical Gardens, which were given this name in the summer of 2011, when the former Lake Gardens were given a 'botanical' designation.

The gardens date back to the twilight of the nineteenth century, when the British colonial Resident General of Malaya, Frank Swettenham, and the British Selangor administration agreed to establish a lush garden and a manmade lake there. The project also obtained the collaborative help of the local Cantonese community under Towkay Chow Ah Yeok, who contributed numerous *chempaka* (a family of evergreens) and orange trees to the parks original plan. After ten years the project was completed with the construction of the Lake Club, an exclusively European club. Carcosa Seri Negara, the former residence of Malaya's Resident-General, was also built within the Lake Gardens. Carcosa also served as the setting of many of the early independence talks prior to Malaya's independence from

Britain in 1957. Today, Carcosa Seri Negara is a part-time wedding venue and a mostly full-time ruin. While the Lake Club opened up to non-Europeans eventually, now named the Royal Lake Club, this was not the only changes that could come to the gardens. While they remain a scenic and serene locale in the heart of a bustling megacity, they now host the city's bird park, butterfly park, and a planetarium. On the outskirts of Perdana Botanical Garden, are Bank Negara, the Bukit Aman Royal Malaysian Police Headquarters (with its own history of fame and infamy), the National Mosque of Malaysia (Masjid Negara), and the Tugu Negara, a national monument to the Malaysian military.

Oceans That Speak: Islam and the Emergence of the Malay World, Islamic Arts Museum Malaysia, Kuala Lumpur, Malaysia, from 13 December 2024 – 15 June 2025.

Red Rivers & Death: The Temiar Orang Asli Fight Against Iron Ore Mining in Kelantan, Forest Research Centre, Perdana Botanical Gardens, Kuala Lumpur, Malaysia, from 14 – 29 December 2024.

Once upon a time, visitors to Bukit Perdana might have entered from the National Train Station, which today still delineates it as a region in Kuala Lumpur from Chinatown. Past the umbrella-resembling Masjid Negara, one begins their ascent by passing one of the widely acclaimed must-see destinations for all visiting Kuala Lumpur, the Islamic Arts Museum Malaysia. It is the largest museum dedicated to Islamic art in Southeast Asia housing more than 10,000 artifacts in 30,000 square metres. Under the patronage of the Albukhary Foundation and the founding and present director Syed Mohamad Albukhary, the Islamic Arts Museum opened in 1998. The building itself is an impressive blend of modern architecture and famed Islamic motifs, sporting an abundance of domes in a variety of styles! The objects themselves are indeed an impressive, spell binding, collection. But overall, the permanent collection lacks curation, a central narrative, or any sense at all. The casual visitor will easily be dazzled by the look of the place but left feeling like they are wandering through a multi-level storage unit, with some spectacular objects, but without any sense of which way to go or how to approach the material. It really is too bad as the objects and the space have a rich

potential that is left unrealised. The gift shop remains one of the most impressive parts of the museum chuck full of artful prints, books, and gifts, at no spared expense!

Because of the Albukhary Foundation's good ties with a variety of international museums and organisations, when a new temporary exhibit comes to the Islamic Arts Museum there is good reason to hold high hopes. Each new temporary exhibition also comes with a beautifully designed coffee table book meant as a bit of an embellishment to take home after a tour of the curation. A few very good items have come to Kuala Lumpur on lease from the world's greatest museums. So, I had great expectation for the 'Oceans That Speak' exhibition.

An oceanic perspective for an exhibition almost promises novelty, especially in relation to the history of Islam and art. Unfortunately, while oceans may indeed speak, it is difficult to ascertain what exactly they have to say. Like the permanent exhibition, this temporary exhibition lacks an overarching narrative to tie all the objects together. Even a chronology of events and issues would have helped. 'Oceans That Speak' also hosts several pieces borrowed from the permanent exhibition. 'Left-over' objects repurposed for a temporary exhibition can be forgiven, especially since most visitors will likely not be that familiar with the whole museum. But without proper curation, what is derivative sticks out like a sore thumb. The information presented is well written, but the exhibition itself just comes across like a decently organised collection of stuff. Yes, the audience is likely to be aware that Malaysia is part of an archipelago, sometimes referred to as the Malay World or Nusantara. What the visitors would like to know is what importance being a part of an oceanic community meant and how that informed this part of the world? Or how Islam is lived and blended into the oceanic world of the Malay Archipelago? Instead, the visitor is left to lurk from piece to piece, learning that in Malaysia there was oceanic trade, particularly in spices, there was Jawi writing, that the Malays did fine wood carvings and elaborate textiles, and that at one point the region was colonised. While the pipe flute music blending of ocean waves heard overhead is inviting, there is not much to keep the audience captivated nor to drive them to engage with the exhibition. It is a shame because it would be good to know what the oceans indeed have to say. The only connective tissue that holds the

exhibition together is merely inferred and somewhat left to interpretation. Perhaps the exhibition means to convey that Islam was the civilising force in the archipelago. But even this is contrived. Perhaps the exhibitors were too afraid of making controversial statements. After all, Malaysian history is contemporaneously quite a matter of debate, not just of sorting fact from fiction, but also in sorting wishful self-fulfilling prophecy from racially informed, revisionist constructed narratives.

The exhibition wants to speak to the prime importance of Islam in the region, but never wants to overstep its bounds. Fair enough, Islam was important for delivering Jawi as the writing system in the archipelago as well as gave a direction for the already artistically developed culture of the region to advance forward. Textiles, intricate and beautiful woodwork, calligraphy, and even artistic copies of the Qur'an demonstrate this without anything being said definitively. But then the exhibition has the audacity to sugar coat colonialism and any sense of history, leading to the conclusion that, perhaps by way of magic, thanks to the oceanic nature of the archipelago, it somehow became a pretty cosmopolitan place. Even though ABIM, the Islamic Youth Movement of Malaysia, has an annual conference on cosmopolitan Islam, it is difficult to find evidence that much of that has ever found a solid home in the Golden Chersonese.

All this can perhaps be forgiven if the facts remain somewhat vague or hard to document. But only a few steps into the exhibition, one notes a simple (deliberate?) error. The famous Terengganu inscription is widely known as the oldest surviving artifact of Islam in Malaysia. The dating of the inscription has been a bit of a historical debate. The 'definitive date of the inscription' was established by the Malaysian Sufi scholar, Naquib Al-Attas, who has a cult following, as 1303. But it was based on a variety of pseudo-historical analysis. But in 2017, a real historian, Ahmat Adam, actually did a proper historical analysis and found the date of the inscription to, in fact, be 1308. The fact that the debate nor the correction (which mind you came with a thorough critical lashing of Al-Attas's techniques) were left unmentioned in the exhibition is a pretty serious slip in a time where truth and facts are constantly under siege from nefarious forces. While the Malay Archipelago is noted as existing between the Indian and Chinese oceanic worlds, the exhibition has little to say about Chinese influence.

A phrase is often passed around in talking about history in Malaysia. *Tanah Air*, literally 'land' and 'water'. It is an excellent approach that has unfortunately been coopted by extremist Malay nationalists. It is a notion of history that accounts for the importance of the land and the waters to the history of the people and the region. It appreciates change in a way anchoring one's history to one homeland does not. It appreciates evolution and the movements of people. The Malay Archipelago has been home to many, some by choice, others by necessity, and others even by violent conquest. All of this is important to the history of the land. A bastardised version of the land and water sees it as all being simply 'Malay'. This is how more extremists elements attempt to build a revisionist history, particularly those beholden to the action and historical exaggeration that is seen in such films as the 2022 favourite *Mat Kilau*. They take the 'my land is my land by conquest' narrative most popularly expounded by western conquerors and take it as good enough for them to use as a tool to perpetuate racial stereotypes and disastrous norms. Malaysian pseudo-historians with PhD's who lean into this realm are a favourite for support and propping up by certain Malay supremacist politicians. In such an atmosphere, we need exhibitions that are beholden to historical fact and stir up questions and discussion within the audience, a discussion and debate that needs to happen in Malaysia in order for us to move forward towards a brighter future. As a centre for public education, museums should have no time for propaganda, they must explore the issues at hand and present what evidence we have. If not, we allow our museums to become tools of the state to the disservice of the people. While the 'Oceans that Speak' exhibition was overall a tremendous disappointment, after exiting the Islamic Arts Museum Malaysia, I proceeded further up the *Bukit* in search of an exhibition with something to say.

As one ascends Bukit Perdana, the foliage only grows thicker as the roads become windier. A sign lets you know that you have entered the domain of the botanical gardens. Aside from the looming and domineering Royal Police Headquarters, the bird park and butterfly park add a much-needed solace from the grating rattle of megacity life. Before one enters the thick of the botanical gardens, a foyer of small buildings line a walkway. One of those buildings is the Forest Research Centre which gained a lot of attention in December 2024. The bulk of the building is a glass walled

space, a large salon, almost made for a small exhibition. Outside the
building is a beautiful jungle garden. On the particular December day I
visited the space, it was filled with three rows of H frame displays featuring
a photo exhibition. It is titled 'Red Rivers & Death' and examines the
struggle between the indigenous Temiar Orang Asli people and the Red
Star Capital iron ore mining company in the northern state of Kelantan.
The exhibition is a collaborative effort between Malaysiakini, an influential
web-based newspaper, with support from the Pulitzer Center's Rainforest
Reporting Grant. The Malaysiakini journalist, S Vinothaa, served as lead
reporter, and the news sites' Azneal Ishak provided the photographs, along
with contributions from the villagers of Kampung Kelaik.

The exhibition is simple, a series of photos looking at the lives of the
Temiar Orang Asli. The photos show young folks playing a local popular
ball game, other villagers in ceremonial attire, and others still fishing and
working around their village. We see beautiful sights of the jungle village,
but then the desolation of that village with muddy roads, torn down trees,
and expanding mining operations. Beyond this we see infographics
showing how the mining operation working upstream from their village

was poisoning their water with chromium, a highly toxic heavy metal to humans. Other graphics demonstrate the dangerous concentration of harmful substances in the water and the villager's blood. While 'Oceans that Speak' was style over substance, this simple, yet elegant exhibition may not have much style, but the substance speaks volumes.

Accompanying the photos is a video put together by the folks at Malaysiakini's News Lab, a fantastic unit that does a great job of breaking down complicated news issues for readers to easily consume with the aid of images and infographic. The video nicely accompanies the photographs, giving a slice of life from one of the Orang Asli tribes, the scattered native peoples of contemporary Peninsular Malaysia. The exhibition also hosts a few items showing the dirtiness of the water consumed by the people of Kampung Kelaik and offers its audience a stamped postcard that can be sent to local MPs, or even directly to the Prime Minister, urging them to take action.

The strength of the story comes in how it is told through the people experiencing it. The whole dilemma kicked off with a tribal patriarch being found dead in a river that he had spent his whole life swimming,

fishing, and bathing in. The patriarch, Angah Alang, who was seventy-six years old, was caught in a flash flood in 2015 which washed a heavy amount of debris from an iron mining operation upstream. The river has thereafter been a mucky red colour. After Angah's death, many villagers began finding lesions on their bodies and their water and food sources appeared tainted, causing sickness throughout the village. Blood tests later confirmed the tribe's worst fears. They had extremely high levels of chromium, a poisonous metal that can stay in the blood for weeks, even months, was found in the villagers' blood. The blood of a nineteen-year-old villager, Azlan, was tested for chromium, aluminium, arsenic, and iron levels. The levels found demonstrated a recent exposure that would put him at risk for severe liver, kidney, and lung damage, as well as higher risks of cancer. While Red Star Capital claimed that they were not leaking any harmful substances into the nearby rivers, subsequent test of the villagers' blood correlated with river water samples at various distances from where the mining was being undertaken.

The tragedy is that this once secluded and natural society has now been damaged in multiple ways by the ongoing mining operation. The video in

the exhibition goes on to not only show how natural beauty is destroyed by these operations, but how it also destroys the way of life for the Orang Asli who now also have cancer to look forward to in the not-too-distant future. The Orang Asli not only have adapted to live in the often-harsh conditions of the forest, they know how to listen to the forest and respect the land and waters of one people to another. When one violates a land or the waters that are not theirs, the tribes come together and work out an arbitration so that justice can be restored. The villagers spoke of being able to listen to the forest and the rivers so that they can live in balance with the natural world they inhabit. But logging and mining companies disturb this peace and there is no one to arbitrate with. What is happening to the Temiar Orang Asli represents a microcosm of the struggle of modernity versus the various indigenous peoples of Malaysia. An ultimate disrespect to both *Tanah* and *Air* – land and water.

While the photos are quite powerful, the exhibition is rather straightforward, but chockablock with information and, especially, a story that demands the audience take action, even if they have no relation to a struggle happening a multiple hour car ride from where the exhibition is

taking place. But the reporting done by Malaysiakini also points out various contradictions in the law. Red Star Capital are essentially abiding by the law while taking advantage of certain loopholes that essentially legalise the poisoning of the land. Meanwhile, the Orang Asli themselves desire greater control of their land and for the government to take greater strides in protecting the land that has been their homes for centuries. The greatest revelation is not that a simple antienvironmental corporation is poisoning an indigenous people but that a history of corruption and a refusal to take stock of numerous historical wrongs has led to a status quo where evil actions are allowed and injustice runs rampant against the environment, the land, the water, and the people of this country. The problem remains that it is hard to identify one 'bad guy' in the overall scenario. While the people of Kampung Kelaik are the ultimate victims, who is to be blamed? Red Star Capital? The Kelantan State Government? The Federal Government? A specific ministry? All of them? It's a complex issue that will require a complex solution.

Calls to action need not be as direct and aggressive as that offered by 'Red Rivers & Death'. But 'Oceans that Speak' could leave one with a

more manageable call to simply 'think' or 'read a bit more into history'. It is a hope that at the very least, whether an exhibition succeeds or fails, that we think about the lands and the waters of the places that we visit or make our homes so that one day they can tell a story beyond what revisionist perspectives or beyond a message of illness, disease, and death. Indeed, oceans, rivers, lakes, and other bodies of water do, as the indigenous people suggest, have much to say. But do we know how to listen and do what is needed to restore the justice denied? With the Malaysian Parliament Complex just being on the other side of the highway from Bukit Perdana, a call to action would not have to be very loud to get to the focal point of change in Malaysia.

ET CETERA

}

ON HALAL DATING APPS

Ghazal Tipu

Are you looking for a spouse? The ideal partner? Then why not try marriage – or halal, as they are known – dating apps? Such as Muzz, Salaams, and Single Muslim. They claim a degree of success in facilitating marriages and, when used in the correct way, provide a practical method for Muslims to find a spouse. But not all is rosy in the halal apps garden.

Alongside matchmaking successes, the digital landscape of halal dating apps comprises dysfunctional individual and collective courting behaviours that bring about harm. Endless profiles create swiping addiction and choice overload. Inconsistent digital dating behaviours reinforce insecure attachment styles, create psychological harm, afford lack of dignity, and diminish accountability. Perhaps most seriously, hookup culture and sexual harms in a world of male entitlement put women at risk of trauma and exploitation.

Islamic etiquette is about returning to our *fitra,* innate nature, and fostering wholesome behaviours. The Prophet's teaching implores the ummah to uphold good character through principles like respect, honesty, and accountability. As the Prophet said, 'the Muslim is the one from whose tongue and hand the people are safe, and the believer is the one people trust with their lives and wealth'. This emphasis on good moral character should also apply to the process and conduct of believers in approaching potential spouses. Nevertheless, the prominent culture of halal dating apps – partially hidden from mainstream Muslim society – goes against the core of Islamic teachings on character, sexual propriety, upholding dignity, and affording emotional and physical safety.

So, we have to move cautiously.

To begin with, we need to acknowledge that there are several challenges to finding a spouse in countries where Muslims are a minority. There are limited public spaces for organic interaction between genders. Dating apps offer a solution; and partially remedy this situation by providing users the ability to reach other Muslims. Different studies have also noted the 'freedom' afforded in finding a spouse. Laurens De Rooij, who works on digital analysis at the Department of Work and Pension, UK, argues that apps offer an 'avenue of agency', allowing 'for young people in potentially conservative environments to choose potential matches with greater freedom, finding someone that satisfies all their potential wants and needs'. He suggests this is particularly the case for women from 'conservative environments'.

How do these apps work? A user first creates a profile on their smartphone. They populate their photos and biographical narrative, as well as other data such as height, ethnicity, educational status, and level of religiosity. After completing their profile, a user is then able to review several profiles a day through a 'swiping' process; swiping right to show interest and swiping left on a profile to reject it. A 'match' is created between profiles if two users swipe right on each other's profile. After a match is created, both users can contact each other directly through instant messaging or voice call. Users can opt for different subscriptions that allow access to potentially unlimited numbers of profiles a day. Whatever your subscription, it is entirely possible to achieve several matches in a short space of time and be in communication with several potential spouses concurrently.

Swiping is the distinguishing feature of modern technological methods of matchmaking, compared to traditional methods of the past in which a would-be spouse – often with the support of a local 'Auntie' - considered a limited number of suitors at one time. Swiping offers innumerable choices. But this comes at a cost. In a psychological sense, as a study lead by Marina Thomas suggests, swiping brings about a Pavlovian sense of reward and the positive reinforcement of getting matches. As such, swiping as an activity is highly addictive, and has become a game or a recreational activity akin to window shopping. Swiping addiction even led someone to bring a lawsuit against Match for creating apps that are

deliberately addictive. This is a timely reminder that dating apps are run by companies who may prioritise profit over wellbeing. Swiping also leads to the psychologically damaging phenomena of choice overload and the illusion of a perfect partner; to the growth of poor interpersonal behaviour patterns and an un-Islamic 'hook up' culture; and to very real dangers to women's sexual safety.

Several studies evidence the negative and crippling psychological effects of too much choice. Tila Pronk and Jaap Denissen's research on the behaviour of sixteen-to-thirty-year-olds found that a higher number of partner options sets off a rejection mind-set. Another study by Jonathan D'Angelo and Catalina Toma found that online daters who chose from a large set of potential partners were less satisfied with their choice a week after making their choice than those who selected from a small set, and were more likely to change their selection. Swiping fuels an illusion of the possibility of selecting a 'perfect' life partner – as if building your own house with its own bespoke features. This false sense of 'build your own human' has the potential of bringing utter disappointment and disillusionment.

Endless swiping is also a problem as would-be potentials may have no real intention of pursuing a match and leave sincere hopefuls unawares. Islam invites us to lower our gaze and be intentional in our relations with others. Encouraged by the ease of 'swiping' for a new 'match', however, many app users engage in hurtful and negative behaviour towards others. Attachment theory helps us to understand and frame some of the more dysfunctional behaviours around online dating. A term coined by the twentieth century British psychologist, John Bowlby, attachment styles are developed through our experience with early caregivers and affect our romantic relationships in adulthood. Those who had a secure childhood and who had their needs met will form healthy and long-term relationships in adulthood. Those whose primary caregivers were inconsistent in childhood may develop an anxious attachment style in adulthood characterised by 'neediness' and low esteem. In contrast, those who were neglected by their caregivers may develop an avoidant attachment style. Their behaviour in adulthood is characterised by being emotionally unavailable and finding discomfort with intimacy.

A host of terms have entered our lexicon since the advent of online dating. These constitute a whole paradigm of online courting behaviours. Ghosting. Breadcrumbing. Benching. Situationships. Love bombing. Zombieing. Arguably, these signify the enabling of insecure attachment styles; or, put another way, halal dating apps potentially enable a cohort of people who unconsciously have no real intention or ability to form a secure long-term relationship.

Despite Islamic rulings on sexual propriety, the wider hookup culture brought about by Tinder does not escape young Muslims. Islam implores us to live wholesome lives and has a particular stance on intimacy before marriage that protects the ummah emotionally, physically, and spiritually. Sexual relationships are to be sanctioned through *nikah*. Like Tinder, however, Muslim dating apps appear to be facilitating pre-marital sex. Such behaviours are a problem for those striving to adhere to Islamic teachings about chastity before marriage. Hookup culture is particularly a problem for young and developing minds. With the endless swiping, provision of choice and focus on physical attraction, what sort of neurology are we hardwiring into the collective young Muslim psyche?

The scale of hookup culture on Muslim apps is difficult to discern. But accounts online provide a glimpse into a world that is not acknowledged in the mainstream Muslim milieu. Social media and internet forums such as Reddit provide further insights into the murkier side of finding a spouse through the apps. One redditor says the lack of guardians (*wali*) and safeguarding made Muzz the 'Muslim version of Tinder'. A Muslim woman on the same forum exclaims: 'these Muslim apps are always geared towards marriage so whyyyy are there men on there trying to hook up?'. She points out that wearing a hijab does not guarantee getting 'respect' from Muslim men. A YouTuber also shares: 'my own experience with Muslim "matrimonial" website was very negative and traumatic, the men expected more of a hookup then actual marriage and ask haram stuff and you get surprised at the photos they sent me that I decided to close it'. A user-generated Instagram page entitled Muzzmatchnightmare evidences Muslims seeking pre-marital sexual encounters and reflects a wider trend of women taking responsibility for creating a safe community for others. Facebook pages have emerged online based in different cities called: 'Are

we dating the same guy?' that allows women to alert others of men who pose a danger to them.

It does seem that the cookie-cutter replication of 'hook-up' dating apps like Tinder is being replicated on halal apps. What makes the behaviours on apps like Muzz particularly sinister is a 'sheep in wolf's clothing' phenomenon. These apps are supposed to be for marriage, but some men are pursuing women for hookups. The prevalence of this phenomenon is not widely known or acknowledged enough by Muslim community and spiritual leaders.

Beyond consensual intimacy, there is also a darker underbelly to Muslim dating apps. Internet accounts reveal the prevalence of sexual assault and aggressive sexual behaviours on Muslim marriage apps. The 'Women United Blog' bravely posted an anonymised account of a woman who was sexually assaulted by a person she met on Muzz (formerly known as Muzmatch). The woman explained that she reported her distressing experience to the police but that 'according to information given to me later by the police, 'Jay' had been allowed to make fake profiles on Muzmatch FOUR times. Despite multiple complaints, Muzmatch have allowed this sexual predator to continue to make fake profiles to have access to vulnerable women like myself.' Following that post, the editor of the blog also posted that more women had come forward who were victims of this perpetrator, as well as other women who were 'abused, attacked and scammed by men they've met on Muzmatch'. The app provides a place to report 'bad behaviour' and officially states it will subsequently warn or permanently ban a member. However, these accounts suggests that apps like Muzz need to create further protocols to safeguard women.

Whatever the official policies or protocols, Muslim women, compared to their white and secular counterparts, may be particularly vulnerable on dating apps. Due to cultural codes around shame and honour, it may be particularly difficult to share such experiences with elders. In Muslim cultures, including South Asian cultures, there are cultural taboos around talking about sex and sexuality. This makes it difficult for Muslim women and men to share their experiences and the scale of the problem is difficult to discern. It leaves one speculating how many other Muslim women are

victims of sexual assault through Muslim marriage apps and an urgent investigation on this matter is strongly advocated.

Despite all the issues and problems, the use of halal dating apps seems to be entrenched and accepted by progressive Muslims as a method for finding a spouse. Yet, the culture that has developed around their use would be ignored at our peril. Inconsistent dating behaviours, hookup culture, and sexual harms ought to make us ask whether and how tradition might prevail over modern methods. More widely in society, public discourse, and internet articles such as 'How to date in IRL' (In Real Life), as well as in-person singles events, suggest the tide seems to be turning away from finding love through technology.

So, what alternatives are there beyond apps and technology?

Muslim should continue to facilitate introductions between their families. Where families facilitate choice and respect their adult children's requirements, the results are usually positive. This is a secure and tried-and-tested method for young Muslims throughout the world. The challenge, however, is for those young Muslims who don't have robust family ties, who may live in large cities – as is increasingly the case – away from their family, or who are newcomers to Islam. In addition, due to different social, economic, and demographic factors, first-generation immigrant families may have few family connections or may have exhausted their connections.

This is why the role of the mosques is important. Mosques ought to be front-and-centre in providing match-making services. Just as churches provide a range of facilities to the community beyond spiritual services, mosques should also do more to lean into their institutional potentialities. Historically, mosques and other Islamic institutions have played a role in facilitating young people to find future spouses and provided matrimonial services. But this role now seems to have diminished. A representative of the Dar ul-Israa mosque in Cardiff provided a potential reason. The match-making services were provided in the past, he says. But the mosque can no longer provide the service as it was difficult to match 'more educated women' with lesser educated men.

But that is hardly a barrier that cannot be surpassed! Mosques need to truly become focus of communities, and step forward to solve some of their problems. They need to do more to mitigate against the harmful

effects of halal dating apps. Since mosques are unlikely to be 'cancelled', they and other Muslim institutions must design interventions to help young Muslims make healthy choices for themselves. Muslim leaders should also continue to push for continually improved safeguarding measures on the sites. Other interventions may include reminding young people to have their wali involved. De Rooij's qualitative study of eleven users of halal dating apps found that 'the first in-person meeting was always in a public place, and for some women, it was seen as important that she be accompanied by another person (often a family member, but not necessarily a male)'.

Having mosque involvement is a start. There could still be limiting factors as mosques themselves are a patriarchal institution. Thus, women-led projects and initiatives could bring to the fore the vulnerabilities facing women on these dating apps and advocate for further safeguarding measures. While these do not seem to exist yet, the Inclusive Mosque Initiative offers mosque services that are tailored to women. User-generated Facebook groups by women asking 'Do you know this man?' indicate that women have introduced their own policing and monitoring measures to highlight and counter sexual violence. Similar initiatives could be started by other Muslim women.

The irony is that from a feminist perspective, dating apps could give women and young girls the agency that they require when facing control or gender-based violence at home. This suggests that there is still a place for halal dating apps, albeit, with more developed and stringent measures as well as the necessary robust safeguarding surrounding apparatus.

Essentially, it is all about creating a culture where it's not a taboo to talk about courtship processes and pre-marital 'relationships'. This will help to create safe spaces in which young Muslims can share with their parents, families, community elders, and spiritual leaders their experiences on marriage apps in real-time so that they can be guided safely with wisdom and insight.

THE LIST

A MOST REFRESHING INVENTORY

'In days of old when Knights were bold', says the much-loved limerick of schoolboys,

and paper wasn't invented
they wiped their arse
with blades of grass
and walked away contented.

There are, as bound to be, various other versions of this little ditty. One replaces paper with toilets, and goes on 'you left your load upon the road'. Not quite, old chum!

Or, perhaps that was the way in Europe during the 'Dark Ages', which were much darker and smellier than we have been told. But elsewhere they knew what to do with their dump; and, more important, immediately afterwords. Given that peoplekind has been shitting since they first made an appearance on the planet, surely they must have worked out what to do with their 'load' before the emergence of toilet paper in the fourteenth century. Although still absent in Europe, where 'medicated paper for water closet' emerged in 1857; and the western style flash toilet made an appearance in the 1860s.

Long before that, there were plenty of proper toilets around the world; and folks used water to clean themselves afterwards. Indoor sewage pipes and toilets in Turkey date back at least to 764 BC as is seen in the castles of the Urartu Kingdom of that period. This is one thousand years before the founding of Constantinople, a city well known for importing Roman cisterns, sewers, and aqueducts and building those into the foundations of the city. Thanks to this early thinking, Constantinople was able to become the largest city of Europe in the Middle Ages. In June of 2021, the first public toilet of the Ottoman Empire was made a museum in the city of

Tokat in northern Turkey. Built in the 1600s, this building was the first publicly available space for crafts people in the Ottoman empire to do their business. Being the first one, it hosted queues that would put the worst's of ladies' room queues to shame. It came to be known colloquially as the *sık dişini helası*, meaning 'hold your pee public toilet'.

So pooing with comfort and sophistication was not necessarily an invention of the British or Western Civilisation! Muslim societies and the ancient societies of Asia and North Africa had long had systems of plumbing and an ethical obligation and dedication to hygiene. In the modern era, it can be said that the non-west has for more superior toilets to those of the west, which have grown lazy and lacking innovation as they wipe with papers of various coarseness and environmental impact!

It is thus fitting that we seek more eco-friendly ways to do our business, explore alternatives to toilet paper, and the ever popular but highly perilous disposable wet wipes. We need, indeed demand, more classy methods of refreshment following the much-required visit to the loo.

In general, toilets in Muslim societies accompany some sort of washing facility, from simple to sophisticated. But it seems rather conclusive that the invention of the seventeenth century French furniture maker, Christophe de Rosiers, otherwise known as the bidet, has become all the rage across the non-western world! While the bidet was once a symbol of high society, innovation and our contemporary era have made it much more accessible. It might just be the solution we need to many of our climate change induced watery woes. Not to mention the gate way to the most superior refreshment available today!

1. The Lota

Before plumbing and the maintenance of good water pressure was the norm of society, there was the lota – an all-round implement for water disseminations. The lota is simply a round jug with a spout. The first lotas, dating back to the second millennium BC, were made from terracotta and clay, but later lotas were largely made from metal, especially copper. While lota has been utilised in a variety of ceremonies from sacred religious practices to weddings and even traditional medicine, it has also gained use as a vessel for pouring water in needy places. As such, it a standard feature

CRITICAL MUSLIM

of most toilets in the Indian Subcontinent, where it is seen as a perfect gadget for the post-loo washing up regime. Lotas across time and cultures come in a wide variety and although shunned by people with stiff upper lips, they have washed the bums of Muslims, Hindus, Buddhists, Sikhs, Jains, Zoroastrians, Christians, Jews, and all matter of religious devotes throughout their existence. Unity can be found in the strangest of places!

2. CuloClean Portable Bidet

A substitute for the lota, this bidet has been noted as being a top choice for backpack travellers or those looking to keep the luggage light! A simple, but elegant design, the CuloClean is a corkscrew plastic plug that you can attach to the top any plastic water bottle. Then simply turn the bottle upside down and squeeze projecting a most refreshing stream of your favourite spring, mineral, or even sparkling water for effective cleansing and comfort! No batteries or electricity needed! For those worried about putting yet further unnecessary plastics into the world, fear not! The makers of CuloClean also sell hygienic bags and reusable bottles so that you can be your eco-friendly best self.

3. Tushy Travel Bidet

This portable bidet is all in one with no need to mess around with lots of parts and assembly. Like the popular accordion-style collapsible water bottles, this silicon bidet collapses for easy travel and even comes with a stainless-steel carabiner clip for easy carry! To use, you simply pull the bidet open and fill it with water. Then flip the angled spicket open, aim, and squeeze to the level of flow you find most useful in refreshing your nether regions. When finished, collapse the bidet back down and see how it fits into most toiletry travel pouches! Great for travel, camping, and dormitories, also available in a wide range of colours!

4. Brondell GoSpa Travel (Handpump) Bidet

While not as sleek as other portable bidets, a proper handpump bidet is just what the doctor ordered for taking care of business after you have

taken care of business. Easily assembled this portable bidet also requires no batteries or electricity, just good old fashioned elbow grease. But the pump on this bidet is specially designed to make wash-up easy for the whole family, even those of us with a weak hand grip. This portable bidet sometimes comes with a collapsable nozzle or can be closed for easy packing when its time to be on-the-go. Holding a greater water capacity than other portable bidets this model gives the most refreshing feeling down there that is guaranteed to last.

5. *The Mosafer Electric Portable Bidet*

Most other portable bidets require work, which for many of us think is the last thing we require to be a part of our loo experience. It is, after all, about relaxing - is it not? Well enter the electric portable bidet. A simple push of the button can adjust stream strength and warmth. And the motor that propels the whole system is quiet, so no need to disturb others should you find yourself in a public latrine. The battery is said to last long, and noted to power through 100 cycles. Each cycle last between thirty and sixty seconds depending on the stream strength setting! And once the battery runs out, fear not, the fast-charge USB plug only takes two hours to reach full strength. The device is also waterproof, which can be quite handy in many of the lavatories available to us around the world. The device comes with its own carrier bag which will easily accompany your other toiletries on the go. A good bum cleaning gizmo for the twenty-first century!

6. *The Standalone Bidet*

Beyond portability, perhaps one's own home toilet could use some modifications And home bidets also come in quite the variety. The standalone bidets are separate fixtures typically situated next to the toilet. Originating in France in the seventeenth century, these fixtures have been a staple in many European homes for generations. You will still find them in some older homes and hotels, or those going for a more traditional or rustic aesthetic. Traditionally, they resemble a low sink or a porcelain bowl and come with controls for adjusting water pressure and temperature. The plumbing is similar to that of a standard toilet, requiring

both a water supply and a drain. This adage will have you feeling like a member of the royal family, as you should, when you visit the john. But it does require some tricky manoeuvres as you have to move from deposit to withdrawal!

7. The Handheld Bidet Sprayers

For those of us without the luxury of space, fear not, more compact additions can be made to pre-existing home toilets. Handheld bidet sprayers, often referred to as *Shattafs* in Middle Eastern countries, or known more colloquially as the 'Muslim Shower', are now *de jure* in Muslim household. These sprayers are similar to a kitchen sink sprayer and are typically mounted on the wall near the toilet or attached to the toilet itself. This is the most common bidet one will find in hotels and most public places, and readily accompany a western toilet bowl or the Asian squatting toilet. They provide a manual control over the water stream, making them versatile for other uses, such as cleaning the toilet. More sophisticated models also allow for temperature control. While they are inexpensive and easy to install, their manual operation might not appeal to everyone. Handheld Sprayers or Shower Bidets will guarantee a most refreshing hygienic polish for bum, toilet seat, and even the floor if you so desire.

8. The Bidet Toilet Seat

For those with the budget, the most convenient and luxurious option is the bidet toilet seat attachment. These seats replace your traditional toilet seat and come with a host of features. These may include heated seats, adjustable water temperature and pressure, various wash modes, oscillating and pulsating stream characteristics, and even air dryers. Electrical requirements are a consideration, as these seats often need to be plugged into a power outlet. The integration of technology (such as heated seats, heated water, massage vibrations, blow dryers, UV sanitization, and so on) in these seats can offer a luxurious and hygienic bathroom experience. Various models exist with retracting bidet spickets and complicated control panels that deliver the best of all possible experience in this best of all possible worlds.

9. The Smart Bidet

Smart bidets represent the pinnacle of bidet technology, incorporating features such as remote controls, programmable user settings, and even connectivity with smart home systems. These bidets provide the ultimate in comfort and convenience, with sensors to adjust water temperature, pressure, and position automatically. They often feature energy-saving modes, self-cleaning mechanisms, and night lights, making them the smart choice for tech-savvy users. Now the smart home is complete! Finally, a bidet that connects to Wi-Fi, if only you can remember the password!

10. The Japanese Toilet

The Japanese Toilet has been widely hailed as the leader in complete refreshment. Since the technology boom in Japanese products in the 1980s and 1990s, Japan has developed a reputation for having the flashiest, and often most esoteric, gadgets on the market. Their bathrooms were not left out of this endeavour. The toilets not only advanced technologically, but were kept beholden to the traditional Japanese culture which holds cleanliness as amongst the top virtues of all. UV sterilisation and sensor drying are a must, but also effort and work are not for the bathroom, let that go on in the outside world. No need to even lift the seat, which is automatic. Lights and even mood setting music are often a feature. And their bidet is state of the art. Refreshment here can be taken for granted as smart-tech blends with numerous buttons, giving way to almost any function the mind can imagine. To these developers, not only is the toilet a sacred space, but one of the highest quality that ought to be considered a human right. The future is indeed here. So, why not loo in the twenty-second century and beyond!

Enjoy!

CITATIONS

Endless Shores by Ebrahim Moosa

I have used the following sources in this article: Persis Berlekamp, *Wonder, Image, and Cosmos in Medieval Islam* (Yale University Press, 2011); Anne Carson, 'Kinds of Water.' *Grand street* 6, no. 4 (1987): 177. https://doi. org/10.2307/25007020; Fredrick C Copleston, *A History of Philosophy*. 8 vols. (Image Books, New York, 1963); Don Mattera, *Azanian Love Song* (African Perspectives Publishing, Johannesbrug, 2007); Marcus Milwright, 'Waves of the Sea': Responses to Marble in Written Sources (Ninth-Fifteenth Centuries).' Chap. 13 In *The Iconography of Islamic Art: Studies in Honour of Robert Hillenbrand*, edited by Bernard O'Kane, 211-21. (Edinburgh University Press, 2007); Jalalud Din Rumi, *The Mathnawī of Jalālud'din Rūmī: Edited from the Oldest Manuscripts Available:With Critical Notes, Translation and Commentary,* translated by Reynolds A. Nicholson (Sang-e-Meel Publications, Lahore, 2004), translation used with amendments; Sophocles, and Gilbert Murray. *The Antigone* (Oxford University Press, 1941); and Encyclopaedia Iranica, 1/1, p. 27, available online at http://www.iranicaonline.org/articles/ab-i-the-concept-of-water -in-ancient-iranian-culture

Rango's Ordeal by Liam Mayo

I have mentioned the following works, in order of appearance, in this essay:
Friedrich Wilhelm Nietzsche, and Douglas Smith, *The Birth of Tragedy* (Oxford University Press, 2000); M Kaika, M. 'Dams as symbols of modernization: The urbanization of nature between geographical imagination and materiality', *Annals of the Association of American Geographers*, 96(2), 276-301 2006; Margaret Cook, *A river with a city problem:A history of Brisbane floods*. (University of Queensland Press, 2023); Benedict Anderson, *Imagined Communities: Reflections on the Origin and Spread of Nationalism* (Verso, London, 1983); Henry Miller, *Tropic of Capricorn*

(Grove Press, New York, 1961) Pg. 64, E R Dodd, *The Greeks and the Irrational* (University of California Press, 1951); Rob Nixon, *Slow Violence and the Environmentalism of the Poor* (Harvard University Press, 2011); Marshall Berman, M. (1988). *All that is solid melts into air: The experience of modernity.* (Penguin, 1988); G Deleuze and F Guattari, (1987). *A thousand plateaus: Capitalism and schizophrenia* (University of Minnesota Press, 1987); K Wittfogel, *Oriental Despotism: A Comparative Study of Total Power*, (Yale University Press, New Haven, 1957); Karl Marx, *Capital: Volume* I, translated by Ben Fowkes (Penguin Classics, 1976; See particularly Chapter 1, 'Commodities,' and Chapter 4, 'The Fetishism of Commodities and the Secret thereof'); Henri Lefebvre, *The production of space.* (Blackwell, 1991); Cook, M. (2023). *A river with a city problem: A history of Brisbane floods* (University of Queensland Press, 2023) p. x.; Gaston Bachelard, (1983), *Water and dreams: an essay on the imagination of matter*, trans Edith R. Farrell. (The Pegasus Foundation, 1983); Herman Melville, Moby-Dick (Penguin Classics, 2003, Original work published 1851)

The Sea and the Quran by Luke Wilkinson

The works cited include: Abdallah Rothman, *Developing a Model of Islamic Psychology and Psychotherapy: Islamic Theology and Contemporary Understandings of Psychology* (New York: Routledge, 2022); C. G Jung and Sonu Shamdasani, *The Red Book: Liber Novus*, (W. W. Norton, 2009); Mohammad Ali Shomali, *Self-Knowledge,* edited by Muhammad Legenhausen (Mahdiyar Publishers, 2006); Travis E. Zadeh, *Wonders and Rarities : The Marvelous Book That Travelled the World and Mapped the Cosmos* (Harvard University Press, 2023).

The quotations are from Reynold Alleyne Nicholson, *The Mathnawí of Jalálu'ddín Rúmí*, Vols 1&2 (Konya Metropolitan University, 2004) L505, L2063-2064, L570-577; and from Toshihiko Izutsu, *Sufism and Taoism: A Comparative Study of Key Philosophical Concepts.* (University of California Press, 1984) pp. 141-149, 488-489, p15.

I have also used Seyyed Hossein Nasr et al, *The Study Qur'an: A New Translation and Commentary* (HarperOne, 2015); and Imam al-Ghazali, *The*

Revival of the Religious Sciences), Vol. 21, *Translated by Walter James Skellie* (Islamic Texts Society, Cambridge, 2010).

Water is Gaia by Christopher Burr Jones

Amongst others, I have consulted with following sources: S M Absar, 'The future of water resource management in the Muslim world', *Journal of Futures Studies*, 17(3), 1-20 2013; K A Ingersoll, *Waves of Knowing: A Seascape Epistemology* (Duke University Press, 2016); D Mueller-Dombois, 'The Hawaiian ahupua. a land use system: Its biological resource zones and the challenge for silvicultural restoration'. *Bishop Mus. Bull. Cult. Environ. Stud*, 3, 23-33 2007; D Mueller-Dombois, 'The Hawaiian ahupua. a land use system: Its biological resource zones and the challenge for silvicultural restoration'. *Bishop Mus. Bull. Cult. Environ. Stud*, 3, 23-33 2007; C Sagan and A Druyan, *Pale blue dot: A vision of the human future in space* (Ballantine Books, 2011); K W Seo et al, 'Drift of Earth's pole confirms groundwater depletion as a significant contributor to global sea level rise 1993–2010' *Geophysical Research Letters*, 50(12), 2023; and Jet Propulsion Laboratory, 'Astronomers Find Largest, Most Distant Reservoir of Water. Jet Propulsion Laboratory', California Institute of technology 2011, which can be accessed at https://www.jpl.nasa.gov/news/astronomers-find -largest-most-distant-reservoir-of-water/

Shariah in a Sinking City by Wietske Merison

John Augustin, 'A Watery Onslaught from Sea, Sky and Land in the World's Fastest-Sinking City.' *Mongabay Environmental News*, April 27, 2020. https://news.mongabay.com/2020/04/a-watery -onslaught-from-sea-sky-and-land-in-the-worlds-fastest-sinking-city/. P H van de Brug, 'Malaria in Batavia in the 18th Century.' Tropical Medicine & International Health 2, no. 9 (1997): 892–902. Ueli Brunner, 'The Great Dam and the Sabean Oasis of Ma'rib.' Irrigation and Drainage Systems 14 (2000): 167–82. Alasdair Glennie, 'Indonesian River Clogged with Chemicals Dumped by Textile Factories.'
Mail Online, April 10, 2014. https://www.dailymail.co.uk/news/article-2601944/Indonesian-river-clogged-toxic-chemicals-dumped-

textile-factories.html. Green Warriors, Indonesia, The World's Most Polluted River, Documentary. Première Lignes, 2018. Dian Tri Irawaty, 'Jakarta's Kampungs: Their History and Contested Future.' MA Thesis, University of California, Los Angeles, 2018. https://escholarship.org/uc/item/55w9b9gg. Marsely L Kehoe, 'Dutch Batavia: Exposing the Hierarchy of the Dutch Colonial City', Journal of Historians of Netherlandish Art 7, no. 1 (January 2015). Lytton John. Musselman, Figs, Dates, Laurel, and Myrrh: Plants of the Bible and the Quran. (Timber Press, Portland, 2007). Christina Thornell, 'Why Jakarta Is Sinking', Vox, February 22, 2021. https://www.vox.com/22295302/why-jakarta-sinking-flooding-colonialism.

Ocean Dreams by Jeremy Henzell-Thomas

Laleh Bakhtiar's *Sufi: Expressions of the Mystic Quest* is published by Thames and Hudson (1976), and Michel Chodkiewicz's *An Ocean Without Shore* is published by the State University of New York Press (1993). A collection of *hadith Qudsi* can be found in *40 Hadith of Imam al-Nawawi* (numerous editions). See also: Jeremy Henzell-Thomas, 'Journey to Islam', in *Narratives of Conversion to Islam in Britain: Male Perspectives,* edited by Yasir Suleiman, Prince Alwaleed Bin Talal Centre of Islamic Studies, University of Cambridge, 2015; 'DNA: A Personal Story.' *Critical Muslim 40, Biography,* Autumn 2021, 145-158 and 'A Stick with Two Ends'. *Critical Muslim 51, Desire,* Summer 2024, 23.

Water as Metaphor by Naomi Foyle

Discover your free water drinking rights in the UK at https://www.bbc.co.uk/news/uk-39881236 and learn more about contemporary interpretations of Heraclitus in the entry 'Heraclitus' by Daniel W. Graham in *The Stanford Encyclopaedia of Philosophy* (Winter 2023 Edition), Edward N. Zalta & Uri Nodelman (eds.) at: https://plato.stanford.edu/archives/win2023/entries/heraclitus/.

The Book of Genesis and Jeremiah are quoted from the King James Bible. The ancient Sumerian myth of The Huluppu-Tree can be read in *Inanna*

Queen of Heaven and Earth: her Stories and Hymns from Sumer by Diane Wolkstein and Samuel Noah Kramer (New York: Harper and Row, 1983). *river / run: an ecopoetic trilogy* (Dorchester: Capefarewell, 2024) by Helen Moore is a trilogy of longform landscape ecopoems about British rivers and Atlantic Salmon written in collaboration with artists and scientists. Gaston Bachelard also writes about 'the water of sleep' in *The Poetics of Reverie: Childhood, Language and the Cosmos*, translated by Daniel Russell (Boston: Beacon Books, 1969). *A River Dies of Thirst (Diaries)* (London: Saqi Books, 2009) translated by Catherine Cobham, and with a preface by Ruth Padel, is a collection of Mahmoud Darwish's diary entries from the painful year of 2006, when Israel attacked Gaza and Lebanon. 'Gold in the Water' by Alinah Azadeh, can be found on her Substack account: https://alinahazadeh.substack.com/p/gold-in-the-water. 'The Drowned Ship' by the late Mourid Barghouti, appears in his collection *Midnight and other poems* (Todmorden: Arc Publications, 2008), translated by Radwa Ashour, with a preface by Ruth Padel. 'Saint of the Source' by Bejan Matur appears in her book *How Abraham Abandoned Me* (Todmorden: Arc Publications, 2012), translated from Turkish by Ruth Christie with Selçuk Berilgen, and a Poetry Book Society Recommended Translation.

Derek Lin's eloquent summary of Chapter Eight of the *Tao Te Ching* can be found at https://taoism.net/the-seven-virtues-of-water/. 'The Election, Lao Tzu, A Cup of Water' can be found on Ursula K. Le Guin's website: https://www.ursulakleguin.com/blog/119-the-election-lao-tzu-a-cup-of-water?rq=way%20of%20water. A full synopsis and sample chapter of *Popular Resistance in Palestine; A History of Hope and Empowerment* (London: Pluto Press, 2011) can be found on Mazin Qumsiyeh's website: http://qumsiyeh.org/popularresistanceinpalestine/. The University of Chichester gave me a grant from its 2023 Research Innovation Fund to co-facilitate the workshop 'You & I: Poetry, Palestine & Israel' with Hugo Filipe Lopes at A Casa Dos Poetas 2023, an Anglo-American poetry festival held in Silves, the Algarve. *Poesia de Resistência Palestiniana* (2023) a journal edited by Hugo Filipe Lopes featuring Palestinian and Israeli poets in Portuguese translation, can be found at https://drive.google.com/file/d/1nLi4_LxmZ0Yu59ZMQIz2u-zQj2Ohn06f/view. Work by forty-two Israeli poets including Yehuda Amichai, Tuvia Ruebner, Yitzhak Laor, and Dahlia

Ravikovitch appears in *With an Iron Pen: Twenty Years of Hebrew Protest Poetry* (Albany: State University of New York, 2009) edited by Tal Nitzan and Rachel Tzvia Back. Naomi Shihab Nye is quoted from her email to me of August 20th, 2024. Atef Alshaer, Farid Bitar, Basman Derawi and Lucien Zell can be found on Facebook. Michal Rubin has two poetry collections forthcoming from Fomite Press (USA) in 2025.

My anthology of Palestinian poets, *A Blade of Grass: New Palestinian Poetry* is published by Smokestack Books, 2017. I quote Atef Alshaer from his introduction to *Out of Gaza* (Smokestack Books, 2024), which he co-edited with Alan Morrison.

Charged with Enchantment by John Liechty

The Lake Isle of Innisfree is from W.B. Yeats's collection *The Rose*, published in 1893.

Records of Iowa corn production in bushels per acre can be found at: https://publications.iowa.gov/50060/1/graphic_summary_iowa_corn_oats_yields_1940_OCR_.pdf

Soil erosion in Iowa and other Midwestern states is discussed in a 2021 article by Becca Dzombak appearing in *The Smithsonian Magazine*: https://www.smithsonianmag.com/science-nature/scientists-say-nations-corn-belt-has-lost-third-its-topsoil-180977485/

T S Eliot quotes are from *Collected Poems 1909-1962* (Faber & Faber, London, 1963); Passages from Lao Tzu are from *The Way of Life According to Lao Tzu,* Witter Bynner translation published in 1944, which is easy to find online. *The Diviner* is from Seamus Heaney's *Death of a Naturalist*, published in 1966. Joseph Campbell's *The Hero with a Thousand Faces*, published in 1949, is a rich study of overlapping stories, myths, and legends. I read it years ago, and have undoubtedly drawn from it. *The Water of Life* and similar tales are from *The Complete Grimm's Fairy Tales*. Pantheon Books: New York, 1972. Quotes from the *Bible* are from either the New Jerusalem or Revised Standard versions.

Ezekiel 47 describes a vision of water flowing from the Temple through the middle of the city and building into a river... The vision is taken up again in Revelation 22.

Robert Louis Stevenson's 12-day journey across America on an immigrant train is described in an essay called *Across the Plains*, from a collection by the same title published in 1892. Other wors include:

Edward Abbey, *Desert Solitaire: A Season in the Wilderness* (McGraw-Hill, New York, 1968) and
Gary Snyder, *No Nature* (Pantheon Books, New York, 1992).

Ben Ehrenreich's 2011 article *Drip, Jordan* gives a shocking idea of the cost of Making the Desert Bloom. It can be read online at: https://harpers.org/archive/2011/12/drip-jordan/

The hadith on giving water is discussed at: https://www.abuaminaelias.com/dailyhadithonline/2017/07/23/best-sadaqah-water-thirsty/

The ritual offering 'yonchap' is described by Karma Phuntsho at: https://texts.mandala.library.virginia.edu/text/y%C3%B6nchap-water-offering
The enormous quantities of water needed to power search engines, the Internet, and AI are raised in a 2020 article by Nicole Kempis at https://earth.org/water-needed-to-power-the-internet/

Documents of Dispossession by James Brooks

All quotes from films are from the author's notes taken during screenings. Edward Said's remark is from his article 'The Morning After', *London Review of Books*, 21 October 1993. Harold Pinter's poem, 'Meeting' (2002), can be read at http://www.haroldpinter.org/poetry/meeting.html.

Masafer Yatta by Liam McKenna

A translation of the Israeli Supreme Court's decision in the Masafer Yatta case (Abu Aram & Ors v Minister of Defence, HCJ 413/13) has been

published online by the Jerusalem-based human rights organisation B'Tselem: https://www.btselem.org/sites/default/files/2022-05/ 20220504_hjc_413_13_hcj_1039_13_masafer_yata_ruling_eng.pdf. The descriptions of the villagers as 'invaders' appear at paragraph 38.

Professor Eliav Lieblich's analysis of the Israeli Supreme Court's decision was published on the German legal blog Verfassungsblog: https:// verfassungsblog.de/wrong-to-the-core/. Further commentary can be found in the legal note published by Diakonia International Humanitarian Law Centre, based in Jerusalem: https://apidiakoniase.cdn.triggerfish.cloud/ uploads/sites/2/2022/05/Legal-Note-Masafer-Yatta-May-2022.pdf.

The transcript containing Ariel Shanon's 1981 comments in relation to Masafer Yatta has been published online (in the original Hebrew only) by the Akevot Institute for Israeli-Palestinian Conflict Research: https:// www.akevot.org.il/en/news-item/document-revealed-by-akevot -ariel-sharon-instructed-idf-to-create-training-zone-to-displace- palestinians/.

Yaakov Havakook's comments on the Israeli Supreme Court's judgment were reported by Yuval Abraham in +972 Magazine: https:// www.972mag.com/anthropologist-masafer-yatta-firing-zone/.

The row about the filmmakers' speeches at the Berlin International Film Festival was reported in the Guardian, as well as other newspapers: https://www.theguardian.com/world/2024/feb/27/ german-minister-says-she-was-only-applauding-israeli-filmmaker-at- berlinale.

The reference to 'everyday evil' is to Ilan Pappé's article 'Everyday Evil in Palestine: The View from Lucifer's Hill' (2021) I(1) Janus Unbound: Journal of Critical Studies 70-82, available online: https://journals. library.mun.ca/index.php/JU/article/download/2319/1832/8244.

Last Word On Halal Dating Apps by Ghazal Tipu

I have mentioned the following studies:

Jonathan D'Angelo and Catalina Toma, 'There are plenty of fish in the sea: The effects of choice overload and reversibility on online daters' satisfaction with selected partners', *Media Psychology* 20, no. 1 (2017): 1-27. The research can be accessed at https://doi.org/10.1080/1521326 9.2015.1121827

Laurens De Rooij, 'The relationship between online dating and Islamic identity among British Muslims', *Journal of Religion, Media and Digital Culture* 9, no. 1 (2020): 1-32. The study can be found at https://doi. org/10.1163/21659214-bja10010

Andrew Porter *et al.* 'Swipe Left on Sexual Harassment: Understanding and Addressing Technology-Facilitated Sexual Violence on Dating Apps', *Journal of Interpersonal Violence*, 0(0). This study can be accessed at https://doi.org/10.1177/08862605241265672

Tila Pronk and Jaap Denissen, *'A rejection mind-set: Choice overload in online dating'*, *Social Psychological and Personality Science* 11, no. 3 (2020): 388-396. This study can be accessed at https://doi.org/10.1177/194 8550619866189

Marina Thomas et al, '99+ matches but a spark ain't one: Adverse psychological effects of excessive swiping on dating apps', *Telematics and Informatics* 78 (2023): 101949. This can be accessed at https://doi. org/10.1016/j.tele.2023.101949

Elisabeth Timmermans and Cassandra Alexopoulos, 'Anxiously searching for love (among other things): attachment orientation and mobile dating application users' motives and outcomes', *Cyberpsychology, Behavior, and Social Networking*, 2020, 23(7), 447-452. This study can be accessed at https://doi.org/10.1089/cyber.2019.0542

The 2017 survey from Match was quoted from https://www. singlesinamerica.com

CONTRIBUTORS

● **Alev Adil**, writer, artist and literary critic reviews for the *Times Literary Supplement* ● **Shani Alexander** is a journalist based in London ● **James Brooks** is a science journalist ● **Khuda Bushq**, a Pakistani-American and part-time Malaysian, has just completed his thesis entitled 'Netflix and Chill' ● **Naomi Foyle**, poetry and fiction editor of *Critical Muslim*, is a well-known science fiction writer ● **Abigail George**, South African novelist, screenwriter, and poet, is the 2023 winner of the Sol Plaatje European Union Poetry Prize ● **Jeremy Henzell-Thomas** is a Research Associate and former Visiting Fellow at the Centre of Islamic Studies, University of Cambridge ● **Christopher Burr Jones** is Senior Fellow of the Centre for Postnormal Policy and Futures Studies ● **C Scott Jordan** is Deputy Editor of *Critical Muslim* ● **John Liechty**, a retired teacher, divides his time between Spain and Morocco ● **Iftikhar H Malik**, Professor-Emeritus, Bath Spa University, is a Trustee of the Royal Historical Society and the Oxford Union Society ● **Liam Mayo** is a seasonal lecturer in social sciences and humanities at the University of the Sunshine Coast in Australia ● **Liam McKenna** is seeking admission to the Bar in London ● **Wietske Merison**, an artist and a Muslim chaplain, is an Associate Fellow at the Indonesian International Islamic University ● **Ebrahim Moosa** is Mirza Family Professor in Islamic Thought and Muslim Societies, University of Notre Dame ● **Steve Noyes** is a British (and Canadian) Muslim writer living in Sheffield ● **Saadia Peerzada**, a poet from Kashmir, is a graduate student of English at the University of Massachusetts, Amhert, US ● **Ghazal Tipu** is a writer and corporate communications professional based in Cardiff ● **Luke Wilkinson** is pursuing a PhD in Theology and Religious Studies at the University of Cambridge, and working on the history of Muslim-Christian relations in Malta, where he grew up.

Critical Muslim is published quarterly by C. Hurst & Co. (Publishers) Ltd. on behalf of and in conjunction with Critical Muslim Ltd. and the Muslim Institute, London.

All editorial correspondence to Muslim Institute, Canopi, 7-14 Great Dover Street, London, SE1 4YR
E-mail: editorial@criticalmuslim.com

Critical Muslim 53

Water